Best Practices in Planning Strategically for Online Educational Programs

Best Practices in Planning Strategically for Online Educational Programs is a step-by-step guide to developing strategic plans for creating and implementing online educational programs within higher-education institutions. From conception to execution and assessment, the successful management of purposeful online educational programs in colleges and universities carries increasing importance and a unique set of requirements. This book enables administrators and faculty to:

- identify the opportunities and challenges presented by online education for institutions based on their histories, missions and market positions
- develop a roadmap for creating and implementing a strategic plan
- provide guidance for assessing the plan and insight into the iterative nature of planning

With computer networked-based technologies gaining ground in traditional private and public institutions, this critical volume is the first to apply the principles and practices associated with strategic planning specifically to online educational programs.

Elliot King is Professor and former Chair of the Communication Department at Loyola University Maryland, USA. He is the author or co-author of seven books and has written extensively about the application and impact of new computer and communication technology since the 1980s. He is a co-founder of Loyola's Master of Arts program in Emerging Media, an online program.

Neil Alperstein is Professor in the Communication Department at Loyola University Maryland, USA. He is Founding Director of its Master of Arts program in Emerging Media, an online program, and is a leader in the use of educational technology in the classroom. He is the author of the book *Advertising in Everyday Life* and of numerous book chapters and scores of scholarly articles.

Best Practices in Online Teaching and Learning

Series Editor Susan Ko

For a full list of titles in this series, please visit: www.routledge.com/Best-Practices-in-Online-Teaching-and-Learning/book-series/BPOTL.

Best Practices for Teaching with Emerging Technologies by Michelle Pacansky-Brock

Best Practices in Online Program Development: Teaching and Learning in Higher Education by Elliot King and Neil Alperstein

Best Practices for Flipping the College Classroom edited by Julee B. Waldrop and Melody A. Bowdon

Best Practices in Engaging Online Learners through Active and Experiential Learning Strategies by Stephanie Smith Budhai and Ke'Anna Brown Skipwith

Best Practices for Teaching with Emerging Technologies 2e by Michelle Pacansky-Brock

Best Practices in Planning Strategically for Online Educational Programs by Elliot King and Neil Alperstein

Best Practices in Planning Strategically for Online Educational Programs

Elliot King
Neil Alperstein

Routledge
Taylor & Francis Group

NEW YORK AND LONDON

First published 2018
by Routledge
711 Third Avenue, New York, NY 10017

and by Routledge
2 Park Square, Milton Park, Abingdon, Oxon, OX14 4RN

Routledge is an imprint of the Taylor & Francis Group, an informa business

Library of Congress Cataloging-in-Publication Data
A catalog record for this book has been requested

ISBN: 978-1-138-93618-8 (hbk)
ISBN: 978-1-138-93619-5 (pbk)
ISBN: 978-1-315-67700-2 (ebk)

Typeset in Minion Pro
by Apex CoVantage, LLC

From Elliot: To Lila and Brooklyn, who are already learning so much online

From Neil: To Nancy, my love and guiding light

Contents

Preface

Strategic planning did not come easily or naturally to higher education in general, and, because of the variations in the ways in which online education has been integrated or perhaps grown up as a stepchild of traditional education, it too has faced its own unique difficulties when it comes to strategic planning. Although strategic planning developed as a result of the maturation of the corporate enterprise, for higher education, strategic planning emerged as a result of crisis, particularly due to the rising cost of a college education, among other factors, as it became important for leadership at colleges and universities to steer their institutions on a course that helped maintain their vitality. However, institutions of higher education and corporations are very different entities, and, as such, strategic planning did not and still does not fit easily into the management of colleges and universities. As higher education has become "big business," stakeholders, including boards of trustees, demand that the institutions they serve operate under sound business principles, making strategic planning a necessity.

Online education in its current iteration has grown in response to a number of factors, including the cost of attending a four-year institution, as the cost of tuition, room and board as well as additional fees now tops $50,000 per year in many private institutions. But cost isn't the only determining factor regarding the growth of online education, as the demographics of those who seek a college degree have also changed, including older students whose life stage and responsibilities are quite different than the average undergraduate. Additionally, the development of newer technologies, like learning management systems, alter the infrastructure of the typical college campus, as instructors can teach without physical boundaries, offering courses to students in different time zones within the United States and serving international students as well. These factors, among others, have changed aspects of institutional life, requiring that online education, like the broader institution in which it exists, needs to plan strategically as well.

This book turns strategic planning into a process-oriented approach by referring to it as planning strategically. Furthermore, the concept of planning strategically is placed within the broader context of strategic planning for the entire institution, which may be a top-down effort, one led by the academic vice-president and executed by the deans, for example. Strategy for online education, however, works most effectively through what may be referred to as planning from the middle. Planning from the middle implies that strategy can be developed at the school, department, small group or individual level. Therefore, this book serves as a practical guide for those involved in planning online programs at the department, school or college level, and it serves those whose institutions place online education in an ancillary virtual space, an eCampus so to speak, separate from the physical campus. The planning processes described in the following chapters serve as a handbook that places online education within the mission of the larger institution. The book adopts the language and steps utilized in corporate strategic planning so they may be applicable to online programs, from developing a program mission and vision, setting goals and objectives, as well as developing outcomes to ensure successful execution of the plan. The book employs a variation on what corporate planners would call a SWOT analysis that is useful for determining an online program's place within the increasingly competitive space of online education. There are practical examples of the planning process available that demonstrate how these tools may be applied. The book concludes that strategy ultimately is not just a management activity; rather, the thesis of the book is that planning strategically is at base a communication activity.

The book is comprised of seven chapters:

Chapter 1—Modern Strategic Planning and Management in Higher Education
Chapter 2—The Practice and Practical Problems of Strategic Planning in Higher Education
Chapter 3—Planning Strategically: An Overview
Chapter 4—Vision and Mission
Chapter 5—Scanning the External Environment
Chapter 6—Techniques for Planning Strategically
Chapter 7—Getting It Done

Chapter 1, "Modern Strategic Planning and Management in Higher Education," traces the development of strategic planning as a management discipline, beginning in the 1960s. Strategic planning developed as a response to changes in the business environment in the United States. As many major corporations expanded and as leadership of those companies transitioned from entrepreneurial founders to professional managers, strategy began to drive corporate shape, nature and growth. Originally, strategic planning was conceptualized as a primary function of senior management, as it provided an essential methodology for senior managers to guide an organization to remain competitive and thrive. The chapter roots the development of strategic planning in higher education in a time of crisis. With the end of the baby boom, there were fewer students of traditional college age. Correspondingly, the cost of attending college was rising, and many colleges and universities began to face financial pressures that they were not prepared for or equipped to handle. In the same way that it was seen as a vehicle to enable companies to remain competitive, strategic planning became a vehicle for colleges and universities to respond to the changing environment. As in the corporate world, the entry of strategic planning into the management of colleges and universities served to empower senior leadership, placing on senior management the responsibility for ensuring the ongoing vitality of an institution. The chapter points out that in practice strategic planning has been an uneasy fit in the academic world. The structure, culture and competitive landscape of higher education are different than those of the corporate world, and those differences have a significant impact on the effectiveness of strategic planning in higher education. Nevertheless, under pressure from accrediting agencies and other external stakeholders, strategic planning has become a routine activity in many colleges and universities.

Today, as in the 1970s, colleges and universities are in a period of great change. Online education has emerged as one of the primary factors both as a cause of the changing landscape and as a response. Strategic planning can help colleges and universities realize the full potential of their online educational opportunities. That plan must take place at two levels—institutionally and programmatically. On the programmatic level, many of the standard techniques used in strategic planning are not effective, as they do not reflect the position of online education in traditional colleges and universities. Moreover, since in many cases online education has been introduced into higher education on an ad hoc basis, each institutional setting calls for an approach appropriate to local circumstances. In many cases, instead of simply empowering senior management, strategic planning on the programmatic level has to be lateral and collaborative. In many ways, strategic planning for online education needs an innovative set of tools and techniques.

Chapter 2, "The Practice and Practical Problems of Strategic Planning in Higher Education," reviews the changing culture for strategic planning in higher education generally followed by an overview of the standard strategic planning process. The chapter outlines the specific terminology—the language of strategic planning—that allows planners to effectively communicate with stakeholders. The process described in this chapter allows those who are planning online programs to match their strategies to those of the university's planning process, to be able to determine those flashpoints where both the university and online education mesh. The chapter describes the challenges that relate to fitting the strategy for online education into the overall university strategic plan. Although the strategic plan for online education may be constructed separately and, in some cases, even independent from the overall university strategic plan, it must be constructed, presented and executed in a way that aligns with the university plan, or else the road to implementing the plan will be strewn with obstacles and the path the success will be more difficult.

Chapter 3, "Planning Strategically: An Overview," takes the standard approach to strategic planning and turns it on its proverbial head by exploring the basic principles of planning strategically, which is described as a subtle but critical shift in the way we think about planning. The chapter explores the basic principles involved in planning strategically as opposed to strategic planning. It describes the benefits and strengths of planning that take place at the middle levels of an organization rather than as an instrument of control from the senior management of the organization. The chapter presents the preliminary steps needed to begin planning strategically—building a planning network—and it advances a "planning from the middle" approach.

Chapter 4, "Vision and Mission," will define the difference between a mission statement and a vision statement and then explore the role that mission and vision statements have come to play in the planning process. The chapter explores the nuances of developing a mission statement first by examining their use in the corporate and non-profit sector, and then it examines how they have been modified in their application in higher education. The chapter will then present a strategy for developing effective mission and vision statements for online education, regardless of the specific circumstances on a given campus. This section on crafting a mission statement for online education has three components. First, it will examine a set of existing university strategic plans and suggest ways in which online education can be justified within the context of the plan. Then, the chapter will detail several specific processes that can be followed to develop a mission and a vision statement for online education. Finally, it will propose strategies to assess the strengths and weaknesses of departmental and program mission statements.

Chapter 5, "Scanning the External Environment," reviews the basic components of a SWOT analysis, a standard means by which corporations position themselves relative to the competition. SWOT—which stands for "strengths, weaknesses, opportunities and threats"—is explored through several of the trends that have had an impact on the macro environment for online education. These trends significantly shape the institutional receptivity to online education and new online initiatives.

Following the analysis of the major factors shaping the overall environment for online education, the chapter explores using SWOT-like approaches to planning strategically for online education. The exploration has two components: the first component is a survey of the competitive contours of online education, and the second aspect looks at ways to assess institutional readiness for online education. Institutional readiness is a critical concept as it turns a critical eye on what a college or university actually has the capacity to do. The chapter concludes by laying out the role the SWOT analysis plays in planning strategically. Although those responsible for charting the future of online education at any specific campus must always be alert to and aware of the larger environment in which they operate, in most routine situations and in their day-to-day activities, they may not have the institutional authority or resources to respond to the macro environment, either by taking advantage of a perceived opportunity or by responding to a perceived threat. Consequently, for planning from the middle, the more micro-level analysis of institutional and departmental strengths and weaknesses, particularly those associated with a targeted objective or goal, represent a more useful application of a SWOT analysis. The targeted analysis can help focus planning on goals that have a greater likelihood of actually being achieved.

Chapter 6, "Techniques for Planning Strategically," describes why the context and environment for online education within institutions of higher learning is more suitable for planning strategically than strategic planning. A toolbox of practical resources is presented that provides an integrated approach for planning strategically based on the use of the Simple Rules Paradigm, along with critical success factors analysis, force field analysis, present state/future state gap analysis and scenario planning. Finally, a case study regarding the implementation of accessibility standards and UDL (universal design for learning) principles based on planning strategically from the middle is presented.

Chapter 7, "Getting It Done," contrasts the experiences developing online education programs at Tufts University and the University of Southern Indiana as a backdrop to the exploration of the types of leadership needed to advance online education regardless of the starting point or specific institutional circumstances. It investigates the need for leadership, strategic thinking and communicating strategically. The chapter describes communications vehicles and approaches that can be utilized to help build support for online education and encouraging faculty engagement. An assessment of the potential for planning strategically from the middle of the organization for online education is presented.

Based on the Generational Model presented in our previous book, *Best Practices in Online Program Development*, this book views online education as being in stages of maturation—what we refer to as generations—at various institutions, whether they be large or small, private or public, or whether online education is central to the university or an ancillary function. But in order for online programs to flourish, those who take responsibility for the development of such programs need to learn to play by the rules established by the broader institution in which online programs operate. What that means is that online programs need to move from their initial ad hoc formulation toward employing strategic processes that help to more firmly root online programs within the management orientation of today's institutions of higher education. This book is geared toward those individuals and groups engaged in online program development that take responsibility for planning strategically. The processes described in this book will help their programs mature and ensure the future for online education within the institution.

Acknowledgments

In our previous book, *Best Practices in Online Program Development*, we introduced the Generational Model of Online Program Development that outlines the stages of program development for online education programs. In this book, we put that model into practice as we set out to describe how to move from ad hoc development toward a more systematic and sustained approached for online education programs. We have learned much from our own experience in the process of creating and managing an online graduate program, and that experience, along with the experiences of those interviewed for this book, represents the best practices in planning strategically for online programs.

First, we would like to acknowledge and thank our colleagues in the Department of Communication at Loyola University Maryland who have participated directly in planning strategically. You have all been wonderful and supportive colleagues on our online journey. We would like to thank Dr. Jeffrey Barnett, Associate Dean for Social Sciences at Loyola, who has been supportive of our online M.A. program in Emerging Media. We are indebted to Dr. Thomas Scheye, Distinguished Service Professor of English and former provost at Loyola, who helped us understand the critical difference between strategic planning and planning strategically.

We would like to thank the many people who we interviewed, including Naomi Boyer (Polk State University), Tracy Chapman (Creighton University), Patrick Connell (Tufts University), Jay Field, (City College of San Francisco), Megan Linos (University of Southern Indiana), Kevin Minch (Truman State University), Susan Rudasill (Florida State University), Gary Shouppe (Columbia State University) and John Sloop (Vanderbilt University) as well as our friends and colleagues at the Online Learning Consortium, at whose Accelerate! conference we presented different aspects of the research that formed the foundation of this book. We would like to thank Susan Ko for including us in the Best Practices series and all the people at Routledge, in particular Alex Marsulis and Daniel Schwartz for their patience, hard work and support in making this book a reality.

Neil would like to thank Dr. Estabon Mezey and Dr. Michael Choti, who saved his life. It has been a remarkable ten years being cancer-free that have allowed him to continue as a productive scholar, teacher, husband, father and grandfather.

Elliot would like to express his appreciation for the medical miracle that has allowed our continued collaboration. As well, Elliot would like to acknowledge his good friend Dr. Sharon Nell, who was the right person at the right place at the right time to open the door for us to establish Loyola's first online program.

Finally, we would like to thank all those who read this book. There are some who say that all education will at some point be online. While that may be an overstatement, we believe it is true that education will continue to be driven by technological developments that will continue to change and hopefully enhance the way students learn. Whether it be through the future development of artificial intelligence, through virtual or augmented reality or through the contributions of cognitive science, we believe the strategic processes and practices that we have written about in this book will be useful as you develop online education programs at your institutions.

1

Modern Strategic Planning and Management in Higher Education

In the spring of 2014, the Harvard Business School unveiled a new educational initiative, HBX. Its initial mandate was to offer three foundational business courses—financial accounting, business analytics and economics for managers (Borchers 2014). The launch had several noteworthy elements. First, it was the Harvard Business School's first foray into education below the graduate level. To be eligible to participate in HBX courses, students needed only to be pursuing an undergraduate degree. Second, HBX represented the business school's first online educational offerings. Harvard, in conjunction with the Massachusetts Institute of Technology, was at the forefront of the development of Massive Open Online Courses (MOOCs) with the development of what it called the edX platform; the business school created HBX.

HBX represented the outcome of a well-publicized debate between two of Harvard's most prominent business professors about how the school should strategically respond to the potential and growth of online education, which, according to some observers, was perhaps the most important strategic decision the school faced since its founding in 1924 and adopted the case study method of instruction (Useem 2014). At the same time, online platforms like edX, Coursera and Udacity were attracting hundreds of thousands of students as well as the attention of venture capitalists. Premier educational institutions such as Stanford University were jumping into the arena. Highly prestigious universities like the Georgia Institute of Technology were experimenting with putting entire degree programs online. How should the Harvard Business School respond, if at all?

On one side of the debate was Michael Porter, seen by many as the leading authority on competitive strategy. Porter's book *Competitive Strategy* (Free Press, New York), published in 1980, has been cited as one of the ten most-influential management books of the twentieth century by the Academy of Management (Bedeian and Wren 2001). His book *Competitive Advantage* (Free Press, New York), published in 1985, became something of a bible to business managers (The Economist 2008). On the other side was Clay Christensen, who, with his 1997 book, *The Innovator's Dilemma* (Harvard Business Press, Cambridge,

MA), positioned himself as the primary theorist of what has come to be called "disruptive innovation." Over time the concept of "disruption" has become the mantra for those in organizations who advocated change.

In Porter's view, organizations gain competitive advantage in one of two ways: either they can offer their products to buyers more efficiently (that is, at a lower cost), or they can differentiate their products from their competitors (The Economist 2008). Christensen held a different perspective. The theory of disruptive innovation suggests that new competitors can challenge the major players in established markets by entering overlooked niches, often those whose profitability is lower, or niches that do not meet the needs of the most demanding buyers of the entrenched suppliers. In this paradigm, established companies often overreach the needs of many customers, offering more features on products than many customers need and with prices that are too high and out of the reach of those who did not need such robust products. After entering the market through an underserved, low-cost niche, new entrants can move upstream while keeping the advantages they developed in profitably, filling those underserved corners of the market and forcing the incumbents to respond; as such, the established market has been disrupted by innovation (Christensen et al. 2015).

With the growth of online education, business schools looked like a market that was ripe for disruption. Although Harvard and other top-ranked schools offered prestige and alumni networks, the education offered by business schools themselves often was not highly differentiated. In fact, the curricula of most respected graduate schools of business meet standards dictated by the Association to Advance Collegiate Schools of Business (AACSB) or other accrediting agencies. Moreover, since many business schools use the case study method of instruction pioneered by the Harvard Business School when it was established

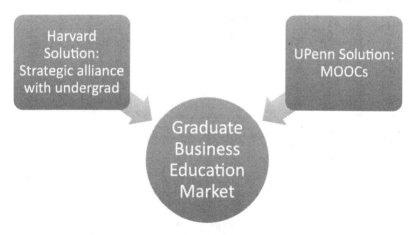

Figure 1.1 Disruptive Forces in Higher Education

more than 90 years ago, the in-class experience frequently is not all that different from school to school. Finally, attending the Harvard Business School is expensive, very expensive. In 2015, the full program cost more than $120,000 in tuition and fees, putting it out of reach for many prospective students even if they could win acceptance.

Not surprisingly, Christensen believed that Harvard Business School should disrupt its own model and embrace the opportunity online education offered to provide a Harvard experience to many more people at a much lower cost. Indeed, in 2011 Christensen had taught an online course about disruptive innovation through the University of Phoenix that reached 130,000 students. In one of his classes, Christensen presented the Harvard Business School as a case study, raising the question: would HBS end up like Blockbuster Video, which was made obsolete by streaming services such as Netflix, a classic disrupter in the Christensen typology? One of the suggestions that emerged in the class challenged the status quo by crafting a strategic response: put the business school's entire first-year curriculum online. Michael Porter was skeptical of that approach. In 2001, he wrote an article about strategy and the Internet in which he suggested that on balance the widespread deployment of the Internet had, to that point, hurt companies' abilities to establish sustainable operational advantages. More worrisome, it had reduced profitability as well. The Internet could help a company achieve a competitive advantage only if the Internet efforts were a complement to the traditional ways of competing and not set apart from established operations. The Internet should be interwoven into existing strategies and buttress established advantages, from Porter's perspective (Porter 2001).

The Harvard Business School Model

When it came to making a strategic decision for the Harvard Business School, Nitin Nohria, the dean of the business school, leaned more toward Porter than Christensen. He geared HBX toward a new market, undergraduate students. Unlike MOOCs, HBX charged tuition, though not nearly as much as a residential course might cost. And, at first, students who completed the three initial courses received what they called a credential of readiness (CORe). The program had two strategic objectives. The first was for Harvard Business School to reach students it had not served in the past, instead of addressing the needs of its traditional markets of graduate students and executive education, which combined generate nearly $250 million in annual revenue. While not lowering the price of a Harvard business education, HBX's second objective was to generate additional revenue. Indeed, the core principle underscoring HBX was that it would not be a substitute for an MBA and it would be self-sustaining. Its courses would also have to embrace the case study method of learning. In other words, HBX courses would somehow embody the business school's traditional educational values and methods but be delivered to a new market and at a lower cost but not for free. HBX also had a systematic implementation strategy. At its launch, HBX courses were offered only to students in Massachusetts. Since then, Harvard has inked deals with several elite liberal arts colleges such Amherst, Wellesley, Bowdoin and Williams. It is also partnering with corporate clients and universities in other countries. It is opening the program to older students and offers it as a pre-MBA boot camp. Finally, it has begun to offer up to eight credits through the Harvard Extension School for CORe classes.

Harvard Business School's strategic response to online education is hardly the only option. For example, the Wharton School at the University of Pennsylvania opted for a different approach. In 2012, almost on a lark, Peter Fader, a Wharton professor, created an introductory course in marketing that was offered as a MOOC on the Coursera platform. Three years later, more than 300,000 people have taken the course, and nearly 100,000 have taken a second course he developed that focused on customer analytics. And Fader wasn't alone. In that period, more than 2.7 million people have enrolled in Wharton's 18 MOOCs, with 54,000 receiving verified certificates of completion, which initially cost $49. The price for the verification was then raised to $95 and then $149. The school also issued more than 32,000 verified certificates of completions in specializations, in which students take four courses for $595. Within three years, Wharton's MOOCs were generating more than $5 million annually.

MOOCS, SPOCS and Nanodegrees

In the wake of the response, the Wharton School decided to invest more heavily in MOOCs and other online offerings only loosely tied, if at all, to its traditional MBA and executive education programs. The school began developing two dozen new courses including what it calls Specialized Private Online Courses (SPOCs), for which it planned to charge $3,700 in tuition. Fader pioneered the SPOC concept for a course that explored the strategic value of customer relationships, which was limited to 30 students. The Wharton School's dean, Geoffrey Garrett, felt that online education could play a different strategic role than the one at Harvard. He saw a four-fold opportunity. The investment in MOOCs could bolster Wharton's global brand. It provided a Wharton education to students who would never be able to attend classes on the university's Philadelphia campus. The courses could identify people who may be good candidates for the traditional MBA program. And, in a discipline in which a textbook might cost as much as $200, it could generate a lot of revenue. Did Penn take the right strategic path? Or would building an alternative to a traditional Wharton education, costing less and being more accessible, cannibalize its core business? Or did Harvard make the right strategic moves? Or will Harvard eventually become like Barnes and Noble, suffering in its competition to Penn's Amazon? Conversely, can both strategies work?

Asking the question is more important than determining the precise answer. As Clayton Christensen noted, disruption generally attacks the high end of the market last, so even if Harvard's strategy were wrong, the mistake would not be known immediately. But, if both Harvard and Penn and other top-tier business schools have had to develop a strategy to address the development of online education, so too do most all the mid-tier and other schools of business, particularly as overall enrollments in traditional MBA programs, particularly part-time programs, drops (Nishihara and Everitt 2014) (figure 1.1). Of course, the same pressures that online education applied to business schools extends to all corners of higher education. All colleges and universities have to determine how they are going to compete given the new opportunities available online. Indeed, the growth of the new entrants into online education has been impressive. By the end of 2015, more than 35 million people had signed up for at least one online course through a MOOC provider. As significantly, MOOC platforms such as Coursera and edX were developing a successful business model by pioneering their own credentials such as nanodegrees (Udacity) and specializations (Coursera) (Shah 2015). Finally, MOOC providers began working with traditional colleges and universities to open the doors and lower the costs for more students, such as edX's partnership with Arizona State University to create the Global Freshman Academy (GFA), which offers a full palette of university-level first-year courses online for $200 per credit. Total cost for one year of credit is under $6,000. Moreover, GFA has an open admissions policy. Anybody can attend (Lewin 2015). Earlier, Arizona State University had shaken up the academic world by concluding a deal with Starbucks in which the coffee chain offered all its employees full tuition to enroll in any of ASU's 49 four-year, online degree programs (Howard 2015).

Online Education Is Decentralized

The majority of colleges and universities have some online courses or online educational programs available in some disciplines (Allen and Seaman 2013, 20). But in most cases, online program development at many institutions has been ad hoc, decentralized and episodic. Not infrequently, the online offerings in many universities are segregated in continuing education and professional development divisions and kept apart from the main academic enterprise. The impetus for creating online courses and online programs can come from many different stakeholders in the university ranging from individual professors to non-academic administrators and even, in some cases, boards of trustees, depending on the particular circumstances of each institution (King and Alperstein 2015). While most colleges and universities have at least begun to experiment with online education, few have created a systematic approach to online education or developed a strategy to address and manage the opportunities and challenges online education presents, especially as it relates to the traditional activities within the academic enterprise. A strategic planning process for online education can be particularly formidable, because every college and university has its own identity, a sense of self, history, development tradition and mission. Every college and university believes that it addresses the needs of specific student populations from defined geographical areas, even within particular programs, or perhaps schools that see the world as their geographic area. Ironically, five years before the launch of HBX, Harvard Business School's dean Nitin Nohria had been asked at a meeting of faculty and staff when the business school would begin offering online courses. New on the job, Nohria replied, "Not in my lifetime" (Nohria 2015). Since that time, the shape and nature of online education has changed. And as the debate between Michael Porter and Clay Christensen about the correct strategy for online education at Harvard Business School demonstrated, fashioning the correct response is complex. But one thing is certain. Every college and university needs to develop a strategy for online education that is compatible with its unique set of circumstances.

The Concept of Competitive Strategy

As Michael Porter observed in his seminal 1996 article "What Is Strategy, " in the 1970s and 1980s, Japanese automobile manufacturers grabbed a significant share in the United States car market, largely at the expense of the big-three U.S car makers, which had long dominated world markets. The "Japanese invasion," as it was then referred to, shook the confidence of U.S. manufacturers. Not only were Japanese cars, which had been long derided since their entry into the American market in the 1950s and early 1960s as being poorly manufactured and cheap, now perceived to be superior in quality to American-made cars; they also cost less than U.S. brands. The big-three auto manufacturers were losing market share and were clearly on the defensive. But the Japanese success, Porter argued, was the result not of a superior strategy but of better operational efficiency, which leads to greater productivity—i.e., higher-quality cars at lower costs. Understanding the difference between operational efficiency and strategy is critical to successful planning. Operational efficiency is applied to the activities and groups of activities in which an organization engages. In a manufacturing business, for example, efforts at operational efficiency may be focused on the assembly line, the process of taking orders, or the link between orders and production. In higher education, operational efficiency efforts could target recruitment, student retention or the link between the two. Operational efficiency can lead to better outcomes, but, since others can learn the same techniques and processes, operational efficiency by itself cannot lead to a sustainable competitive advantage. Moreover, as competitors benchmark against each other, they begin to look more and more alike, and their distinctions fade.

An example in higher education of an operational change that can lead to a temporary advantage that cannot be sustained is the growth of SAT-optional admissions for undergraduates. Bates College was the first school to drop the requirement for a SAT test. It did so in 1969, and for nearly four decades just a handful of schools followed suit. But starting around 2010 more and more schools decided to go the test-optional route, and by 2015 approximately 850 colleges and universities no longer required standardized testing as part of the admission process, including major institutions like George Washington University and Brandeis University (Anderson 2015). The first schools that moved to an SAT-optional structure could recruit to a broader range of students who were otherwise qualified to attend but who, for whatever reason, did poorly on standardized tests. That advantage, however, has dissipated as other colleges and universities take the same route. As Porter observed, everybody can imitate operational improvements.

Strategy Starts With Positioning

According to Porter, an ongoing competitive advantage can be realized only if an organization does things differently. "The essence of strategy," Porter wrote, "is choosing to perform activities differently or to perform different activities than rivals do" (1996, 64). A strategy starts with positioning. A company, for example, can choose to deliver only a subset of products that its competitors offer. It can opt to serve only a specific segment of customers. Or it can work to reach its customers differently. Porter calls those positions variety, needs and access (figure 1.2).

A strategy involves the creation of a unique and valuable market position through different activities. To achieve that position and to define those activities, a strategy involves creating a series of trade-offs—if an organization does one thing, it cannot or should not do another—which can protect it from

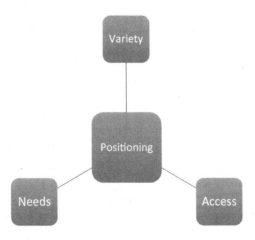

Figure 1.2 Elements of Positioning

competitors imitating its place in the market. By deliberately limiting and focusing its activities to a specific realm, an organization can differentiate itself in a way that provides an ongoing competitive advantage. In short, developing a strategy involves choosing what to do and what not to do. And it involves ensuring that there is a good fit between all the activities that support the organization's position. Strategies rely on systems of activities, systems that are unique to the organization, because they are based on the unique trade-offs the organization has made. In Porter's view, organizational structures, systems and processes need to be tailored to be strategy-specific (1996, 74). In summary, a strategy involves developing a unique position supported by an interlocking system of specific activities that involve clear trade-offs compared to its competitors.

The appeal of Porter's definition of strategy for higher education is obvious. In the United States, there are approximately 1,500 to 2,000 colleges and universities that offer B.A. degrees or above (not including another 800 institutions that offer degrees in only one field, such as medical schools) and another 2,000 or so institutions that offer two-year degrees (Carnegie Classification 2015). Obviously, not every college or university can appeal to every potential student. Since 1973, the Carnegie Foundation for the Advancement of Teaching (and now the Indiana University Bloomington's Center for Postsecondary Research) has long grouped institutions according to six dimensions, among them the nature of the educational program, the degree of research conducted and student profiles. However, these classifications, updated in 2015, do not really capture the potential character of the educational experience at any specific institutions (Carnegie Classification 2015). Carnegie classifications do not adequately define any particular institution. Each institution, regardless of its classification, can and does define itself. Moreover, many institutions see themselves as combining several elements of different Carnegie classifications. For example, major Ivy League universities are clearly major research institutions, but they also house undergraduate liberal arts colleges. And it is not unusual for the liberal arts college to be seen as the centerpiece of the institution, even if the college is dwarfed by other activities. The question is, what role should online education play in that self-definition?

The Growth of Corporate Strategic Planning

Porter's vision of competitive strategic planning is derived from a more general conception of strategy and the growth of strategic planning in the corporate world, which emerged as a management discipline in the 1960s. Perhaps the Rosetta stone of strategy is *The Art of War* written by the Chinese warrior-philosopher Sun Tzu more than 2,000 years ago. In the book's 13 chapters, Tzu lays out the need to assess the situation prior to an attack, to develop a plan of attack, to identify appropriate tactics, and to be flexible and adjust to changing conditions, and other elements needed to achieve victory. But *The Art of War* is more than a handbook of military tactics. Tzu asserts that the greatest victories are those achieved without fighting any battles at all (Art of War Quotes n.d.). In other words, if a country, and by extension any organization or entity, could properly assess its situation and flexibly pursue an appropriate series of tactics and maneuvers, it could successfully achieve its goals, often without conflict with its competitors.

From Hannibal to Napoleon to George Patton, military strategy has an ancient and honored pedigree. But strategy did not emerge as a corporate management discipline until the mid-1960s with the publication of *Strategy and Structure: Chapters in the History of the American Industrial Enterprise* by Alfred Chandler (MIT Press, 1962), who was then on the faculty at the Massachusetts Institute of Technology and who some credit as being the founder of contemporary business history. In the book, Chandler investigated four major manufacturers of the era—E. I. du Pont de Nemours and Company; Standard Oil of New Jersey; General Motors; and Sears, Roebuck and Co.—all of which had grown rapidly in the first part of the twentieth century and moved away from being monolithic, centrally managed, single location operations into multi-unit, semi-autonomous divisions that operated under a corporate umbrella (Hindle 2009). His hypothesis was that the rapid growth served as the catalyst for changes in the organizational structure of each of those companies and dictated their organizational form. As the leadership of each company competed to expand their businesses, the organization of the company changed to accommodate the growth.

Strategy Dictates Organizational Structure

What he discovered was more complicated. While to some degree organizational structure followed its own dynamic, to a greater extent, a company's strategy dictated its organizational structure. Because the leaders of these companies wanted to aggressively grow, they established an internal structure that facilitated that growth. In other words, Chandler argued that strategy preceded structure. The companies he examined established several layers of management ranging from field units to the general office (or what is today called the C-level suite). Strategy—such as adding product lines in the case of General Motors; moving into new market areas such as Standard Oil and Sears, Roebuck; and buying competitors—was determined in the general office and played the largest role in the corporation's success. Chandler's insights had such a dramatic impact, because the book was published at a critical junction in the history of American industry. As companies grew in size, top-level management became more and more removed from day-to-day operations. Moreover, an era dominated by larger-than-life "titans of capitalism" such as John D. Rockefeller seemed to be drawing to a close. Managers rather than the founding families increasingly ran the manufacturing and retailing giants of the second part of the nineteenth century, but the parameters and impact of managerial control, and what was to take the place of visionary leadership, was not yet clearly established, particularly for companies that had far-flung operations (Drucker 1954). Chandler's book not only put the development of an overall strategy clearly on the agenda of senior management; it posited that a sound strategy coupled with an appropriate structure supporting the strategy was the essential element of corporate success. This contradicted Drucker's view that decentralized management of large corporations was more efficient than centralized command-and-control oriented operations. In Chandler's analysis, top management shaped the future of the organization through the development of strategy.

The themes found in Chandler's book were expanded in Igor Ansoff's 1965 book *Corporate Strategy*, which was intended to provide a blueprint for practical strategic decision-making. Ansoff, a management consultant and eventually founding dean and professor of management at Vanderbilt University who some have described as the "father" of strategic management, developed or expanded upon several key concepts that serve as the foundation for strategic decision-making and management. Perhaps Ansoff's most significant insight was that strategy—as opposed to other types of choices made within organizations such as decisions about policies, programs and procedures—always required new and fresh decisions based on the current environment in which an organization operated. As conditions changed, and conditions were always changing, strategy had to be reviewed and altered accordingly. Other kinds of decisions could be delegated to various management levels, but strategic decision-making was the domain of senior management (Easy-Strategy.com n.d.). The same year that *Corporate Strategy* appeared, content about strategic planning was incorporated into the curriculum at the Harvard Business School (Floyd and Wooldridge 2000, 6).

Fundamentals of Strategic Planning

The original formulation of strategic planning had several fundamental concepts. Perhaps most importantly, it emphasized midrange and long-term planning rather than current success or simply the efficiency of ongoing operations. One of the primary tasks of top management was to regularly look forward and lay out the course to achieving a known future state. Secondly, to a large degree, the idea of strategic planning and management severed planning from the formal budgeting processes. Companies typically used the budgeting process to set goals and objectives for the coming year and several years beyond. Strategic planning principles called for a much more expansive and in-depth process, one that perhaps could not be conducted annually. And in the same way that strategy defined structure, strategy also provided the rationale for revenue and expense projections.

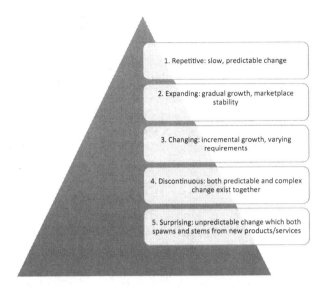

Figure 1.3 Ansoff's 5 Levels of Environmental Turbulence

Moreover, the approaches to strategic planning that developed when the concept first began to take hold in corporate America required that companies carefully assessed the environment in which they operated. From this viewpoint, understanding the notion of environmental turbulence is critical to fashioning a successful strategy. Ansoff described five levels of environmental turbulence ranging from markets that were changing at a slow and predictable pace to those that were expanding rapidly and in unforeseen and unanticipated ways (1965) (figure 1.3).

For a strategy to achieve its goals, it must respond to the environment in which the company is operating. Coupled with the notion of environmental turbulence is the idea that companies must always be changing. If an organization's management believes that it will continue to operate in the way that it always has, there is little compelling reason to invest time and effort into planning. Engaging in a strategic planning process assumes that the organization will take some set of actions geared to achieving a defined outcome (Kastens 1979). Finally, the first wave of strategic planning in corporate America relied on what came to be called a formulation-implementation structure or process. In it, senior management formulated strategy while other parts of the organization were responsible for its implementation. In its most stripped down format, strategic planning in this period argued that after surveying the environment, a centralized group of senior executives can determine a specific course of action for the next three to five years and then shape and reshape the organization to execute the strategy to achieve their vision.

Framework for Strategic Planning

The formulation-implementation framework is still the dominant approach to strategic decision-making processes, but it holds several potentially inhibiting factors that often make it hard for organizations to successfully execute their strategy and leads to many strategic plans having little impact on the actual future course of the organization (Mintzberg 1987). Indeed, shortly after the need for strategic planning was placed on the managerial agenda, a long list of reasons why the planning process often does not work emerged (Steiner 1979, 287–298). Among the most common pitfalls for a strategic plan is that the strategic vision of senior management does not align with the way a company or organization actually runs. All companies have corporate cultures that consist of well-established patterns of behavior, and many of these patterns are very entrenched. People like to complete their tasks in ways to which they have become accustomed and resist change. Since strategic planning implies change, employees sometimes feel threatened, or they feel that senior management is out of touch with the way the work actually gets done. Front-line employees may feel that the strategy has been hatched by a small coterie of people in the upper management suite and the boardroom with little regard for the people who are actually "doing the work" (Schwartz and Davis 1981). If senior management cannot get "buy in" from the employees through effective and ongoing communication, effectively executing a strategic plan may be unlikely, if not impossible.

The potential gap between the people charged with developing the plan and the people charged with executing the plan is just one of the potential pitfalls in the path to the development and implementation of a successful strategic plan. Another major challenge stems from the idea that strategic planning implies a certain degree of rationality. As strategy is a decision-making process—what to do and what not to do—the idea is that those responsible for crafting a strategy will make a series of appropriate decisions based on the evidence they have gathered, and then the organization as a whole will execute those decisions. But a lot of businesses run in more of a reactive and ad hoc manner. For example, a garage-based entrepreneur or hobbyist develops a small, relatively inexpensive computer, and, in turn, the entrenched competitors like IBM have to respond quickly. Or an engineer in a lab discovers a use for a type of adhesive that didn't work as expected, and Post-it Notes starts generating huge amounts of money for 3M. Many markets are, as Ansoff noted, unpredictable, and it is difficult to plan for the unforeseen. Also, large organizations are political in nature. While the typical strategic planning framework assumes that senior decision-makers will make data-driven decisions, different units and people at various levels within organizations use the strategic planning process to enhance their positions and increase the resources available to them. As with all political processes, winners and losers emerge, and a wide range of factors such as interpersonal networks, the social capital people or units have and individual persuasiveness can have an significant impact on strategy development and execution and, in practice, sometimes not in a positive way. Finally, senior managers may fundamentally misread the environment in which they operate. The leadership of the big three American automakers could not anticipate the oil shocks that made cars that could travel further per gallon of gasoline more attractive in the marketplace leading the way for Japanese auto manufacturers to penetrate the U.S. market. The executives at Digital Equipment Corp., the largest manufacturer of what were called mini-computers, simply did not recognize the threat personal computers posed to their business. In the case of Digital Equipment, such myopia proved fatal.

Parallels Between Business and Higher Education

Many of the obstacles to successful strategic planning in the business world are magnified in the academic environment. Universities are very complex institutions. The gaps between senior administrators, boards of trustees, faculty and other staff are often great, and the vision, goals and priorities of the stakeholders do not line up with each other; sometimes they clash. Universities embody powerful but conflicting impulses toward both tradition and change. And while the competitive environment in higher education is significantly different than in most other organizational environments, in many ways, college and universities, or at least subsets of colleges and universities, do compete with each other for students, resources, and prestige, among other things. But that competition is not viewed as direct competition, as is the case among automobile manufacturers or mobile phone manufacturers, for example. A student who goes to Harvard, for example, is not necessarily a student who was lost by Yale, in the same way that a person who bought a Toyota represents a lost sale for Ford. Despite these organizational challenges, over the past 30 years, strategic planning in higher education has become more commonplace.

Strategic Planning in Higher Education

The need for strategic planning in higher education is rooted in the period between 1880 and 1910, when the structure of the contemporary university was established. It was in that period that universities transformed from being relatively small institutions that provided a fixed liberal arts education to a small group of a socially elite individuals to complex entities that supported graduate and professional schools. As that change took hold, institutions of higher learning began to view the discovery of knowledge as an important part of their mission and generally began to redefine their educational missions.

During this period, a wave of new universities endowed by benefactors such as Johns Hopkins, Leland Stanford, John D. Rockefeller (who provided the initial funding for the University of Chicago) and others were established, and the

Growth of the Modern University

Mid-nineteenth century—higher education embraced teaching practical arts along with traditional classical liberal arts.

Early Twenteeth century—colleges and universities transformed into research centers charged with creating new knowledge and serving as gatekeepers to an array of professions.

1960s—colleges and universities opened their doors to women and other underserved populations.

2000s—saw the growth and development of online education programs.

Figure 1.4 Growth of the Modern University

leading educational institutions like Harvard found themselves both competing with these newly established institutions and experimenting with new ways to educate their own students. The business of higher education became much more complex, and efficient management became more critical for a college or university to survive and thrive. College and university administrators had to balance the competing interests of the faculty, students, staff, alumni and bene-factors. The Harvard of 1925 was in many ways a different university than the Harvard of 1850 (Veysey 1965).

While the basic structure of contemporary higher education took shape in the period between 1870 and 1910, in many ways, the kind of growth and expansion that characterized American industry in the first half of the twenti-eth century was replicated in higher education in the post–World War II era. With the G.I. Bill, not only was a university education suddenly within the reach of a much larger percentage of the population, but a college degree came to be viewed as an essential component for upward mobility and a chance at reaching the American dream. Enrollment at state universities and university systems expanded dramatically. For example, prior to World War II, the student populations at the typical state university ranged between 3,000 and 6,000 stu-dents. By 1970, the Ohio State University at Columbus, for example, had more than 50,000 students. Guided by a master plan published in 1960, California's multi-campus university system had more than 150,000 students at ten cam-puses. A second system consisting of state colleges was also formed; it had more than 200,000 students (Thelin 2004). Exploding student growth was only one part of the equation in the rapid transformation of higher education in the post-war period. During WWII, universities contributed heavily to the war effort, particularly in terms of research for military purposes. The Manhattan Proj-ect started at the University of Chicago, the University of California provided management of Los Alamos, and the first modern computer was developed at the University of Pennsylvania, just to name a few contributions. As a result, in 1947, the six-volume *Higher Education for American Democracy*, in addition to calling for increased access to higher education through the establishment of community colleges and increased federal aid, proposed that federal funding for scientific research in a wide range of fields should continue at universities both private and public. Although research had joined the mix of higher education in the United States in the second half of the nineteenth century, the federal government's entry as a funder for basic research provided a major new source of revenue and prestige for colleges and universities that invested in building their research capacities (Graham and Diamond 1997).

College athletics represented another domain of rapid growth in the post-war period. While the commercialization of college sports was being decried as early as the 1920s, in the 1950s two developments completely changed the rules of the game. First, the NCAA negotiated a major television contract putting college football and basketball on the glide path to become major revenue producers for colleges and universities with major athletic programs. Sports became more than an amusement for students and alumni, as they became a major marketing tool to attract new students as well. Secondly, the NCAA formalized a system of athletic scholarships, and, for the first 20 years, schools and universities could offer as many athletic scholarships as they chose, but scholarships could not be withdrawn if the student-athlete stopped playing. The management of athletic scholarships changed the competitive landscape for college sports as the Ivy League schools and other top research institutions declined to offer scholarships and ceased to be competitive on the playing fields (Thelin 2004).

Expansion of Higher Education

By the 1960s, as Clark Kerr, the president of the University of California noted, the systems for which he was responsible had an operating budget of $500 million and a construction budget of more than $100 million. The University of California had operations in more than 100 locations and ongoing activities in more than 50 countries. And the university employed more people than IBM. It included a huge hospital system and managed the largest colony of primates in the world. Within the huge number of activities under the umbrella of the University of California, only about one-third of its expenditures were actually linked directly to teaching (Kerr 2001). While the University of California is an extreme example, throughout the 1960s and 1970s there was a huge expansion throughout the higher education landscape. Colleges and universities became co-ed, and local commuter colleges that largely served single cities became regional universities. State universities and state university systems also increased in size and reach. As the higher education experience became more commonly residential, colleges and universities had to build classrooms, lecture halls, and dormitories and provide food services. More buildings were constructed on campuses between 1955 and 1974 than in the previous 200 years

(Keller 1983, 9). As prospective students became more willing, able and eager to leave home to live at school for their undergraduate education, colleges and universities had to ramp up their marketing and recruitment activities. As the federal government and other agencies stepped up funding for research, many institutions became primary engines of economic growth in their regions with deep connections to local and even national companies and industries. In short, colleges and universities became complex organizations whose activities reached far beyond the classroom and the laboratory.

Not surprisingly, as universities grew in size and scope, the principles of strategic management began to migrate from the corporate world to the campus. Perhaps the first sustained effort at understanding strategic management in higher education was George Keller's "Academic Strategy: The Management Revolution in American Higher Education" (1983). Ironically, Keller introduced his clarion call to colleges and universities for the need to adopt and incorporate modern management techniques with a litany of challenges that are as relevant in 2016 as they were when the book was first published in 1983. Smaller schools were failing economically and even having to close their doors while large, prestigious institutions—including New York University, Columbia University, and Brown University, among others—were being forced to take extraordinary measures such as dipping into their endowments or seeking outside support to right their fiscal ships. With an aging professoriate and the large number of baby boomers who attended college drawing down, there were fewer college-age individuals, and among them fewer students were interested in the liberal arts. Additionally, tuition and associated costs were escalating, making it more and more difficult for students to afford to attend college for four straight years (Keller 1983, 2–14) (figure 1.4).

Active Change-Oriented Management

In short, Keller called for a more active, change-oriented management style in higher education with more hands-on leadership that could transcend the historic divide and, not infrequently, animus between an institution's faculty and its administration. He contended that those responsible for the future of the institution had to attend more closely to market trends, the competitive landscape, and general environmental factors and well as a specific school's history and its traditions and mission to be able to navigate the rocky shoals in which higher education found itself (Peterson 1984, 663).

Keller argued that the senior administrative leadership in the academic world, specifically university presidents, must play a more active role in shaping the direction of their institutions, if those institutions were to survive. The book is replete with stories of strong leaders such as Stephen Joel Trachtenberg at the University of Hartford and Colin Campbell at Wesleyan University in Middletown, Connecticut. The former was what Keller described as a motley collection of formerly independent colleges that banded together under one structure a mere 20 years earlier and was still struggling to find its place. The other was an academically prestigious university that seemed to be potentially heading toward bankruptcy. In both cases, the presidents of each institution crafted and executed plans to put their universities on solid footing, and the plans worked (Keller 1983, 44–52). Despite the successes to which Keller pointed, efforts to incorporate strategic planning processes and disciplines into higher education did not go smoothly in many places (Hinton 2012, 7). While strategic plans were often well-conceived, well-researched and clearly conceptualized, the largest barrier to the introduction of modern management principles to higher education was that the organizational culture in academia was completely different and at times antithetical to corporate organizational culture and those differences were accentuated by strategic planning. For example, one of the pillars of strategic planning is that planning is the domain of senior management. In the university setting, the faculty does not concede that senior administration has the authority or even the right to set the direction of an institution, nor, in many instances, is it clear that university presidents can impose their will on the faculty.

Additionally, most organizations are geared toward a central activity or goal and organized in a way that is supposed to successfully achieve that central outcome. If a company produces widgets, for example, the engineering department is responsible for designing great widgets. The manufacturing department is oriented to producing great widgets, marketing promotes the widgets, the sales department sells the widgets, and so on. Each department is expected to interact with the others to allow the company to reach its objectives.

Colleges and universities, on the other hand, have been described as "loosely coupled" organizations (Weick 1976)—the idea being that while the activities of each part of an organization may be responsive to the actions in other parts of the university, those units of the organization responsible for specific actions also retain their own identity and, to some degree, their independence. In practice, each part of the university has its own separate set of goals and objectives related to the central mission of the institution; however, they are only loosely tied to the other parts of the organization. The athletic department, for example, must be responsive to the academic project of the university; however, on a day-to-day basis and sometimes even over the long term, in many ways it acts autonomously. From such a perspective, most colleges and universities can be viewed more or less as a collection of relatively independent fiefdoms, each moving in its own direction and at its own pace. On one level, the goals, aspirations, needs and hopes of the advancement department are related to the overall academic mission of the university, but its activities, on an ongoing basis, do not overlap much with, let's say, the records department, or enrollment management, whose activities also are related to the overall academic mission of the university. Looked at another way, a university's athletic identity often is independent of its academic identity, though each is responsive, in some way, to the other. Loosely coupled organizations present significant challenges for traditional management practices, including strategic planning. According to Weick, loosely coupled organizations lack several characteristics upon which conventional management theory depends. Organizational units are not highly inter-dependent; goals and strategies to achieve those goals are not necessarily congruent; and the activities of each unit are hard to coordinate (Weick 1982). Given the general difficulties in managing the loose confederation of departments and offices, importing strategic planning and management concepts closely associated with corporate management makes the transition challenging. Strategic planning in the corporate world is based, at least theoretically, on market data. Historically, most colleges and universities did not have access to similar or comparable information. At best, the initial efforts at strategic planning in higher education, which were geared to clarifying an institution's mission, prioritize the allocation of resources and promote an organizational focus, which had little impact on the ongoing activities of many institutions. At worst, such plans became sources of conflict among different units and led to, among some, disillusionment, as faculty and staff invested time and energy, creating documents whose recommendations were never likely to be acted upon in any meaningful way (Hinton 2012). Overall, in its first several iterations, strategic planning did not appear to be a good fit for higher education, and there were very few examples of a strategic planning process that led to genuine transformation in higher education (Rowley et al. 1997).

External Drivers for Strategic Planning

Despite the serious cultural barriers and resistance to strategic planning and management in many institutions of higher education, along with the lack of many visible success stories in the early efforts to apply strategic planning techniques, the concept continued to be attractive to many stakeholders for several reasons. First, although perhaps strategic planning could not be applied holistically across the institution, many of a college or university's functions are primarily business operations. For example, dorms need to be built and maintained. Essential services need to be offered to students and other stakeholders. With the goal of ameliorating many of the strategic planning issues faced by institutions of higher learning, in 1965, the Society for College and University Planning was established, providing an institutional home for those in the university tasked with the planning process. Perhaps more importantly, since the 1980s, accrediting agencies, federal and state governments, and even boards of trustees have become increasingly interested in measuring institutional effectiveness and accountability, with a focus on outcomes rather than on adherence to standards (Carter-Smith 2015, 7). The attention to outcomes has led to the requirement for universities and colleges to develop self-assessment mechanisms including academic program reviews. Strategic planning has become one of the expected activities in which significant outside stakeholders expect universities and colleges to engage (Dodd 2004).

The forces of change identified in the 1980s, during the first wave of strategic planning in higher education, have not abated, and in many ways they have intensified. Issues such as affordability, access, changing demographics, learning outcomes, value of a college degree, and workplace readiness, among others, continue to be hotly debated (Spellings 2007). Despite the wholesale restructuring of higher education, the fear that many universities and colleges would go out of business, despite what many pundits have been predicting since the early 1980s, has not materialized. However, many institutions of higher learning do face serious financial constraints and budgetary limitations. Finally, over the past 20 years, a range of new delivery mechanisms for higher education has emerged. The 1990s and 2000s witnessed explosive growth of for-profit universities, funded largely by loans to students by the federal government. Since the 2000s, online education has attracted millions of students to online programs sponsored by established colleges and universities and to entrepreneurial ventures such as Coursera and Udacity, as well as through alliances among various players (Allen and Seaman 2016, 4). Institutions are under considerable pressure to respond to changes that are taking place in higher education, so, despite the limited success, strategic planning remains a viable vehicle for doing something.

Old Challenges Remain

While the pressure to change in higher education has intensified over the past 20 years, and strategic planning and management is potentially a tool to help manage that change, the institutional barriers to employ strategic planning and management have not dissipated. Colleges and universities are remarkably resilient institutions that, in many cases, are able to harness significant resources to stay afloat. To illustrate such resilience, in 2015 the board of trustees of Sweet Briar College, a 114-year-old institution, unanimously voted to shutter the school, citing a worsening financial condition stemming from declining enrollment and the inability for students to pay the full tuition. On the surface, Sweet Briar would seem to be an institution that, given the current trends in higher education, should not be able to survive; it is very small—only around 750 students. Sweet Briar is located in a rural area in Virginia. And it is a single-sex school. A large number of single-sex colleges merged in the last great wave of change in academia during the 1960s and 1970s, when co-education became standard. But a group of Sweet Briar's alumnae opposed the recommendation, wrested control of the board of trustees and committed to raising $12 million to keep the college open. The following year, Sweet Briar reported a record number of applications, and the school had a new lease on life (Diersing 2016). The

Sweet Briar example demonstrates that the competitive landscape for higher education is still dramatically different than other marketplaces. In business, a small competitor, analogous to Sweet Briar, would likely fall by the wayside. But colleges and universities are not directly comparable to other kinds of enterprises. And while colleges and universities do have to respond in some way to the changes in the environment around them, the nature of those responses can be very different than the responses of organizations and institutions in other sectors. The net result is that while many institutions are facing serious financial pressures, there have been very few outright collapses and closures over the past ten years (Selingo 2013): "Of the 1,640 private nonprofit institutions in the United States, only 33 have closed in the last 20 years" (Warren 2016). In his letter to the editor at the *New York Times*, David Warren, president of the National Association of Independent Colleges and Universities, was responding to an article that reported "the number of four-year, nonprofit public and private colleges going out of business could triple, to 15 from five a year, over the next few years" (Hartocollis 2016). That is really not a very high number. And those schools whose financial difficulties have gained widespread attention, such as Franklin Pierce College and Dowling University, have been small institutions. Indeed, colleges and universities are very hardy institutions. Other than the Roman Catholic Church, no other major institutions in Europe or America have been around for 500 to 1,000 years. In the United States alone, 25 colleges and universities founded before 1790 are still in operation today. The traditional universe of colleges and universities is remarkably stable.

On the other hand, while younger and developing countries are investing in expanding their high education offerings, in the United States and Western Europe the traditional public and non-profit segments in higher education have not been the focus of many entrepreneurial efforts, leaving the field to for-profit institutions, which have attracted millions of students but generally are seen as delivering a substandard educational experience. With the emergence of online education, however, that situation is starting to change, as traditional universities large and small add online classes and programs. As opposed to the Christensen model, in which a start-up competitor offers a new product in a niche and then disrupts the existing marketplace, online education has the promise and potential to allow existing institutions to be the disruptive agents. The question is how to manage that process.

The Strategic Challenge for Online Education

Incorporating strategic planning processes into the ongoing management of colleges and universities has proven to be challenging but now is a routine activity for many institutions. Developing strategic plans specifically for online education presents its own set of obstacles. In fact, strategic planning for online education has to take place at two different levels—institutionally and programmatically. First, colleges and universities have to decide what role online education will play in its overall educational project. In other words, where does online education fit in the overall university strategic plan? Second, if online education is incorporated into an institution's long-term strategy, how can the growth of online programs be managed? By every measure, online educational programs are a new entry into the academic universe. How they are to develop also requires strategy and planning. Interestingly, while administrators at most colleges and universities report that they believe online education is critical to their institutions' online strategies, the overall picture has become more complex. Schools that are already involved with online education continue to believe that it will play an important role in their future. But increasingly, however, schools that have not yet begun to offer classes and programs online feel that they may not have to do so in the future. Most of those institutions, however, are small, and, even if they opt out of online education altogether, that would not have a major impact on the overall growth of online education generally (Allen and Seaman 2016, 21–26).

Ad Hoc Online Program Development

The fundamental decision to include online education in the university's overall strategy presumably takes place through the university's regular strategic planning process. But the implementation and growth of online programs can take place at different levels of the institution, which poses a problem that must be resolved if online education is going to reach its potential within the context of traditional higher education. The emergence of online education in traditional higher education has been ad hoc, in which every institution follows its own path. In many cases, the unit charged with continuing education has pioneered online education. Sometimes, programs geared at remedial education and degree completion have been the first to adopt online delivery systems. Professional master's degrees have been an area in which online education has made significant in-roads. Sometimes, a central office is charged with the responsibility for cultivating and promoting online education. In each case, for the effort to succeed and become sustainable, strategic planning needs to take place within the units directly responsible for online education. The need for strategic planning at lower levels in the organization requires rethinking the overall strategic planning process (Floyd and Wooldridge 2000, 38). After all, strategic planning and management was initially conceptualized as a senior management activity, but strategically structuring online education cannot take place solely at a senior administrative level. At the same time, online education requires the coordination of a wide range of departments across the university, from information technology and instructional design to admissions and records to academic support and student life. As it matures, online educational planning should also involve advancement and alumni relations. Consequently, strategic planning at the program level has to be a more horizontal or lateral process than a vertical process. The departments responsible for developing the online educational programs must spend time getting buy-in from others across the university, which may or may not be interested at all in online programs.

Complicating matters, it is not intuitively obvious where the planning process should be lodged. At Harvard, the Harvard Business School struck out on a different plan from the Harvard Extension School. Harvard is also is a partner in the MOOC platform edX. As a university, however, Harvard does not have a singular vision for online education as a part of its overall strategy. Moreover, where the planning process should be appropriately lodged can shift as online educational programs mature. For example, at Tufts University, online education was initially launched at a single school. Over time, the university opted to create a central office to support online educational efforts across the university. At its inception, the office's role was conceptualized solely as a support operation, but, as online education at Tufts expands, that role conceivably could change into a more proactive operation to cultivate and deepen online learning activities.

Online Education: An Uneasy Fit

And strategic planning for online educational programs presents other complications. In the same way that corporate strategic planning has been an uneasy fit in the academic world in general, the strategic planning methods used generally in the academic world need to be modified for online education. Not only can strategic planning for online education not be solely a top-down process; it must be more flexible and nimble than strategic planning in higher education generally. It must address a different set of stakeholders and integrate their roles in a collaborative process. In short, strategic planning on the programmatic level cannot be hierarchical. It must be collaborative. In many ways, just as it is pioneering a new approach to teaching and learning, online education demands a new approach to strategic planning in higher education as well.

Conclusion

Strategic planning emerged as a management discipline in the 1960s, as a response to changes in the corporate environment in the United States. As many major companies expanded, and leadership of those companies transitioned from entrepreneurial founders to professional managers, research indicated that strategy drove the shape, nature and growth of many corporations. Strategic planning was conceptualized as a primary function of senior management. It provided an essential methodology for senior managers to guide an organization to remain competitive and thrive. In the mid to late 1970s, higher education found itself in a time of crisis. With the end of the baby boom, there were fewer people of traditional college age. The cost of college was going up, and many colleges and universities were facing financial problems. In the same way that it was seen as a vehicle to enable companies to remain competitive, strategic planning became a vehicle for colleges and universities to respond to the changing environment. As in the corporate world, the entry of strategic planning into the management of colleges and universities served to empower the senior leadership, placing on senior management the responsibility for ensuring the ongoing vitality of an institution.

In practice, however, strategic planning has been an uneasy fit in the academic world. The structure, culture and competitive landscape of higher education differ greatly from the corporate world, and those differences have a significant impact on the effectiveness of strategic planning in higher education. Nevertheless, under pressure from accrediting agencies and other external stakeholders, strategic planning has become a routine activity in many colleges and universities. As in the 1970s, colleges and universities are in a period of great change. Online education has emerged as one of the primary factors both as a cause of the changing landscape and as a response. Strategic planning can help colleges and universities realize the full potential of their online educational opportunities. That plan must take place at two levels—institutionally and programmatically. On the programmatic level, many of the standard techniques used in strategic planning are not effective, as they do not reflect the position of online education in traditional colleges and universities. Moreover, since online education has been introduced into higher education on an ad hoc basis, each setting calls for an approach appropriate to local circumstances. In many cases, instead of simply empowering senior management, strategic planning on the programmatic level has to be lateral and collaborative. In many ways, strategic planning for online education needs an innovative set of tools and techniques.

References

Allen, E. and Seaman, J. (2013). *Changing Course: Ten Years of Tracking Online Education in the United States*. Babson Survey Research Group and Quahog Research Group. Retrieved from: www.onlinelearningsurvey.com/reports/changingcourse.pdf

Allen, I. E. and Seaman, J. (2016). *Online Report Card Tracking Online Education in the United States*. Babson Survey Research Group and Quahog Research Group, LLC. Retrieved from: www.onlinelearningsurvey.com/highered.html

Anderson, N. (2015, July 27). George Washington University Applicants No Longer Need to Take Admissions Tests. *The Washington Post*. Retrieved from: www.washingtonpost.com/news/grade-point/wp/2015/07/27/george-washington-university-applicants-no-longer-need-to-take-admissions-tests/

Ansoff, H. I. (1965). *Corporate Strategy: An Analytic Approach to Business Policy for Growth and Expansion*. New York: McGraw-Hill.

Art of War Quotes (n.d.). *Goodreads*. Retrieved from: www.goodreads.com/work/quotes/3200649-s-nz-b-ngf

Bedeian, A. and Wren, D. (2001, Winter). Most Influential Management Books of the 20th Century. *Organizational Dynamics*, 29:3, pp. 221–225.

Borchers, C. (2014, March 21). Harvard Business Enters Online Education Fray. *Boston Globe*. Retrieved from: www.bostonglobe.com/business/2014/03/20/harvard-business-school-launches-online-education-program/L2x3xMuBgjR12TLlh01XYO/story.html

Byrne, J. (2015, December 22). Behind Wharton's Massive Bet on Online Learning. *Fortune*. Retrieved from: http://fortune.com/2015/12/22/wharton-online-learning/

Carnegie Classification (2015). The Carnegie Classification of Institutions of Higher Education. *About Carnegie Classification*. Retrieved from: http://carnegieclassifications.iu.edu/

Carter-Smith, K. (2015). Institutional Effectiveness in Higher Education. *Research Starters*. Retrieved from: http://connection.ebscohost.com/c/articles/31962621/institutional-effectiveness-higher-education

Christensen, C., Raynor, M. and McDonald, R. (2015, December). What Is Disruptive Innovation? *Harvard Business Review*, pp. 45–53. Retrieved from: https://hbr.org/2015/12/what-is-disruptive-innovation

Diersing, C. (2016, February 1). Sweet Briar College Gets Record Number of Applicants. *USA Today College*. http://college.usatoday.com/2016/02/01/sweet-briar-record-number-applicants/

Dodd, A. H. (2004). Accreditation as a Catalyst for Institutional Effectiveness. *New Directions for Institutional Research*, 123, pp.13–25. doi: 10.1002/ir.116

Drucker, P. (1954). *The Practice of Management*. New York: Harper and Brothers.

Easy-Strategy (n.d.). Igor Ansoff: The Father of Strategic Planning. Retrieved from: www.easy-strategy.com/igor-ansoff.html

The Economist (2008, August 4). Competitive Advantage. Retrieved from: www.economist.com/node/11869910

Floyd, S. and Wooldridge, B. (2000). *Building Strategy From the Middle: Reconceptualizing Strategy Process*. Thousand Oaks, CA: Sage Publications.

Graham, H. and Diamond, N. (1997). *The Rise of American Research Universities*. Baltimore, MD: The Johns Hopkins University Press.

Hartocollis, A. (2016, April 29). At Small Colleges, Harsh Lessons About Cash Flow. *The New York Times*. Retrieved from: www.nytimes.com/2016/04/30/us/small-colleges-losing-market-share-struggle-to-keep-doors-open.html

Hindle, T. (2009, April 9). Alfred Chandler: The Economist Guide to Management Ideas and Gurus. *The Economist*. Retrieved from: www.economist.com/node/13474552

Hinton, K. (2012). *A Practical Guide to Strategic Planning in Higher Education Society for College and University Planning*. Retrieved from: www.scup.org/page/resources/books/apgsphe

Howard, C. (2015, April 6). Barista to Bachelor's: Starbucks-ASU Partnership Offers Full 4-Year Online College Degrees. *Forbes*. Retrieved from: www.forbes.com/sites/carolinehoward/2015/04/06/from-barista-to-bachelors-starbucks-asu-partnership-offers-full-4-year-online-college-degrees/

Kastens, M. (1979, July–August). The Why and How of Planning. *Journal Managerial Planning*, pp. 33–35.

Keller, G. (1983). *Academic Strategy: The Management Revolution in American Higher Education*. Baltimore, MD: The Johns Hopkins University Press.

Kerr, C. (2001, 5th edition). *The Uses of the University*. Cambridge, MA: Harvard University Press.

King, E. and Alperstein, N. (2015). *Best Practices in Online Program Development*. London and New York: Routledge.

Lewin, T. (2015, April 22). Promising Full College Credit, Arizona State University Offers Online Freshman Program. *The New York Times*. Retrieved from: www.nytimes.com/2015/04/23/us/arizona-state-university-to-offer-online-freshman-academy.html?_r=0

Mintzberg, H. (1987, July–August). Crafting Strategy. *Harvard Business Review*. Retrieved from: https://hbr.org/1987/07/crafting-strategy

Nishihara, N. and Everitt, L. (2014, July 20). Why Interest in Part-Time MBA Programs Is Sagging. *Poets and Quants for Executives*. Retrieved from: http://poetsandquantsforexecs.com/2014/07/20/why-interest-in-part-time-mba-programs-is-sagging/#sthash.8YQ47J4J.dpuf

Nohria, N. (2015, June 22). Online Education: From Skeptic to Super Fan. *HBX Blog*. Retrieved from: www.hbxblog.com/author/nitin-nohria

Peterson, M. (1984, September–October). Review of Academic Strategy: The Management Revolution in Higher Education by George Keller. *The Journal of Higher Education*, 55:5, pp. 662–665.

Porter, M. (1996, November/December). What Is Strategy. *Harvard Business Review*. Retrieved from: https://hbr.org/1996/11/what-is-strategy

Porter, M. (2001, March). Strategy and the Internet. *Harvard Business Review*. Retrieved from: https://hbr.org/2001/03/strategy-and-the-internet/ar/1

Rowley, D. J., Lujan, H. D. and Dolence, M. G. (1997). *Strategic Change in Colleges and Universities.* San Francisco, CA: Jossey-Bass Publishers.

Schwartz, H. and Davis, S. (1981, Summer). Matching Corporate Culture and Business Strategy. *Organizational Dynamics*, 10:1, pp. 30–48.

Science and Engineering Indicators (2012). *Carnegie Classification of Academic Institutions.* Chapter 2: Higher Education in Science and Engineers, National Science Foundation. Retrieved from: www.nsf.gov/statistics/seind12/c2/c2s.htm#sb1

Selingo, J. (2013, April 12). Colleges Struggling to Stay Afloat. *The New York Times.* Retrieved from: www.nytimes.com/2013/04/14/education/edlife/many-colleges-and-universities-face-financial-problems.html?_r=0

Shah, D. (2015, December 29). MOOCs in 2015: Breaking Down the Numbers. *EdSurge.* Retrieved from: www.edsurge.com/news/2015-12-28-moocs-in-2015-breaking-down-the-numbers

Spellings, Margaret (2007). A Test of Leadership: Charting the Future of U.S. Higher Education. Retrieved from: https://www2.ed.gov/about/bdscomm/list/hiedfuture/reports/pre-pub-report.pdf

Steiner, G. A. (1979). *Strategic Planning: What Every Manager Must Know.* New York: The Free Press.

Thelin, J. (2004). *A History of American Higher Education.* Baltimore, MD: The Johns Hopkins University Press.

Thelin, J., Edwards, J. and Moyen, E. (n.d.). *Higher Education in the United States—Historical Development.* Retrieved from: http://education.stateuniversity.com/pages/2044/Higher-Education-in-United-States.html

Useem, J. (2014, May 31). Business School Disrupted. *The New York Times.* Retrieved from: www.nytimes.com/2014/06/01/business/business-school-disrupted.html?_r=0

Veysey, L. (1965). *The Emergence of the American University.* Chicago: The University of Chicago Press.

Warren, D. (2016, May 11). Letter to the Editor, the Future of Small Colleges. *The New York Times.* Retrieved from: www.nytimes.com/2016/05/12/opinion/the-future-of-small-colleges.html?_r=0

Weick, K. (1976, March). Educational Organizations as Loosely Coupled Systems. *Administrative Science Quarterly*, 21:1, pp. 1–19.

Weick, K. (1982, June). Administering Education in Loosely Coupled Schools. *The Phi Delta Kappan*, 63:10, pp. 673–676.

2

The Practice and Practical Problems of Strategic Planning in Higher Education

Strategic planning for online education does not take place in a vacuum. Rather, a strategy for planning online education needs to take place within the larger context of planning in the university or university system as a whole. Consequently, prior to beginning even to conceptualize a strategic plan for online education, the context, culture, climate and processes of strategic planning in higher education must be understood, both generally and specifically at each institution if the plan has any chance of success. In some institutions, those responsible for managing the online educational efforts have been discouraged from creating specific strategic plans for their particular units. The argument against strategic planning in those cases is that any strategic plans for online education would be more appropriately integrated into the overall university strategic plan. Unfortunately, in many situations, insisting that strategic planning for online education be subsumed into the overall university strategic planning process diminishes the likelihood that online education will get the necessary focus and attention needed to create and implement an appropriately detailed, useful and ultimately successful plan.

Overcoming Resistance to Strategic Planning

The potential for resistance to the development of a strategic plan for online education suggests several preliminary and preparatory steps should be taken. Those championing online education must fully understand the conventional strategic planning process and the role of strategic planning within the institution. Stakeholders have to be able to position the strategic plan for online education as a corollary to the university's strategic plan and support the overall university mission, vision and goals. At the same time, leaders of online educational initiatives must be aware and communicate that the strategic plan for online education is distinct, and must take place on its own timeline and with its own structure, which can be independent of the overall university planning process. Before embarking on the hard work of creating a strategic plan for online education, those responsible for the process should fully investigate and understand the planning environment in their institution.

To provide a foundation for building understanding of the local strategic planning environment on an institutional level, this chapter will review the changing culture for strategic planning in higher education generally followed by an overview of the standard strategic planning process. Knowledge and insight into the general strategic planning processes and activities is critical for three reasons. First, strategic planning has developed a specific terminology, almost a language of its own, and being well versed in that language is critical to communicate to the multiple stakeholders of any plan that will be developed and implemented. Secondly, understanding the strategic planning process at the institutional level will allow advocates of online education to determine how best to participate in the university planning process, identify those critical points at which the university planning process can be influenced, and present the strategy of online education as an integral part of the institutional process. Finally, the process for developing a strategic plan, or perhaps more appropriately planning strategically for online education, is derived from the standard strategic planning approaches. Incorporating standard strategic planning language, as well as incorporating planning activities into the strategy for online education, will ground the plan in a well-established management practice.

The review of the general strategic planning process will be followed by an analysis of the challenges that traditional approaches to the planning process pose within the academic setting. The chapter illuminates the difficulty in relying on the overall university strategic plan to provide a blueprint for online education. However, the stewards of online education should capitalize and exploit the areas in which a strategic plan for online education can be linked to the overall strategic plan. Although the strategic plan for online education is separate and, in some cases, even independent from the overall university strategic plan, it must be constructed and presented in a way that aligns with the university plan, or else the road to implementing the plan will be strewn with obstacles and the path to success will be more difficult.

The chapter will conclude with initial insights into ways to modify traditional strategic planning for use by leaders of online educational programs. As noted in Chapter 1, the history of strategic planning in the private sector is marked with expensive failures. Plans are laboriously crafted over a long period of time and released with great fanfare only to wind up on the proverbial dusty shelf never to be consulted and with little impact on the ongoing operation of the organization. Instead of adhering to the plan, major decisions are made opportunistically and ad hoc, which, ironically, are how many decisions about online education are currently made. The goal for planners is to have help guiding the future of the organization. For the advocates of online education, the objective in developing a plan is to cajole the institution at large to appropriately respond to the challenges online education presents to every college and university. This is a critical point and worth repeating: a strategic plan on the institutional level is intended to be a blueprint for the future, and, once crafted, the mandate is to successfully implement the plan. For online education, the product of a strategic planning process is both a blueprint and a persuasive document intended to build alliances with other areas in the university, gather resources and win broader support for a vision of the future.

The Strategic Planning Culture in Higher Education

In the fall of 2007, the Office of Quality Improvement at the University of Wisconsin–Madison, surveyed the members of the National Consortium for Continuous Improvement in Higher Education about their strategic planning process (Cotter and Paris 2007). Fifteen of the approximately 100 members responded, detailing their strategic planning efforts. Among the key findings:

- Only two-thirds of the respondents had a campus-wide strategic plan.
- Sixty percent of those with a strategy have been engaged in planning for ten years or less.
- Many key processes, most notably process improvement initiatives, were not aligned with the plan.

One implication of the study was that although engaging in strategic planning was no longer novel in higher education, by the mid-2000s the process of strategic planning and the discipline to implement strategic plans was not yet deeply rooted in the culture of higher education. At that time, whether strategic planning resulted in demonstrable benefits for a university remained an open question and the subject of considerable debate (Dooris 2002–2003).

The Wisconsin study also revealed some insights into the ways strategic planning in higher education can differ from the role it often plays in the corporate world. For example, strategic plans in the private sector seldom have more than a five-year time horizon, while many university strategic plans exceeded five years. Not infrequently, strategic planning in higher education runs in a ten-year cycle, which, to some degree, often more closely parallels accreditation cycles (Cotter and Paris 2007). As a case in point, the strategic plan for George Mason University, a public university based in Fairfax, Virginia, covers the period from 2014 to 2024. Its most recent accreditation process was completed in 2011 and runs to 2021, with a mid-period review scheduled for 2017. Schedules of this length are not unusual, as both the University of Notre Dame and Vanderbilt University have ten-year plans, as do smaller schools like Utica College.

While many schools do structure their strategic plans to cover a five-year period, the longer timeframes are evidence of one of the primary motivations for colleges and universities to engage in strategic planning processes at all. Rather than an internal, organic process driven by senior management to provide direction to the organization as a whole, as strategic planning has come to be used in the corporate world, in the academic setting, strategic planning often represents more of a response to the demands of external stakeholders such as accreditors and governmental regulators (Jennings and Wattam 1998).

Potentially longer timeframes are not the only way that strategic plans differ in the academic world from the plans crafted in the private sector. On a very fundamental basis, one of the primary raisons d'être for corporate strategic plans is to give senior management the tools to ensure that corporate processes are aligned with the mission, vision, objectives and goals of the company as defined in the strategic plan. Strategic plans, by definition, historically were developed as tools for management control. The Wisconsin survey indicated, however, that in many instances, at least some significant processes in each university had not been successfully aligned with the strategic plan. Moreover, senior management in higher education has fewer levers to ensure that the necessary processes are aligned with the plan.

In the decade or so since the Wisconsin survey was conducted, the internal and external pressures on colleges and universities have continued to mount. Perhaps most challenging, the general economy and the economics of attending colleges and universities have not rebounded since the recession of 2008. While the "sticker price" for tuition has continued to rise, the net revenues for many colleges has remained flat or dropped due to a variety of reasons. To attract students, for example, private colleges and universities have been forced to discount their tuition more aggressively. By 2014, the discount rate for full time first-year students had climbed to 48 percent, a full ten percentage points higher than it had been ten years earlier, according to a survey by the National Association of College and University Business Officers. Despite the rise in discounting, approximately half of the respondents reported declining enrollments in 2013 and 2014 (Woodhouse 2015).

The tuition picture in public universities was no more encouraging. The tuition at a public four-year institution was, on average, approximately 40 percent higher in 2015–2016 than in 2005–2006 (Jennings and Wattam 2015). At the same time, state aid for public universities dropped sharply: in 2015, 47 states were still providing less support for higher education than they had at the beginning of the 2008 recession (Kirst and Stevens 2015). Pricing pressure was only one of the major factors having an impact on colleges and universities. While enrollment at public and non-profit colleges and universities is expected to grow between 2014 and 2025, the rate of growth will be sharply lower than it had been from 2005 to 2014 (Mitchell 2016). At the same time, student demographics are changing dramatically. In 2014, the University of California system announced it had enrolled more Hispanic students for the academic year than ever before. Women continue to represent a larger percent of the undergraduate population, constituting 57 percent of undergraduate students in 2014 compared to 40 percent in the 1970s. Finally, the number of college students over the age of 25 is increasing sharply. In 2009, 40 percent of undergraduate and graduate students were older than 25. That number may climb to 43 percent by 2020 (Holland 2014).

Growth of Online Education

The growth of online education represents a third factor exerting an impact on higher education. The number of students who have taken at least one course online has increased five-fold over the past 15 years, and the rate of increase is much faster than the increase in face-to-face setting (Tyce et al. 2016). But the absolute number of students taking online classes is not the most significant factor. The emergence of online education has had an impact well beyond the development of online-only classes and online-only programs. The increasingly commonplace use of educational technologies in hybrid and blended classes leads some researchers to believe that online technology could potentially lead to a deepening and widening of the entire education experience. The promise of online education is not just as an alternative delivery mechanism; it is also a fundamental driver to improving learning outcomes (VanderArk and Schneider 2012).

These pressures have driven many colleges and universities to increasingly turn to corporate management techniques to better manage the change in the sector. The most visible aspect of this trend is the willingness of institutions of higher education to appoint presidents with little or no academic experience but strong business experience. Colleges and universities ranging from Mt. St. Mary's University in Emmitsberg (a relatively small, private, Catholic university in rural Maryland) and Hampshire College (in western Massachusetts) to huge state universities like the University of Iowa and the University of Missouri have turned to leaders who rose to prominence primarily in the private sector. In 2012, individuals from outside of academia headed approximately 20 percent of all college and universities, up from 13 percent six years earlier (Cook 2012).

The reason for the turn to non-academics to be college presidents is often pretty straightforward. Those empowered to hire college presidents argue that, typically, professional academics are not as capable of dealing with the change in higher education as successful executives from the private sector. Those who favor non-academics to lead colleges and universities feel executives from the business world are better prepared to innovate, control costs and effectively manage a complex institution (McKenna 2015).

While some of those appointments have resulted in high-profile disasters, with the presidents being forced to resign in the wake of controversial events or actions, the trend they represent is firmly in place. Given the pressures building in higher education, colleges and universities are being called on to rethink their business model. And while even the use of the term "business model" can raise objections to some constituencies within academia, in the context of higher education a business model can be conceptualized as the processes, technologies and resources used to deliver value (Soares et al. 2016). In marketing parlance, there is clamor from the government, students, the public and other stakeholders for colleges and universities to better define and deliver on their "value proposition." Over time, as the senior management in higher education responds to that clamor, the role of and need for effective strategic planning will continue to increase.

Approaches to Strategic Planning

In 1993, S. Fredrick Starr, then the president of Oberlin College, argued that the central tenet of strategic planning was to redefine a university's intellectual and moral identity to allow it to align itself with its environment (Starr 1993). There is no small degree of irony in that statement. By the time he expressed that notion, Starr was near the end of his tenure at Oberlin, a tenure that was marked by fierce criticism of him, precipitated by the perception that the president was trying to turn Oberlin into "Harvard of the Midwest." Although during his 11-year administration Starr chalked up several noteworthy achievements including putting the institution on a stronger financial footing, doubling the size of the endowment, strengthening the science curriculum, increasing the size of the faculty and working to diversify the institution, the end of his administration was marred when both the students and the faculty came to question his vision for the college overall. Starr had launched a strategic planning process, drafted by a group called the Strategic Issues Steering Committee, that called for, among other things, the elimination of needs-blind admissions, an increase in the number of merit scholarships, and significant changes in the first-year experience for students. Both students and faculty objected vigorously to the report. Starr stepped down from the presidency within a year of the release of the plan, whose implementation was delayed. The plan was ultimately scrapped entirely (Hansen 2006).

The Process of Strategic Planning

At its base, strategic planning involves three basic processes: organizations must first decide what should reflect the fundamental thrust of organizational activity for a specified period of time (what does a particular organization want to be in the period ahead?); second, they must carefully examine and assess their own organizational capabilities; and, third, strategic planning involves analyzing and understanding the environment in which an organization operates (figure 2.1). Those three processes provide the framework for determining the organizational goals, the steps that need to be taken to achieve those goals, and the measures that will be used to determine if the goals have been achieved.

Traditionally, those processes are incorporated into five steps (Harvard Business Essentials, xvii). First, companies will create a mission statement or a vision

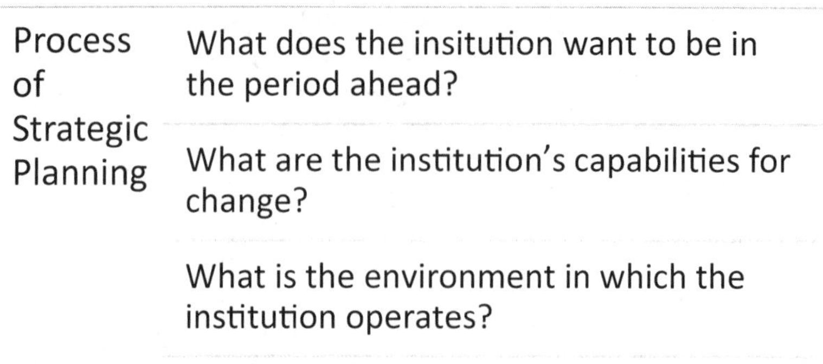

Process of Strategic Planning	What does the insitution want to be in the period ahead?
	What are the institution's capabilities for change?
	What is the environment in which the institution operates?

Figure 2.1 Process of Strategic Planning

statement. The mission statement or vision statement encapsulates the purpose of the organization and what it hopes to achieve for its stakeholders. Next, the strategic planning methodology calls for an analysis of both the internal and the external environment. This activity is often called a SWOT analysis as the organization assesses its strengths, weaknesses, opportunities and threats. The internal and external SWOT analysis is intended to realistically understand the organization's key competencies and capabilities as well as how it matches up to its competitors. Moreover, effective planning involves a good understanding of the external landscape and general environment in which the organization operates. The planning exercise rests to a large degree on successfully determining the most significant changes to which the organization will be compelled to respond over a specified period of time.

The SWOT analysis is followed by the creation of specific goals and objectives to be achieved. The difference between goals and objectives is one of the more confusing aspects of the terminology used in strategic planning, and different experts define the terms differently, and some even flip the meanings of the words. In short, most commonly a goal is an end point that an organization wants to achieve that will help support the overall vision laid out in the mission or vision statement; it is broad and general. Objectives, on the other hand, are the tasks that have to be completed to achieve the goal; they are specific and measurable. For example, a regional university may have a goal to become a nationally recognized university. Among the objectives to support that goal may be increasing the number of applications from specific states as well as distributing the number of students accepted across a broader geographic area than are historically represented.

Once the goals and underlying objectives have been laid out, the tactics needed to achieve the objectives must be determined. Tactics are the specific activities used to fulfill the objectives needed to reach the goal. Let's say one of the goals of a university is to improve its financial stability. One of the objectives to reach that goal is to increase its endowment. One of the tactics then may

Figure 2.2 5 Steps in the Strategic Planning Process

be to enlarge the advancement office to increase fundraising. Another tactic may be to reorganize how the endowment is managed to improve investment returns.

The final step in creating a strategic plan is determining performance measures, which are yardsticks through which tactics, objectives and goals can be gauged. Sticking with the example of improving the financial stability of a university by increasing its endowment, the tactic of enlarging the advancement staff can be measured by the headcount in the advancement office. The tactic of reorganizing how the endowment is managed and the returns the endowment realizes can be easily assessed as well.

All in all, a strategic plan visually often appears like a pyramid (figure 2.2). The mission or vision statement sits at the top. It rests on a select number of goals, which are supported by a larger number of objectives or milestones that must be accomplished to reach the goals. Each objective can be associated with several tactics to achieve the objectives and performance measures to assess the progress to the objectives and ultimately the goals of the plan.

Alternative Planning Models

While the cascading pyramid represents the most common format for strategic planning, it is not the only one. In their book *Strategic Change in Colleges and Universities*, Rowley et al. (1997) developed an alternative model that they characterize as a strategic planning engine. Their model is based on earlier work by Dolence and Norris in which they developed a set of, what they referred to as, key performance indicators (KPIs) and applied them to strategic planning at the University of Northern Colorado and Illinois Benedictine College (Dolence and Norris 1994). Conceptually, key performance indicators consist of a set of measures that gauge the most critical aspects of an organization's performance (Parmenter 2010).

Rather than starting with a vision statement, Rowley, Lujan and Dolence's strategic planning engine starts with developing a set of key performance indicators that can be used to assess the ongoing institutional quality and improvement. For example, student retention or four-year graduation rate can be thought of as a key performance indicator. The engine's succeeding nine steps, however, largely follow the typical corporate planning model. Following the development of the KPIs, institutions conduct internal and external environment assessments followed by a SWOT analysis. At that point, goals, objectives and strategies are formulated and analyzed to understand their potential impact on the KPIs. A plan's success can be judged by the actual improvements measured through the KPIs.

Starting from KPIs rather than a mission statement, Rowley argues, more directly ties planning to the activities most critical to its operation, development and long-term survival. In the place of an aspirational vision, KPI-driven plans start by trying to clarify the expectations of the institution's key stakeholders, and the KPIs are premised measuring actual performance against those expectations. KPIs serve as the links between the strategic plan and the actual operational performance. And they can provide a richer method, grounded in information for comparing the institution to its competitors and its own past performance as well as its view of itself (Rowley et al. 1994). Starting with KPIs instead of a vision statement, a variation to the standard approach to strategic planning, is often promoted both in the corporate world and in higher education.

A gap analysis is a simple management approach that characterizes the differences between the current state of the organization and the desired end state. In general, a gap analysis is a four-step process. The organization must have an honest evaluation of the current state of the organization based on a common set of metrics. The desired future performance must be determined. The exercise is to determine the gap between the current state and the desired state. Once the gaps are identified, strategies can be developed to close those gaps. A gap analysis can be conducted at several points in the strategic planning process. Hussey, for example, proposed inserting a gap analysis after the goals of the strategic plan have been developed but prior to the formulation of the objectives that support each goal (1999). The purpose of the gap analysis is to more clearly delineate both the starting point and the end point of the plan as well as to help clarify the challenges needed to achieve the desired future.

In the corporate world, a gap analysis is most comfortably applied to the revenue projections associated with a strategic plan: a company currently generates X amount of revenue and hopes to increase revenue by a defined amount by a specified date. With the gap analysis in mind, different strategies can be analyzed to determine their role closing the gaps. But a gap analysis can be conducted for any key process, and, consequently, it is particularly useful and appropriate for organizations that have created a functional set of KPIs. Within the planning process, a gap analysis can be conducted for each KPI. In addition to an internal gap analysis, many companies include benchmarking as part of their strategic planning process. Benchmarking consists of identifying specific processes or KPIs, measuring them and then comparing the outcome to an external measure, most frequently competitors or leaders in the area (Collie n.d.). Benchmarking provides a context within which the current performance of an organization can be better understood. It also provides insight into the ways that the leading organization functions, which can inform the gap analysis and help clarify goals or objectives.

On the surface, the methodology for benchmarking is straightforward. The first step is to determine what processes or aspects of the organization are to be measured and to what or to whom the organization is to be compared. Next, the data that will be compared is collected internally and externally, and a gap analysis is conducted. The final step is to create a plan to address the gaps. In practice, effective benchmarking demands a serious investment in time and resources to be done correctly. Not only must data be collected internally, organizations must reach out to the comparative group, which often includes competitors or others in their industry. Because of the potentially competitive and proprietary nature of the information that can be best used for benchmarking, often industry associations such as the Network for Change and Continuous Improvement and the Society for College and University Planning are good venues to collect comparative information in higher education.

Despite the difficulty it may present, the effort to collect benchmarking-oriented information can yield significant benefits. Benchmarking grounds planning in the real-world competitive environment within which an organization operates. It can serve as an educational process in which key players can learn about the best practices in a given area and the circumstances in which those best practices can actually be implemented. Through benchmarking, organizations can learn what other participants in their competitive set are doing as well as better understand the path the organization wishes to follow by gaining insight into those organizations that are ahead of them. Finally, benchmarking adds a sense of realism to what can become a completely aspirational exercise laced with wishful thinking. Done correctly, benchmarking is intentional, outwardly focused, deliberate and oriented toward realistic change.

The Business Model Approach

Since they began to make headway in the corporate world 50 years ago and in higher education 20 to 30 years ago, most strategic planning processes have included some variations of the procedures outlined above. More recently, an alternative approach to guiding investment and transformation in higher education has emerged. This approach focuses on using a business model analysis to empower leaders to make data-informed decisions that align institutional practices with desired outcomes (Soares et al. 2016).

The notion of a "business model" represents a method of framing corporate resources and processes in ways that could be simulated and analyzed and projected (figure 2.3). The term was popularized by Clayton Christensen as part of his more general theory of disruptive innovation. In its simplest form, a "business model" has four parts. It starts with a company or organization's value proposition—in other words, what the company does for its customers so those customers will purchase whatever it is the company is producing. It then looks at what is called the organization's value chain, or the set of processes, resources and partners needed to fulfill the value proposition. The third element in a business model is the profit formula, or, more generally, how the company or organization can organize itself in a sustainable way by ensuring that it collects more in revenue that it costs to produce the product. The competitive strategy is the final component. The competitive strategy lays out how the company or organization will maintain and defend its value proposition.

Working from a business or economic model rather than a comprehensive or traditional strategic plan provides a framework to provide direction for a company or organization. It requires senior leadership to disaggregate the functions of the organization and to determine on a deep and organic level the ways in which value is created and the processes and procedures that support that value creation. Competitive strategy is only one aspect of that approach, though a critical one.

The business model incorporating or operating with competitive strategies has utilitarian potential and flexibility. The idea is gaining traction in higher education for three other reasons. First, such a model focuses policymakers' attention squarely on the bottom line. This is especially important as college affordability continues to be a major political issue. Creating a viable business model, by definition, puts a college or university on a sustainable footing

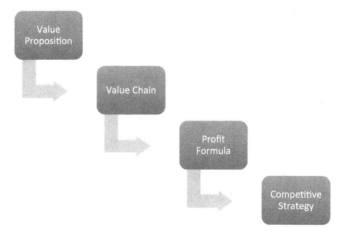

Figure 2.3 Business Model of Strategic Planning

financially. Second, the concept of a business model is very comfortable for the new generation of leadership in higher education that has emerged from the business world. It requires that business leaders understand the costs associated with virtually every area of the institution. Soares et al. (2016) argue, "The required data go far beyond what can be gleaned from financial statements or even from conventional cost accounting. What's needed are structural models that describe how resources are applied to particular activities in sufficient detail to allow in-depth understanding of what's being done at what cost, and 'what-if analysis' of what might be done to effect improvements" (2016). Third, by assessing different activities through their relationship to a business model, colleges and universities can better assess both the need for innovation and the impact of innovation on their operations. Disruptive innovation can lead to change in business models. By recognizing disruptive innovation and incorporating that change into a business model, organizations can both ensure their own viability and potentially gain a competitive edge (Soares and Margetta 2011).

The growth of Southern New Hampshire University provides a vivid example of the dynamic aspects of the business model approach. A decade ago, SNHU was a struggling private university catering to traditional students. It could not differentiate itself in a meaningful way. Then, the school's administration reoriented its focus from the undergraduate program to the small online education program it was running at the time, and it focused on creating value for adult and non-traditional students. The switch involved reworking most of SNHU's policies, practices and procedures. The result was an operation that within six years was generating more the $500,000 in revenue and growing at a rate of 35 percent a year (Christensen et al. 2016). By changing the strategic approach to a business model, SNHU was transformed from being a humdrum also-ran institution to being seen as an exemplar of the future of higher education. The growth of online education is only one indication of changes taking place. The number of non-traditional students skyrocketed over the past decade. At the same time, taxpayer support for higher education dropped. Understanding how those changes impact a college or university's business model can provide insight into the appropriate adjustments the institution should make in order to remain economically viable.

The Balanced Scorecard

In the 1990s, yet another approach to corporate planning emerged—the "Balanced Scorecard," based on two fundamental insights. First, Robert Kaplan and David Norton, the idea's architects, argued that traditional performance measurements in the corporate arena relied too heavily on financial results. Based on a research study in which companies whose intangible assets played a central role in value creation, Kaplan and Norton asserted that if companies were to improve their performance in those intangible areas, measurements associated with those areas had to be integrated into their overall management systems (Kaplan 2010).

The balanced scorecard augmented traditional financial measurements with metrics derived from three additional areas (figure 2.4). The first was internal business processes. The second was the customer, and the final new area was something they called "learning and growth." Measuring internal processes, the authors argued, could help measure efficiency. How well did an organization carry out its essential tasks? Focusing on the customer gauged satisfaction. Was the company delivering on its value proposition? Learning and growth acknowledges that, in many knowledge-based organizations, the employees are the repositories of knowledge and that the knowledge base of the company must be responsive to rapidly changing environments (Kaplan 2010). Or as Kaplan himself put it, "[B]alanced scorecards tell you the knowledge, skills, and systems that your employees will need (their learning and growth) to innovate and build the right strategic capabilities and efficiencies (the internal processes) that deliver specific value to the market (the customers), which will eventually lead to higher shareholder value (the financials)" (Kaplan 2010).

In a short period, the balanced scorecard approach was widely embraced by a diverse set of companies and organizations. According to the market research company Gartner, more than half of all large American companies use a version of the balanced scorecard. A study by the management consultants Bain and Company found it to be in the top-ten management techniques used globally. And the *Harvard Business Review* has listed the balanced scorecard as one of the most important business ideas of the past 75 years (Kaplan et al. n.d.). The warm and relatively rapid acceptance of the concept led to a conundrum and

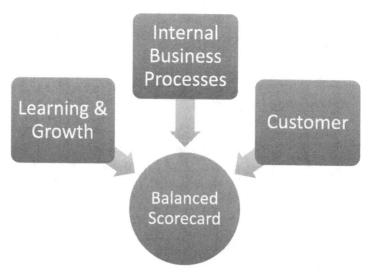

Figure 2.4 The Balanced Scorecard

eventually to the second deep insight to be incorporated into the approach. Since the idea behind the balanced scorecard was to measure the intangible assets of a company to improve performance, the question became: which intangibles should be measured and how should the measurement be done? As Kaplan and Norton worked with companies attempting to implement a balanced scorecard approach, they came to the understanding that there was not one set of generic metrics that would be appropriate for every company. They discovered that many companies, both those that were working well and those that were falling, were already trying to measure things like customer retention and satisfaction, defect rates, and lead times, with varied results. Frequently, those metrics did not capture the most important drivers to guide the direction of the company.

Moreover, the balanced scorecard approach, in Kaplan and Norton's view, was not intended to be a benchmarking-lite approach. Looking at the retail market, it would not necessarily be useful for a low-cost retailer like Wal-Mart to be measured in the same way as a full service retailer like Nordstrom's. Kaplan and Norton's solution was the idea that the metrics by which performance of the intangible elements of the organization could be judged should be driven by the strategic plan. With this breakthrough, the balanced scorecard became a framework through which companies could articulate their strategic objectives. Frequently, companies using a balanced scorecard approach learned to begin the process by describing what they hoped to achieve in each area. Those descriptions could then be turned into statements, often in a specific voice of the stakeholder being addressed, and the particular measures are based on those statements.

But the reconceptualization or re-articulation of strategic objectives is only one of the impacts that the notion of a balanced scorecard has had on strategic planning. Once the strategic objectives were laid out, the links between the objectives and their role in supporting the overall strategic vision could be clarified. Kaplan and Norton called this technique a strategy map. A strategy map is a blueprint that demonstrates how an organization will convert its initiatives and resources, both tangible and intangible, into the desired outcome (Kaplan 2010). According to Kaplan, companies should start their strategy mapping by first determining their destination—what is the vision for the company. The map should then demonstrate how it will arrive at that destination, taking into account the different perspectives involved. Overall, classic strategic planning, creating key performance indicators, benchmarking, creating a business model and the balanced scorecard coupled with strategic mapping share several concepts in common. Each approach is premised on the idea that companies must agree upon a desired outcome: understand both their internal and their external environments, and the craft-specific steps to be taken to succeed in a fluid and changing world. While classic strategic planning serves as the foundation for the other schemes, each approach has a somewhat different emphasis and perspective. But the very fact that different approaches have emerged is evidence of how hard the process is in practice.

Why Planning Fails

For better or worse, the concepts and methodology behind corporate strategic planning have been crossing over into the academic world for the past 30 years. But ironically, strategic planning in the corporate world itself has only met with limited success. Too often, strategic planning processes conclude with large-scale plans that have little impact on the actual operation of the organization. By some estimates, as many as 70 percent of all strategic plans are not successfully executed (Sterling 2003); that number may be generous. Robert Kaplan, who pioneered the concept of the balanced scorecard approach to planning, suggested that as many as 90 percent of all strategic plans fail completely or in part (Leverington 2013). The perceived failure rate for strategic planning is so high that it raises the question: why invest the time in strategic planning at all? The answer is that the benefits for strategic planning can be huge if the major pitfalls in developing and implementing the plan can be avoided. In fact, one of the most pervasively pithy little maxims of business is that "failing to plan is planning to fail."

Writing in *Forbes* magazine, consultants for Aileron, a center geared to helping small business expand that was founded by billionaire pet food entrepreneur Clay Mathile, presented ten reasons why so many strategic plans do not achieve their goal (figure 2.5). The top item on the list is developing a plan just for the sake of having a plan. The idea that companies and organizations should create strategic plans is now deeply embedded into the culture of professional management, but the high rate of failure means that many managers are skeptical about the benefits that strategic planning can produce. Moreover, top leadership may feel that their latitude for decision-making may be constrained by a strategic plan, while managers further down in the organizational hierarchy may not see how a strategic plan relates directly to their department within the organization. Where there is resistance to strategic planning, companies and organizations may perfunctorily go through the strategic planning process without the doing the background work and preparation needed to understand and communicate why the strategic plan is necessary and how it will be applied. If strategic planning becomes a check-the-box exercise for senior management, the likelihood that the plan will have the desired impact fades.

Without a commitment to the planning process, the plan has little chance of succeeding. But an a priori commitment is only the first step in improving the chances for success. In too many cases, after a plan is written, it just winds up proverbially gathering dust on a shelf. The reason so many plans are ignored, according to Kaplan and his collaborators, is that, traditionally, strategic planning processes are carried out in isolation, separate from the ongoing activities of

10 Reasons Strategic Plans Fail	Having a plan simply for plans sake
	Not understanding the environment or focusing on results
	Partial commitment
	Not having the right people involved
	Writing the plan and putting it on the shelf
	Unwillingness or inability to change
	Having the wrong people in leadership positions
	Ignoring marketplace reality, facts, and assumptions
	No accountability or follow through
	Unrealistic goals or lack of focus and resources

Figure 2.5 10 Reasons Why Strategic Plans Fail (Aileron, Forbes.com 2011)

the organization. This gulf means that many strategic plans are never embraced at the level of the organization at which they must be executed. According to their research, two-thirds of the information technology and human resource professionals they surveyed reported that their units are not aligned with business unit and corporate strategies. Around 60 percent of the organizations do not link their financial budgets to their strategic priorities. The compensation packages of 70 percent of the middle managers and 90 percent of the frontline employees are not connected in any way to the success or failure of specific strategic efforts. Fully 95 percent of the workforce does not understand the corporate strategy. And finally, in most settings, Kaplan and Norton observed, senior executive teams spend one hour or less monthly discussing strategy. If the purpose of a strategic plan is to lay out the vision for the organization for the mid- to long-term future, it cannot be effective if people ignore it, do not tailor their efforts to support the plan, and never monitor progress toward the strategic goals (Kaplan et al. 2005).

Clearly, many strategic plans are doomed to fail from the outset. But for others, the planning process itself is flawed. According to the consultants at Aileron, many organizations do not spend enough time understanding the external and internal environments in which they operate and focus too heavily on results. These shortcomings manifest themselves in many different ways. The relationship between the changing external environment and the operating results is at the heart of the dilemma that Clay Christiansen has described as the innovator's dilemma. It is hard to determine what changes in the external environment will actually have a meaningful impact on the long- and short-term results for the company. Changes that may be important for the long-term survival of a company may inflict significant short-term hardships. On the other hand, it is not easy to roll the dice on the corporate future.

The internal assessment of company capacity is just as important as the external environmental scan. Plans cannot succeed if the organization does not have the sufficient resources to accomplish the strategic objectives and the tasks associated with them. Exacerbating the problem, since strategic planning often takes place outside the ongoing day-to-day activities of the organization, strategic planners may not have a full understanding of exactly what the capacity of the organization actually is at a given point or how much investment would be needed to enable the organization to reach a specific goal. Unfortunately, conducting internal and external assessments of the strengths, weaknesses and opportunities for an organization takes time, money and commitment, which are often in short supply in many settings. People are too busy running the business to do research. Consequently, many strategic plans are based on insufficient or faulty data or assumptions. Not surprisingly, if the data and assumptions underlying the plan are wrong, the chance of the plan succeeding is not great.

A major reason that the vast majority of strategic plans fail is that the wrong people are involved in the planning process and the plan's execution. The consultants at Aileron recommend that the people who will actually be responsible for the strategic plan should be involved in the planning process. But depending on the size and scope of the organization, it may or may not be appropriate to include frontline and middle managers in the planning process. After all, strategic planning was launched explicitly as a methodology that enabled senior managers in complex, multifaceted organizations to assert management control over the direction of the company. Strategic planning is a tool for senior leadership to manage operational personnel. While the strategic planning groups cannot be isolated and removed from the ongoing operations of the organization, there is an ongoing debate about who specifically should be on the strategic planning team. Some consultants believe that the chief executive officer should drive the process. After all, the CEO is ultimately accountable for the performance of the business (Simply Strategic Planning n.d.). On the other hand, hard-driving senior leadership can dominate the process and exclude alternative voices, limiting the potential scope of the plan. In addition to representing a wide range of organizational perspectives, without strong leadership the planning process can be diverted and become diffuse. In many ways, strategic planning involves choices—what an organization should do and, conversely, what the organization should not do. In some cases, choosing one course of action by definition precludes an alternative course, but that is not always the case. Strong leadership can help the planning team stay focused on the most important decisions. Strong leaders are needed to communicate and sometimes to spearhead the plan's implementation. For a plan to work, ongoing communication has to take place through several channels and over the plan's entire time period (Everse 2011). The initial step is for senior management to find ways to effectively communicate the strategy throughout the organization, and the message should have three parts. First, the organization's leaders must demonstrate how the strategic plan supports the organization's overall mission. The ongoing mission anchors most organizations, and, for the strategy to make sense to the employees and other stakeholders, it must clearly align with the mission. Secondly, top management must demonstrate commitment to implementing the plan. Important decisions have to be justified in terms of the strategic plan. Finally, senior management must communicate the plan to division and unit managers and frontline employees in a way that makes the impact of their specific activities clear and appropriate. Frequently, strategic plans do not drill down to the activities employees actually carry out on a daily basis. And the relationship between individual jobs and tasks and the overall performance of the company is not intuitively obvious (Everse 2011). For a strategic plan to succeed, all parties must understand it and buy into the vision. Unfortunately, according to a study conducted by the Metrus Group, only about 14 percent of the employees in a company typically understand their organization's strategy and direction (Witt 2012).

Ensuring that the strategic plan is understood throughout the organization is only one facet of the communication process. For a strategic plan to actually have an impact, it must be monitored, measured, and reviewed, and the different units and departments have to be held accountable to the tasks, goals and objectives laid out in the plan itself. Follow-up has to be regular, ongoing and meaningful. Some consultants argue that meeting to monitor the strategic plan and measure progress toward the goals should take place as frequently as every month. Without that kind of ongoing attention and follow-through, 70 to 80 percent of the goals in a strategic plan will not be reached (Baldwin n.d.).

The final reason so many strategic plans fail to achieve their aims is organizational inertia. Godkin and Allcorn describe three sources of organizational inertia—insight inertia, action inertia and psychological inertia (2008). Insight inertia is the inability to respond to changes in the environment or organizational behavior. People don't change because they do not recognize the factors that are driving the need for change. Their perception of the external environment is incomplete or flawed, or systematic surveillance has been curtailed or ceased altogether. For example, in the late 1970s, Digital Equipment Corp. was the second-leading computer manufacturer in the country. When the personal computer was created, DEC's CEO did not perceive the need for such a small computer, famously telling a World Future Society meeting in 1977 that he did not see any reason why somebody would need a computer in their home. Around 20 years later, DEC was sold to a personal computer manufacturer. Action inertia occurs after an environmental scan has been completed. Even if appropriate data has been collected and the drivers of change are identified and understood, too frequently the organizations cannot move fast enough to respond to the need for change in a timely fashion, generally due to a failure of management. Responses can be poorly conceived or designed or not successfully implemented. Or managers may assume that certain actions to address changes in the external environment won't work, given the specific context.

The final source of organizational inertia is psychological. Many people don't like change. Employees are comfortable in the way they perform their tasks, and they do not see themselves as the stewards of the organization generally. They just want to do their jobs to the best of their abilities. If they do not clearly understand the reasons for change and they are not given the proper incentives and motivations to change, they may resist doing things differently. If inertia is an anathema to strategic planning and organizational change, ironically it can overtake the strategic planning process itself. As Clay Christensen noted, most managers do not have a competency in strategic planning, and, once they have a strategy that seems to work for them, they want to stick with that strategy and not change it (Christensen 1997). It is important to note that inertia is not the same as paralysis. Inertia is not the inability to respond but the inability to respond effectively or appropriately; management consultant Donald Sull refers to it as "active inertia" (Sull 1999). Active inertia is an organization's predilection toward adhering to and reinforcing existing patterns of behavior. Sull describes four components of active inertia. The first is blinders or the inability to see the environment in new ways or identify meaningful changes. The concept of blinders explains why generals often strategically plan to fight the last war rather than the next one. The second source of active inertia is routines or tendency to continue to implement processes as they have been traditionally been implemented. The third component is what Sull calls shackles or the aversion to calling into question existing relationships with an organization's key stakeholders. And the final piece is dogma, or the slavish adherence to corporate culture. At times, strategic planning challenges all of those components, but frequently inertia is more powerful.

Many formidable challenges and barriers stand in the way of crafting and implementing a successful strategic plan. The plan may not align with the actual operation of the organization. Senior management may not be committed to the plan. The plan may not be successfully communicated throughout the organization or effectively monitored and measured. It may be impossible to overcome the different dimensions of organizational inertia. At best, once those factors come into play, the plan will not be able to deliver its full benefits. At the most extreme, those factors can have a negative impact on the long-term survival of the organization.

The Challenges of Planning Processes in Higher Ed

While necessary, successful strategic planning is difficult to effectively realize in the corporate world. With that in mind, successful strategic planning is made more difficult, because of the organizational nature of the academic world. As suggested in Chapter 1, organizationally, colleges and universities are not naturally structured to support traditional strategic planning, so it is not surprising that the processes typically associated with strategic planning present unique complexities when they are attempted in institutions of higher education. In fact, every aspect of strategic planning is more difficult in the academic world than in the corporate world. Moreover, the procedures, techniques and sequences generally laid out for strategic planning in the corporate world cannot be easily modified to fit higher education. Every step in the best practices of strategic planning—from developing the core strategic planning team to developing a vision statement based on the organization's mission statement, to conducting an internal and external analysis of the organization's strengths and weaknesses, opportunities, and threats, to implementing and reviewing the plan—are carried out differently in higher education. For example, as Rowley et al. note, most of the management literature about strategic planning is premised on the idea that senior management, particularly the chief executive officer, will drive the process. Even George Keller, who first propagated that idea that colleges and universities should embrace the principles of strategic planning, argued senior administration officials should drive the process (Rowley et al. 1997). But most traditional colleges and universities, Rowley noted, operate according to the principles of shared governance. In fact, the core activities of colleges and universities—teaching and research—are controlled not by senior management but by the faculty, which jealously guard their prerogatives in this arena.

A Participatory Planning Model

A top-down model for strategic planning, Rowley argued, simply won't work in academia since it ignores the institutional context of most universities. The alternative he proposed is a participatory model in which faculty and administrators form working groups to address the issues raised through the strategic planning process. This approach has also been described as the communicative approach to strategic planning, where the objective is to solicit broad input from stakeholders with the goal of building strong buy-in for the final plan (Willson 2006). As with the other approaches to strategic planning described in this chapter, this approach is problematic. First, the process of selecting the subject areas that will form the foundation of the strategic process and its outcome have to be agreed upon. The potential here is to tilt the outcome of a strategic plan into a pre-ordained direction, which can damage the credibility of the plan, particularly among those groups who do not see the emerging strategic direction as supportive of their interests. Faculty and administrators in many colleges and universities do not, on a routine basis, work together. These working groups have to be constructed, determine their own agenda, and then execute their tasks. Typically, the relationships between the faculty and administrators in a university, particularly those working outside of academic affairs in areas such as administrative services or student life, are complicated at best. Since teaching and formal learning stands as the central activity of virtually every college and university, members of the faculty not infrequently feel that their voices should have additional authority in any planning processes. The recommendations of working groups in which the faculty voice is not adequately represented may be critically evaluated by the faculty.

But the issue of the composition of the working groups for strategic planning using the participatory model in higher education is more complicated that simply ensuring adequate faculty representation. University faculties are not monolithic and don't speak with a single voice. Perspectives vary among faculty members from different disciplines and schools within the university. It is not hard to imagine that the views of professors of accounting could feel differently on a range of issues than professors of philosophy, to use a very stereotypical example. Moreover, the perspectives of tenured and untenured faculty (people who have been at an institution for a long time versus those who are newer) and a host of other factors influence any specific faculty member's input into any working group. Finally, participation in a time-consuming process like strategic planning is not integrated into the incentive structure for faculty members in most colleges and universities. The pressures to produce research and to be effective teachers often lead many faculty members to conclude that they don't have the time to participate. Paradoxically, faculty support is essential for any strategic plan to succeed (Sanaghan 2009). Given the limitations of the impact of working groups, Rowley suggests that strategic planning committees should also convene open forums and targeted question-and-answer sessions to engage as wide a representation of views as possible. And many strategic planning processes in colleges and universities ultimately wind up involving a huge percentage of the university community. Indeed, according to Allen and Baker, over 400 of Widener University's 1,000 full-time employees were directly involved in the deliberations involved in the strategic planning process, and hundreds more took part in town hall meetings, departmental meetings held to address planning, in addition to an array of other feedback opportunities (2012). While potentially usefully, all of these steps add time to the preliminary parts of the planning process. And having overly broad participation in creating a strategic plan carries risks as well, particularly the possibility that the institutional goals will become obscured by the goals of specific units or departments in the eyes of the participants associated with those units or departments (Goldman and Salem 2015).

In most cases, the responsibility to facilitate broad-based input into the strategic planning process falls to a coordinating committee of some sort. In the corporate world, the central coordinating team for strategic planning may consist of eight to 12 people (Gable 1998). In contrast, a study conducted by Hanover Research found that the strategic planning committees in the universities averaged 25 members and that those members came from all quarters of the university including senior administration officials, students, staff and faculty. Members of the coordinating committee varied widely in their levels of experience, institutional authority, commitment to the university as an institution both personally and professionally, and experience and skill in working within that environment (Hanover Research 2014). Ensuring that the members of the coordinating committee have an appropriate voice in its deliberations requires sophisticated management skills.

Finally, the communicative or participatory approach to strategic planning can take an extraordinary amount of time. For example, in light of the perceived shortcomings of earlier strategic planning processes, Cleveland State University adopted a communicative approach to planning in 2005. The entire planning process, however, took three years to complete (Hill et al. 2009). Given the degree of ongoing work from so many different areas within the university and from so many individuals, it is difficult to sustain that kind of planning process on an ongoing basis. In the corporate world, strategic plans generally run from three to five years. But if the process itself takes three years to complete, the plan's time period must be significantly longer for the plan to have impact. In fact, when Hill et al. reported about the process at Cleveland State in 2009, they noted that it was still too early to determine if the plan was driving substantive institutional change four years after the strategic planning process had been launched.

Mission Statement Challenges

Clearly, even the first step to simply craft an effective and efficient procedure for strategic planning in higher education is not a simple task. The pre-planning for the process could take months, and, given the rhythm of the academic calendar, a one-semester delay can easily turn into a year. And once the pre-planning is completed and the effort gets underway, none of the other steps in the corporate model fits neatly into the academic environment well. For example, one characteristic of strategic planning in the corporate world is that the vision statement for the strategic plan should be grounded in the organizational mission and encompass the organization's core values (Hussey 1999). The place of the mission statement in the academic world, however, differs greatly from the mission statement in the corporate world. Moreover, colleges and universities do not have nearly the same latitude, as private enterprises have to remake themselves in light of changing market conditions.

Multiple factors constrain the ways that colleges and universities can reshape their mission, and those restraints also limit the flexibility in creating a vision statement for a strategic plan. The first is that private companies have one primary stakeholder—their owners or shareholders—who can remake the business as they see fit. Colleges and universities have multiple stakeholders, and the boards of trustees or other governing boards do not have nearly the flexibility and freedom of those working in the private sector. Consider a company like General Electric, for example, which started in 1892 as a power and lighting company. GE grew over the years to become a manufacturing conglomerate with units active in transportation, communication, medical devices and more. In the mid-1980s, however, with Jack Welch as chairman of the board and CEO, GE's largest division by far was its financial services operations. Following the financial crisis of 2008, CEO Jeffrey Imelt decided to shed most of GE's financial services and concentrate on high-margin industrial operations. By 2015, GE was touting itself as a software company that built stuff. Its focus was to create the operating system for industry.

While colleges and universities clearly evolve over time and the rise of online education and other factors have triggered a period of turmoil, for most institutions the rate and direction of change cannot be nearly as rapid and decisive as what occurred at even a huge company like GE. A university's mission is defined not only by its board of trustees but by history and traditions, often safeguarded by its alumni, its faculty as well as external forces such as accrediting and credentialing agencies and the state governments for public institutions. Indeed, in many areas, the overall parameters that define adequacy of the educational offerings are determined not by individual institutions but by outside agencies charged with setting standards. Moreover, mission statements play a different role in higher education than they do in the corporate world. Historically, if universities had mission statements, and many venerable institutions including Harvard University do not, they were long and complex (Hinton 2012). They include long descriptions of the founding of the university, aspirations for their students, the values to which the institution adheres and additional information. They often run for a page or more. Currently, the mission statement for the University of Wisconsin is 425 words in length. Those kinds of "comprehensive" mission statements present two problems for strategic planning, Hinton argued. First, because they were so long and complex, it was difficult to identify the specific elements in the mission statement with which everybody agreed that could then serve as the foundation for the university's activities. When accrediting agencies began to use how well a university's activities aligned with its mission, the lack of specificity in the mission statements became even more problematic. The second dilemma posed by comprehensive mission statements, according to Hinton, was that they could lead to "mission creep." Colleges and universities would find themselves devoting resources to activities beyond their primary mission—activities that were secondary but nonetheless mentioned in the comprehensive mission statement. An accrediting agency could view "mission creep" as evidence that the institution was not using its resources effectively.

In response, as alignment with the mission statement became a factor in the accrediting process, many institutions began to streamline their mission statements, often creating a corollary statement of values to describe how the institution functions to supplement the mission statement. The shorter mission statement, in turn, focuses on what the university actually does. For example, when the University of Rochester created the first mission statement in the institution's 160-year history in 2009, it settled on ten words—"Learn, Discover, Heal, Create—and Make the World Ever Better," which is short enough to put on a tee shirt (Kiley 2011). But shorter, more succinct mission statements also present problems as the basis for creating vision statements for strategic plans in higher education. To a large degree, these mission statements do not differentiate one institution from another in any meaningful way. A survey conducted by Gallup found that the mission statements of 50 institutions of higher education were remarkable similar regardless of the type or size of the college or university or whether they were public or private status, land-grant status or religious affiliation, or for-profit or not-for-profit status (Dvorak and Busteed 2015). Not surprisingly, educational excellence, training leaders for the future, nurturing lifelong learning and serving the community or similar platitudes are part of the mission statements of a majority of colleges and universities (Ozdem 2011). The mission statement of many colleges and universities do little to distinguish one institution from another. Brand identity among institutions of higher education, to use marketing terminology, is based not on a unique mission but on factors such as location, cost, class size, history and tradition and other non-educational factors. But those characteristics are the very ones that are, with good reason, being stripped away from the overall university mission statements. If a strategy, in part, is meant to differentiate one entity from its competitors, in many cases the mission statement of the university, though a necessary starting point, does not provide a strong enough direction for a strategic plan.

What Are Strengths? What Are Weaknesses?

In the standard corporate strategic planning process, an analysis of the internal and external strengths and weakness, opportunities and threats (SWOT) follows the crafting of the vision statement. But conducting a SWOT analysis in a higher-education setting poses just as many if not more complications as trying to ground the strategic plan's vision statement through the university's mission statement (or lack of mission statement, as the case may be). For an external analysis of strengths and weaknesses, opportunities and threats, the first hurdle to overcome is identifying who the competition truly is. Colleges and universities can have a wide range of competitive sets within which they can situate themselves. There are Carnegie Classifications and the U.S. News & World Report rankings. There are athletic leagues. There are the institutions within which one college has a lot of cross-applications with another. And there are schools with which there are long-standing rivalries or connections, academically or athletically.

Traditionally, students select the school that they plan to attend along a wide range of variables including academic excellence and admissions policies, cost, program offerings, student life, geography, tradition, family history and more. Not only do all those variables come into play, but they can change for undergraduate and graduate programs, among different departments and according to the different kinds of experiences schools offer. The decision to attend a college is much different than the decision to buy a car for example. Moreover, prospective undergraduate students often compare colleges outside of any clearly defined set as they are not sure what they are really looking for, making it hard for colleges and universities to know exactly with whom they are competing. And student decisions are often made on factors well beyond the control of a specific institution (Morse 2013).

With the growth of the residential college experience over the past 40 years and online education over the past ten years, the market for higher education operates on a national and international level. For example, West Virginia University hired William Brustein to map out a global strategy for the school (The Chronicle 2016). Traditional liberal arts colleges recruit nationally, and even state universities work hard to attract out-of-state students who pay higher tuition rates than state residents. In some respects, higher education is a Hobbesian all-against-all marketplace. Since every college can potentially be competing with every other university, creating meaningful points of comparison can be difficult and in some ways arbitrary. Even mapping an institution's competitive position can be extremely complex (D'Aveni 2007). Of course, a SWOT analysis is typically not restricted to understanding the competition and the competitive landscape. It can also be used to assess internal and external processes and to compare them to industry standards and best practices, which can be seen as an application of the same concepts as benchmarking. But the path to creating a culture of benchmarking in higher education has been long and far from smooth. When a handful of colleges and universities first began to explore creating benchmarks in the early 1990s, within a short period of time more than 600 different processes and functions, primarily administrative, were identified. And the benchmarking process often consisted of simply asking an amenable institution about its experience with that process.

By the mid-1990s, benchmarking through consortia became more prevalent. Colleges and universities with a common interest in improving a specific function, such as handling of student records, formed groups, working together to develop what could be considered best practices. Often these consortia are made up of an array of colleges and universities from two-year community colleges to elite private research institutions. The most difficult aspect in this approach is defining processes in ways that can be meaningfully measured and compared. The central conundrum in using benchmarking for a SWOT analysis as the basis for a strategic plan is that for the exercise to be most beneficial it should encompass what can be called the core competencies of the organization—those processes through which the organization creates value and serves its constituents and stakeholders. The core competency of institutions of higher education at every level is teaching and learning, with many schools having the added mandate of research and creating new knowledge. Teaching and learning is a very difficult, if not impossible, process to benchmark, particularly among institutions with different mandates, standards, student bodies and brand-image and traditions. Research is often benchmarked according to the number of grants an institution receives or the quantity of scholarly output rather than the impact of the research itself. Finally, consortia-based benchmarking efforts can be very expensive (Epper 1999).

Undertaking a meaningful SWOT analysis may be beyond the reach of many colleges and universities. For an external environmental scan, it is difficult to determine an appropriate comparative set that will encompass a broad range of processes and indicators. For an internal analysis, establishing and identifying best practices for a meaningful set of practices that have a significant impact on the operation of the university is not a trivial task, and it can be expensive as well. Finally, undertaking an in-depth SWOT analysis can uncover a dizzying number of weaknesses and threats. For example, for the purposes of a SWOT analysis conducted by an engineering college in India as part of its strategic planning process, the institution was grouped into four broad areas to examine—people, products (i.e., facilities), processes, and product. A two-day workshop returned with more than 30 weaknesses and threats in the process area alone. While undoubtedly a useful exercise, determining the most critical areas to address, incorporating those ideas into the format of a strategic plan and engineering buy-in from stakeholders who were intimately involved with the processes in question, but not the way they were identified as weaknesses and threats, was a complicated task (Ozdem 2011).

Measuring Progress

Of all the steps in a strategic planning process, the most critical is the implementation and measurement of the plan. As Sandy points out, the lifecycle of many strategic plans is one of "bold initiatives (that) often remain lifeless prisoners in plans books that are rapidly filed away" (Sandy 1991, 30). But once again, the challenges posed in higher education to successfully implement a strategic plan are greater than those posed in the corporate sector. Strategic planning consultant Erica Olsen identified the 11 most common pitfalls that block the effective implementation of a strategic plan (n.d.) (figure 2.6). Each of the potential pitfalls is exacerbated in the academic world. According to Olsen, the most common reason that strategic plans are not implemented in the corporate world is that nobody in the organization takes ownership of the plan and drives it forward. In the corporate world, generally senior management has the responsibility to communicate the strategy to middle-level managers and frontline personnel. A critical part of that process is for management to communicate the metrics by which the employees' performances will be measured as a part of the organizational effort to achieve the plan (Gallo 2010).

In the academic world, the organizational lines of communication are not as clear or defined as they are in the corporate setting. In most settings, the president or chief academic officer of a university, even if he or she claims ownership of the plan, cannot dictate to faculty to alter the way they conduct themselves in light of a new strategic plan. Indeed, while contractually faculty members owe their primary professional loyalty and allegiance to the university with which they are associated at any point of time, that loyalty and allegiance may be balanced against their commitment to their academic discipline or field of study and other external activities (Little 2010). Moreover, many members of the academic community have either formal or informal security of employment, further complicating the process of instituting a strategic change across an institution.

The fact is that if one of the primary reasons to implement a strategic plan is to respond to shifts in the overall competitive environment by planning and managing change efficiently (as Lloyd Armstrong, former provost and vice president for academic affairs at the University of Southern California, has noted), the unusual position of senior faculty as both managers and producers of the core product—education—is only one of the headwinds change agents face. U.S. higher education has a laudable reputation around the world, which many see as confirmation that what they specifically are doing right now is working. In short, many people believe that what they are doing at any moment in time is successful and altering what they are doing will lower the quality of the offering. In addition Armstrong argued that the multiple mandates of many universities for excellence in teaching, research and student development,

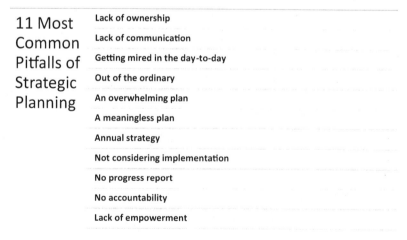

Figure 2.6 11 Most Common Pitfalls of Strategic Planning (Olsen n.d.)

particularly for undergraduate education, means that colleges and universities are deploying multiple business models, as well as adding the complexity of trying to manage three models within the context of one organization, which may create a situation in which none of the models can be optimized. Not infrequently, different parts of the organization may be in conflict with others. Given these underlying tensions, it may be impossible to implement a single vision for a college and university in a way that supports the different models. (Armstrong n.d.). The reward and incentive system in place in higher education is not conducive to facilitating change. Faculty evaluation prizes individual achievement and professional autonomy, and there is little to motivate faculty members to take risks on new ventures if the rewards are not clearly presented. A system to reward experimentation and risk taking is not in place in other parts of the university either (Lane 2007). In review, despite the perceived need for strategic planning, in the corporate world often it does not achieve the desired or anticipated results. And the obstacles in the way of success in strategic planning in higher education are even greater. Many of the traditional steps used in strategic planning in the corporate world do not map comfortably onto the structure, traditions and ways of operating in higher education.

Strategic Planning for Online Education

Even though many observers believe that strategic planning has been largely ineffective in higher education, the concepts that animate the effort have become increasingly ingrained in higher education, particularly among senior administrators (Luke 2014). As Benjamin Ginsberg pointed out in his book *The Fall of the Faculty: The Rise of the All-Administrative University and Why It Matters*, nearly every college and university now engages in some sort of strategic planning process. The work product of these efforts, in Ginsberg's view, is a document that cobbles together a version of the university's mission with a vague vision, a laundry list of goals and action items without identification of the sources or the resources to implement them. To a large degree, the plans primarily serve as instruments for senior administrators to try to assert control over their institutions that are unwieldy and difficult to manage. Strategic plans among universities are often not very distinct and do not serve to differentiate the institutions from each other. So it is not surprising, Ginsberg contends, that most strategic plans are quickly forgotten and have little impact on their respective institutions (Ginsberg 2011).

Given the difficulties involved in the strategic planning process generally, trying to incorporate strategic planning for online education into that process would be problematic if not impossible. Most of the challenges identified that stand in the way of successful strategic planning at the institutional level are more intense when it comes to planning for online education. Bypassing the issue of creating a vision for online education for the moment, conducting an environmental scan and internal and external SWOT analysis is beyond the reach of most institutions. The emergence of online education changed the competitive landscape even among colleges and universities that believe they have developed a coherent set of institutions with which they like to compare themselves. Internally, online education has to compete for resources with other programs, and what seems like a weakness for online education—the need for face-to-face advising prior to enrolling in classes, for example—may seem like a strong suit for other programs. And implementing a strategic plan for online education is even more daunting. The services that go into delivering an online program are dispersed across the university. Those resources, ranging from the technology infrastructure to the admissions process to student services, are not generally managed or supervised by the same people who manage the online educational offerings.

While the specific processes traditionally associated with strategic planning may not be appropriate for strategic planning for online education, the growth of the strategic planning culture in higher education has provided those people responsible for the development of online education with three valuable—indeed, critical—resources. First, the prevalence of strategic planning has established an atmosphere and environment in which planning is a familiar concept. When administrators of higher-education programs talk about planning for the future, it is a familiar concept. Whether or not it has been done poorly, planning is not a foreign or unusual idea. Strategic planning has created a common language. When people talk about vision, goals, objectives, environmental scans and so on, those concepts are increasingly well understood by the different stakeholders involved, particularly stakeholders upon whom the administrators of online educational programs rely for resources. While it may be difficult to actually ascertain the strengths and weaknesses, opportunities and threats that online education on a specific campus may face, the language itself is useful in trying to analyze the internal and external environment. Finally, for many online educational programs, the institutional strategic plan provides both a starting point and a vehicle for integration of the strategic plan for online education into the overall operation of the university. If many strategic plans can be seen as instruments of control for senior administrators, then, to be effective, ultimately any plan for online education has to be in harmony with the institution's overall strategic plan. At the bottom line, planning for online education should take place outside the overall institution strategic planning process but be mindful of and consistent with the university efforts to plan strategically.

Conclusion

The challenge for those responsible for developing online educational programs is to take the concepts and language used in institutional strategic planning and fashion them into a process that can effectively chart the future. The process must be nimble and efficient. It cannot take the six months to two years that institutional strategic planning often takes in higher education. To some degree it must be ongoing, as the contours of online education are changing rapidly. And frequently, the strategic plan for online education should not be comprehensive. While planning for online education should address the future, in most cases the outcome of the planning process will not be able to touch on every aspect of the long-term future. The output of the plan will not be a total answer about what to do over the next two, five or ten years, but it can provide guidance regarding future needs on an ongoing basis.

The inclusive communicative approach that most colleges and universities take for overall strategic planning may not be the most suitable for online education. The communicative approach is used for campus-wide planning on the belief that if many people are involved in the planning process, it will be easier to win their buy-in when the plan is ultimately developed. The larger the number of people involved, the greater the sense of ownership for the plan overall, or so the theory goes. And while that theory has never been fully tested, on an institutional level the inverse seems to be true. If a plan is constructed by a small group of planners, it has little chance of success. For many of the critical service providers, however, online education is too low a priority to invest much time and effort in a planning process. Many of the stakeholders in online education have their own departmental priorities and initiatives. Online education is only one claim on their time, and it is often competing with other, more urgent priorities from other parts of the university.

Finally, the work product of the planning process in online education is different from a traditional strategic plan. Instead of developing a blueprint, replete with a collection of tasks to be completed in support of goals and objectives designed to execute a specific vision, the result of planning for online education should be a persuasive document, a tool to enlist other stakeholders in the vision for online education and to gather resources. Effective planning for online education uses the language and trappings of traditional strategic planning to gather support for this new approach to higher education.

References

Aileron (2011, November 11). 10 Reasons Why Strategic Plans Fail. Forbes.com. Retrieved from: https://www.forbes.com/sites/aileron/2011/11/30/10-reasons-why-strategic-plans-fail/#73480c4586a8

Allen, J. and Baker, J. (2012). Building an Institution Worthy of Its History: The Evergreen Strategic Plan at Widener University: Faculty and Staff Began to See Accreditation (and Accountability) as Something Truly Meaningful. *Planning for Higher Education*, 40:2, pp. 48–58.

Armstrong, L. (n.d.). *Barriers to Change and Innovation in Higher Education*. TIAA CREF Institution. Retrieved from: www.tiaainstitute.org/public/pdf/barriers-to-innovation-and-change-in-higher-education.pdf

Baldwin, D. (n.d.). *Follow-Through—the Key to Strategic Planning Success*. Center for Simplified Strategic Planning. Retrieved from: www.cssp.com/CD0908b/StrategicPlanningFollowThrough/

Christensen, C. (1997, November/December). Making Strategy: Learning by Doing. *Harvard Business Review*, 75:6, pp. 141–156.

Christensen, C., Hall, T., Dillon, K. and Duncan, D. (2016, September). Know Your Customers' "Jobs Be Done." *Harvard Business Review*, 94:9, pp. 54–62.

The Chronicle of Higher Education (2016). Global Strategist Joins E. Gordon Gee at West Virginia U. Retrieved from: www.chronicle.com/article/Global-Strategist-Joins-E/237740

Collie, S. (n.d.). *Benchmarking in Higher Education, Office of the Vice President for Management and Budget, University of Virginia.* Retrieved from: www.virginia.edu/processsimplification/resources/Benchmarking%20Nov%20%203.pdf

Cook, B. (2012, Spring). *The American College President Study: Key Findings and Takeaways.* American Council on Education. Retrieved from: www.acenet.edu/the-presidency/columns-and-features/Pages/The-American-College-President-Study.aspx

D'Aveni, R. (2007, November). Mapping Your Competitive Position. *Harvard Business Review*, 85:11, pp. 110–120.

Dolence, M. and Norris, D. (1994, Summer). Using Key Performance Indicators to Drive Strategic Decision Making. *New Directions for Institutional Research*, 82, pp. 63–80.

Dooris, M. J. (2002–2003). Two Decades of Strategic Planning. *Planning for Higher Education*, 31:2, pp. 26–32.

Dvorak, N. and Busteed, B. (2015, August 11). It's Hard to Differentiate One Higher Ed Brand From Another. *Business Journal, Gallup.* Retrieved from: www.gallup.com/businessjournal/184538/hard-differentiate-one-higher-brand.aspx

Epper, R. (1999, November/December). Applying Benchmarking to Higher Education: Some Lessons From Experience. *Change*, pp. 24–31.

Everse, G. (2011, August 22). Eight Ways to Communicate Your Strategy More Effectively. *Harvard Business Review*. Retrieved from: https://hbr.org/2011/08/eight-ways-to-energize-your-te

Gable, C. (1998). *Strategic Action Planning Now: A Guide for Setting and Meeting Your Goals.* Boca Raton, FL: St. Lucie Press, p. 9. Retrieved from: www.hanoverresearch.com/media/Strategic-Planning-in-Higher-Education-%E2%80%93-Best-Practices-and-Benchmarking.pdf

Gallo, A. (2010, June 24). Making Your Strategy Work on the Frontline. *Harvard Business Review*. Retrieved from: https://hbr.org/2010/06/making-your-strategy-work-on-t

Ginsberg, B. (2011, July 17). The Strategic Plan: Neither Strategy Nor Plan But a Waste of Time. *The Chronicle of Higher Education*. Retrieved from: www.chronicle.com/article/The-Strategic-Plan-Neither/128227/

Godkin, L. and Allcorn, S. (2008). Overcoming Organizational Inertia: A Tripartite Model for Achieving Strategic Organizational Change. *The Journal of Applied Business and Economics*, 8:1, p. 82. Retrieved from: www.na-businesspress.com/Godkin.pdf

Goldman, C. and Salem, H. (2015). *Getting the Most Out of University Strategic Planning: Essential Guide for Success and Obstacles to Avoid.* Rand Corp, p. 9. Retrieved from: www.rand.org/content/dam/rand/pubs/perspectives/PE100/PE157/RAND_PE157.pdf

Hanover Research (2014). Best Practices in Strategic Planning. Retrieved from: https://intranet.ecu.edu.au/__data/assets/pdf_file/0004/711499/Hanover-Research,-Best-Practices-in-Strategic-Planning,-May-2014.pdf

Hansen, J. (2006, March 10). Back in the Day: The Strategic Plan. *The Oberlin Review*. Retrieved from: www.oberlin.edu/stupub/ocreview/2006/03/10/news/article10.html

Hill, S., Kogler, E., Thomas, E. and Keller, L. (2009). A Collaborative, Ongoing University Strategic Planning Framework: Process, Landmines, and Lessons: Planners at Cleveland State University Describe That Institution's Highly Communicative and Participatory Strategic Planning Process. *Planning for Higher Education*, 37:4. Retrieved from: https://www.questia.com/library/journal/1P3-1758049271/a-collaborative-ongoing-university-strategic-planning

Hinton, K. (2012). *A Practical Guide to Strategic Planning in Higher Education.* Society for College and University Planning. Retrieved from: www.scup.org

Holland, K. (2014, August 28). Back to School: Older Students on the Rise in College Classroom. *NBC News*. Retrieved from: www.nbcnews.com/business/business-news/back-school-older-students-rise-college-classrooms-n191246

Hussey, D. (1999). *Strategy & Planning: A Manager's Guide.* New York: John Wiley & Sons Inc., pp. 22–24.

Jennings, D. and Wattam, S. (1998). *Decision Making: An Integrated Approach.* London: Financial Times Management.

Jennings, D. and Wattam, S. (2015). *Trends in College Pricing 2015.* Trends in Higher Education, College Board 2015. Retrieved from: https://trends.collegeboard.org/college-pricing/highlights

Kaplan, R. (2010). *Conceptual Foundations of the Balanced Scorecard*. Working Paper 10-074, Harvard Business School. Retrieved from: www.hbs.edu/faculty/Publication%20Files/10-074.pdf

Kaplan, R. and Norton, D. (1996, January–February). Using the Balanced Scorecard as a Strategic Management System. *Harvard Business Review*, 76. Retrieved from: https://hbr.org/2007/07/using-the-balanced-scorecard-as-a-strategic-management-system

Kaplan, R. and Norton, D. (2000, September 1). Having Trouble With Your Strategy: Then Map It. *Harvard Business Review*. Retrieved from: https://hbr.org/2000/09/having-trouble-with-your-strategy-then-map-it

Kaplan, R. and Norton, D. (n.d.). *Balanced Scorecard Basics*. Balanced Scorecard Institution, Strategy Management Group. Retrieved from: http://balancedscorecard.org/Resources/About-the-Balanced-Scorecard

Kaplan, R., Norton, D. and Sher, G. (2005, October). The Office of Strategy Management. *Harvard Business Review*, 83:10, pp. 72–80.

Kaplan, R., Norton, D. and Sher, G. (n.d.). *Who Is Involved in Strategic Planning?* Simply Strategic Planning. Retrieved from: www.simply-strategic-planning.com/who-is-involved-in-strategic-planning.html

Kiley, K. (2011, June 20). Saying More With Less. *Inside Higher Ed*. Retrieved from: www.inside-highered.com/news/2011/06/20/colleges_pare_down_mission_statements_to_stand_out

Kirst, M. and Stevens, M. (2015). *Remaking College: The Changing Ecology of Higher Education*. CA: Stanford University Press.

Lane, I. (2007). Change in Higher Education: Understanding and Responding to Individual and Organizational Resistance. *Journal of Veterinary Medical Education*, 34:2. Retrieved from: www.ccas.net/files/ADVANCE/Lane_Change%20in%20higher%20ed.pdf

Leverington, K. (2013, June 4). 90% of Strategies Fail? Where to Begin. *Kirkleverighton.com*. Retrieved from: http://blog.kirkleverington.com/?p=901

Little, A. (2010, June 17). Further Thoughts on Loyalty. *Historiann*. Retrieved from: https://histori-ann.com/2010/06/17/further-thoughts-on-loyalty/

Luke, J. (2014). *Effective Strategic Planning for Disruptive and Challenging Times*. Higher Education Commission. Retrieved from: http://cop.hlcommission.org/Leadership/luke.html

McKenna, L. (2015, December 3). Why Are Fewer College Presidents Academics. *The Atlantic*. Retrieved from: www.theatlantic.com/education/archive/2015/12/college-president-miz-zou-tim-wolfe/418599/

Morse, R. (2013, July 31). Freshmen Students Say Rankings Aren't Key Factor in College Choice. *U.S. News & World Report*. Retrieved from: www.usnews.com/education/blogs/college-rankings-blog/2013/01/31/freshmen-students-say-rankings-arent-key-factor-in-college-choice

Olsen, E. (n.d.). Avoid the 11 Strategic Implementation Pitfalls. *On Strategy*. Retrieved from: http://onstrategyhq.com/resources/avoid-the-11-strategic-implementation-pitfalls/

Ozdem, G. (2011, Autumn). An Analysis of the Mission and Vision Statements on the Strategic Plans of Higher Education Institutions. *Educational Sciences: Theory & Practice*, 11:1, pp. 1887–1894.

Parmenter, D. (2010). *Key Performance Indicators (KPI): Developing, Implementing, and Using Winning KPI's*. Hoboken, NJ: John Wiley & Sons Inc.

Rowley, D., Lujan, H. and Dolence, M. (1997). *Strategic Change in Colleges and Universities*. San Francisco, CA: Jossey-Bass Publishers.

Sanaghan, P. (2009). *Collaborative Strategic Planning in Higher Education*. Washington, DC: National Association of College and University Business Officers.

Sandy, W. (1991, September/October). Avoid the Breakdown Between Planning and Implementation. *The Journal of Business Strategy*, pp. 30–33.

Simply Strategic Planning (n.d.). Retrieved from: http://www.simply-strategic-planning.com/

Soares, L. and Margetta, J. (2011, June 28). *Morgan Guiding Innovation in Higher Education; How to Manage the Emerging Changes in College Delivery Center For American Progress*. Retrieved from: www.americanprogress.org/issues/labor/news/2011/06/29/9868/guiding-innovation-in-higher-education/

Soares, L., Steele, P. and Wayt, L. (2016). *Evolving Higher Education Business Models: Leading With Data to Deliver Results*. Washington, DC: American Council on Education. Retrieved from: www.acenet.edu/news-room/Documents/Evolving-Higher-Education-Business-Models.pdf

Starr, S. F. (1993, Fall). A President's Message to Planners. *Planning for Higher Education*, 22:1, pp. 16–22.

Sterling, J. (2003). Translating Strategy Into Effective Implementation: Dispelling the Myths and Highlighting What Works. *Strategy and Leadership*, 31:3, pp. 27–34. Retrieved from: www.smocksterling.com/comm/pdf/SS-C-013.pdf

Sull, D. (1999, July/August). Why Good Companies Go Bad. *Harvard Business Review*, 77:4, pp. 42–50.

Tyce, H., Puckett, J., Wilson, J. and Pagano, E. (2016, March). Five Trends to Watch in Higher Education. *BCG Perspectives*. Retrieved from: www.bcgperspectives.com/content/articles/education_public_sector_five_trends_watch_higher_education/?chapter=2

VanderArk, T. and Schneider, C. (2012). How Digital Learning Contributes to Deeper Learning. *GettingSmart.com*. Retrieved from: http://net.educause.edu/ir/library/pdf/CSD6152a.pdf

Willson, R. (2006). The Dynamics of Organizational Culture and Academic Planning. *Planning for Higher Education*, 34:3, pp. 5–17.

Witt, D. (2012, May 21). Only 14% of Employees Understand Their Company's Strategy and Direction. *Blanchard LeaderChat*. Retrieved from: www.google.com/#q=William+Schiemann+strategic+plan

Woodhouse, K. (2015, August 25). Discounting Grows Again. *Inside Higher Ed*. Retrieved from: www.insidehighered.com/news/2015/08/25/tuition-discounting-grows-private-colleges-and-universities

3
Planning Strategically
An Overview

Just before the turn of the millennium, the dean of the College of Pharmacy and Health Sciences at Creighton University in Omaha, Nebraska, had what he thought was an interesting idea that potentially could have a major impact for his school. He decided to launch two online educational programs: one was a transitional doctorate in physical therapy (DPT), a degree that was just beginning to gain traction in the profession; and the other, a doctorate of pharmacy (D. Pharm), a credential that was growing in popularity as the entry level degree for pharmacists. It was a bold, even visionary, idea. After all, Creighton had just implemented its first comprehensive online learning management system, WebCT, a couple of years earlier (History of Technology n.d.).

Technologically, the programs he facilitated were not very sophisticated, consisting primarily of readings and online discussions. The central information technology unit at Creighton supported the courses and related services, but the College of Pharmacy and Health Sciences provided the instructional design for the classes. The programs themselves were hosted on the college's, not the university's, servers. And the administrators launching the programs were so unsure of their viability that they devised an exit strategy if they didn't work out. After all, they had a responsibility to the students who took the risk of enrolling. But not only did the programs survive; they flourished. Over the ensuing years, the reach of online education at Creighton has grown, where, in 2016, the university offers more than 20 certificates as well as bachelor's, master's and doctorate degree programs in the health sciences, business, education, ministry and more. Together these programs serve thousands of students. Creighton's online graduate programs are advertised across the country on National Public Radio and elsewhere, dramatically increasing the university's academic footprint and profile.

To facilitate growth, the Center of Academic Innovation at Creighton was created and is now broadly responsible for supporting online education across the university. It guides departments and colleges in program development. It trains faculty to teach online and provides instructional design services. It ensures that the quality of online education meets the necessary standards and is consistent with Creighton's overall academic mission and Jesuit traditions. In short, the Center for Academic Innovation serves as the central address for institutional planning and administrative support for distance education at Creighton. But the road from offering two programs using relatively rudimentary online technology in a single school within the university to a broad set of offerings being nationally advertised and supported by a central organization that serves the entire university community was not a straight one. In many ways, where Creighton found itself in 2016, with a plethora of online offerings, could not have been anticipated or even imagined in 1999. More than a decade after the first programs came online, the university did not have any defined policies or specific procedures that governed online education. The initiatives for online programs came from many different sources including bottom-up ideas from interested faculty and top-down efforts from administrators in different quarters in the university. Some of Creighton's schools opted to establish their own online programs. Others chose to work with third-party vendors to create online programs. And while some faculty members were interested in online education, a not-insignificant number were vehemently opposed. Interestingly, however, the forces that have come to shape online education at Creighton were not set in motion because online education was embraced as an element of the university's strategic plan. On the contrary, in 2013, Creighton released "One Creighton: Bridging to a Greater Future," its new strategic plan, which called for an increase in full-time enrollment from 7,800 to 9,500 students. The strategic plan projected much of the expansion to be driven by the number of online students, adult learners and professional programs (Perry 2014).

The plan's release sparked a heated controversy and overt resistance across the campus. In March 2015, the Faculty Council, the body at Creighton charged with representing the views of the faculty members at the university level, unanimously passed a resolution of no confidence in the strategic plan, asserting that despite widespread consultations across the campus during the plan's development, the process was not adequately transparent. Moreover, among other complaints, the faculty claimed that the plan's goals were not specific enough to allow the Creighton community to understand the direction in which the university was moving (Perry 2015). Ultimately, not only was the strategic plan itself scrapped, but the planning committee associated with it was replaced. When he took office in July 2015, the incoming president, Rev. Daniel S. Hendrickson, S.J., announced that he would be modifying the strategic planning process at Creighton and discontinued the Creighton Strategy Team. He also indicated that he would develop other approaches for developing and implementing strategic initiatives in the future (Henrickson 2015). But even as the strategic planning process at Creighton became mired in controversy, and even though the support for online education was one of several points of contention in the plan, Creighton has been able to continue to develop and expand its online educational program. The Creighton example demonstrates that while strategic planning for online education must be responsive to and in some ways be aligned with overall strategic planning processes, leaders of online education can, and should, effectively work independently of campus-wide strategic planning. Moreover, while the standard concepts used by strategic planners (developing a vision; conducting an internal and external SWOT analysis; creating goals, objectives and tactics; and then implementing the plan) are essential to understand, those concepts may be modified or refashioned to fit the specific context for online education. Instead of following the standard process for building a comprehensive strategic plan, the aforementioned concepts may be of general use to leaders of online education. This chapter explores the basic principles involved in planning strategically as opposed to strategic planning, a subtle but critical shift in perspective. It describes the benefits and strengths of planning that take place at the middle levels of an organization rather than as an instrument of control from the senior management of the organization. The chapter presents the preliminary steps needed to begin planning strategically—building a planning network.

Planning Strategically Versus Strategic Planning

In their book *Built to Last*, Jim Collins and Jerry Porras examined iconic companies that had outperformed their competitors and flourished for extended periods of time. They examined such well-known and well-respected companies as 3M, Motorola, Procter & Gamble, Merck, Nordstrom, Sony and Disney, which had turned in excellent sustained financial results for decades. They then compared those companies to competitors that had not fared as well (figure 3.1). The goal of their research was to identify what those companies had in common that allowed them to prosper and thrive over the long term as their competitors fell by the wayside (Collins and Porras 1994). As could be expected, Collins and Porras found several fundamental, or what they described as timeless, principles and patterns to which the successful companies they studied seemed to adhere and the patterns of success they had in common. It was a myth that these visionary companies succeeded by developing brilliant or complex strategic plans. Many of their greatest, most-successful initiatives came from experimentation, trial and error, and accident. Rather than the result of foresight and planning, their achievements were based on their willingness to act expeditiously when opportunities presented themselves and to accept that sometimes they would fail (Collins and Porras 1994).

As it turns out, many great organizations are not fundamentally guided by strategic plans, as the formal strategic planning processes can hamstring an organization, among other reasons (Linn 2008). First, formal strategic planning can be very taxing on an organization's resources both financially and in terms of time. Second, for many of the most important stakeholders, the planning process may be considered secondary to their other responsibilities.

5 Reasons for Strategic Planning Failure	Insufficient resources
	Strategy is a secondary effort
	Too many goals and objectives and lack of prioritization
	Strategy as politcal football
	Strategic process cannot account for the unexpected

Figure 3.1 5 Reasons for Strategic Planning Failure (Collins and Porras 1994)

Third, there simply may be too many goals and objectives, and the tasks associated with them or the goals and objectives may be poorly prioritized, and they may simply overwhelm the organization. Fourth, a strategic plan can become a political football in the competition for resources among different operational units. Instead of appropriately guiding the activities of the company, the strategic plan becomes a locus of inter-departmental jockeying and the accumulation of organizational power. And fifth, by definition, strategic planning means making choices. When an organization opts to move in one direction, by definition it is not moving in another. With plan timeframes ranging from three to five years (and frequently longer in higher education) and the need to allow a strategy to mature, produce the desired results, and have an impact, a strategic plan can impede or even present an obstacle to an organization's ability to react to unexpected or suddenly urgent changes in its environment. As Collins put it in his book *Good to Great*, plans need time to build their momentum. On the one hand, companies or organizations that jump from strategy to strategy damage their chances for success (Collins 2001). On the other hand, companies or organizations that are too locked into a specific vision may miss important opportunities or fail to react to important threats to their business model.

Planning strategically, in contrast, takes the same concepts as strategic planning but deploys them in a more nimble way. Like strategic planning, planning strategically still involves setting priorities. It still relies on analyzing the internal and external environments for strengths and weaknesses, opportunities and threats. And it still orients stakeholders to a long-term vision. But instead of trying to create an all-encompassing path forward, it suggests that stakeholders should be strategic about the areas they chose to address in their planning. After a guiding vision is established and the internal and external environments are sufficiently understood, the critical questions posed in planning strategically are: What can be done now? What can be done next? What can be done that will actually move the program toward fulfilling its vision? What are the obstacles to be overcome in order to successfully take those steps? Is it possible to overcome those obstacles, and, if so, how?

And unlike strategic planning, which by its very nature is a cyclical process—create the plan, implement the plan, assess the plan, create the new plan—planning strategically is ongoing. If a culture and discipline of planning strategically is developed and nurtured correctly, planning can take place on an ongoing basis and be applied to a wide variety of problems and challenges, ranging from small issues to major new directions, as well as aspirational goals. The idea of implementing continual planning in a strategic way rests on the following assumptions. First, the mission or vision for a specific unit, company or organization is generally fixed and relevant for a significant period of time. In contrast, the internal and external environments are always in flux, and thus they should always be under surveillance. Consequently, new opportunities and new challenges can present themselves at any time. By planning strategically, the planning process can be ongoing and run in parallel with implementation. As one plan is being implemented, others, concerning different parts of the online educational project, can be brought into focus. At all times, however, planning strategically means that the planning effort can always be focused on aspects and elements of the program that can make an important difference.

Planning strategically should not be confused for operational planning. Unlike operational planning, planning strategically is not reduced to just being tactical or short term. It can be used to develop and support the long-term organizational vision or mission. It can be applied to all different time horizons, long, mid and short term. Planning strategically is an approach to knitting together the mission, vision and objectives of the company with the routine activities needed to achieve them. Perhaps most importantly, planning strategically can

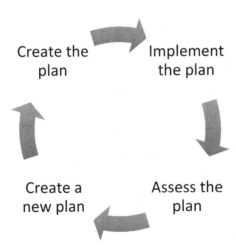

Figure 3.2 Strategic Planning Process

be conceptualized as an ongoing communication process between one group within an organization and other stakeholders, including senior management (Surbhi 2015) (figure 3.2).

Planning From the Middle

The concept of planning strategically grew in part from the realization that the most important organizational knowledge on which a company relies to achieve its most fundamental and basic goals is often lodged in the functional departments rather than in senior leadership. As Floyd and Wooldridge argued, people in the middle levels of an organization are uniquely positioned between the priorities set by senior management and the operating realities of a competitive arena (Floyd and Wooldridge 2000). This unique perspective offers several advantages to thinking and planning strategically. For example, while senior management controls how the resources of an organization are deployed, those closer to the operational front lines have a better understanding how resources are developed, cultivated and actually used. In short, organizational knowledge is more firmly grounded at the operational level, and it is the people who are closest to the front lines who actually know what the front line looks like.

Over the past 20 years, several studies have suggested that anchoring strategic planning processes in the middle of the organization rather than at the senior levels resulted in better operational outcomes and higher performance. Various explanations have been offered for those findings. First, researchers like Henry Mintzberg, Cleghorn Professor of Management Studies at McGill University, argued that the concept of strategic planning was based on a mistaken notion that the planning process could be separated from actual implementation. Mintzberg described traditional strategic planning as "intended strategy," because it captures an organization's intention—what an organization wants, hopes and plans to do. But the world is too complex and unpredictable for the "intended strategy" to unfold as anticipated. Actual strategy emerges through the collision of those "intentions" with the real world. Mintzberg calls what results from the clash of the intended strategy with actual events the "emergent" or "realized" strategy (in Rivera 2012). In other words, despite the mission and vision statements or goals and objectives formalized in a strategic plan, inevitably the environment will force the organization to zig and zag in many different directions as it responds to different events and circumstances. The organization's actual strategy is defined by the impact of the zigs and zags on the professed goals and objectives.

With that in mind, it is the people in the middle of the organization that are responsible for many of the ongoing decisions taken in response to shifting realities. Consequently, they play a critical role in the emergent, realized or actual strategy, with or without the acquiescence or even knowledge of senior management. In fact, since they are the ones charged with executing the amalgamation of tasks required for the ongoing organizational activity, people in the middle are actually in the best position to modify a vision in light of the real operating condition. People in the middle of the organization are guardians of the possible and the actual, rather than the ideal or the aspirational, putting them in the pivotal position in determining a realistic, achievable plan as well as its success (Elliott n.d.). While people in the middle of an organization assert a lot of control over day-to-day functions and activities, that is not their only impact on strategy. They often play a critical role when companies and organizations undertake the kind of formal analysis that serves as the foundation for strategic planning. For example, in a study of the use of formal analytical processes used for 27 strategic issues in three organizations with different organizational structures, Ann Langley, a professor of management at HEC Montreal and the holder of the Canada research chair in strategic management in pluralistic settings, found that analytical processes were carried out in a linear context; that is, somebody initiated the analysis, somebody else conducted it and yet another party received the analysis. But formal analysis, she found, had several dimensions (figure 3.3).

Not only was formal analysis geared to information discovery, communication, direction and control, but its importance also came from symbolic reasons such as presenting a specific image to an external stakeholder or exuding the impression that something is being done. Perhaps surprisingly, she found that formal analysis did not necessarily lead to better decision-making. It did, however, lead to social integration and could serve as a glue to bind the organization together. At the bottom line, the communication, control and direction, and symbolic aspects of formal analysis may be as important or even more important than the information gathering and recommendations. The interaction associated with formal analysis reflects that organizations are made up of multiple groups that socially interact with each other in complex ways (Langley 1989). But the most important finding is that projects that include line managers in their planning and analytical processes have a much higher potential to succeed, if they are valued participants in the communication processes associated with the analysis (Ginzberg 1978). Other observers are even more adamant about the relationship between those in the middle of the organization and the successful outcomes of a plan. Alan Bracke, a training and management consultant, argued that middle managers determine if a strategy succeeds or fails and consequently must be given a strategic role in any organization (2004).

Figure 3.3 Dimensions of Formal Analysis

Ironically, in many ways, planning from the middle is much more compatible with the organizational structure in higher education. As noted in Chapter 1, institutions of higher education can be generally conceptualized as loosely coupled organizations. That is, many of their units operate autonomously or semi-autonomously, and actions in one part of the organization have little or no formal impact in another part of the organization and are often taken without regard to their impact in other parts of the organization. Indeed, in many settings in higher education, people in one functional unit may have little idea of what another unit does or even its direct contribution to the organization's mission, if any. The links between the units are poorly understood, and the forces that can integrate those units into a unified vision of the whole organization are weak compared to those forces animating each unit (Gilmore et al. 1999). Put another way, the links between what it takes to create a world-class athletic program and its relationship to building a world-class physics department, let's say, are not intuitively clear.

As so many units and subunits within a college or university operate relatively independently of each other, they are well positioned to develop their own strategic visions and can, under the right circumstances, take the steps needed to achieve those visions. In order to succeed, the aspirations of the individual units, over time, have to be harmonized with the overall vision and mission of the institution. But on a routine basis, planning strategically often can be more effective at the unit or subunit level in many colleges and universities. In actuality, individuals, to achieve their goals, can use the proven principles in planning strategically.

Challenges in Planning From the Middle

Given the organizational structure of many colleges and universities, planning strategically at the unit or subunit level seems intuitively appropriate. But given the history and development of strategic planning generally and strategic planning in higher education in general, many barriers to planning strategically at the unit or subunit level have emerged. Perhaps the most significant initial barriers to planning strategically are cultural and political. As discussed in Chapter 2, strategic planning in higher education has not been demonstrably effective and often is considered by many in the academic community as either a waste of time or a vehicle for senior administrators to try to assert their control over the direction of the institution and, as a corollary to the assertion of control, something to be ignored or, in the worst case scenario, resisted. Against that background, many middle-level administrators and faculty members do not think it is within their domain to engage in strategic planning processes. And this attitude is not limited to academe. Within many corporations, middle managers limit their involvement in acting strategically because they do not see that as a part of the responsibilities, nor do they believe that senior management expects them to do so.

In a study of 262 middle managers, Saku Mantere, of the Swedish School of Economics and Business Administration, investigated the four-fold typology for middle-level managers' engagement with strategic processes. Based on the work of Wooldridge and Floyd, he suggested that middle managers could primarily implement a top-down strategy, modify a top-down strategy, synthesize information and pass it on to senior management and suggest alternatives. He examined under what conditions middle managers engaged in any of those activities, which he called "strategic agency." He defined "strategic agency" as an "individual's capacity to have a perceived effect upon the individual's own work on an issue the individual regards as beneficial to the interests of his or her organization" (Mantere 2008, 298).

He identified seven factors that enabled middle managers to become active participants in strategic activities. Those factors were narration, contextualization, resource allocation, respect, trust, inclusion, and refereeing. Taken together, middle managers were willing to think, act and plan strategically based on the following: felt that senior management welcomed their voices and listened to them; the activities taking place in the middle of the organization would be integrated into the overall picture for the organization; senior management could clearly explain the reasons for the strategic choices they make; and, ultimately, the resources would be available to implement those decisions. Clearly, those conditions do not exist in many organizations, including most colleges and universities, but they provide a blueprint for successfully getting started with planning strategically. In fact, the first challenge in planning strategically from the middle is creating space for that kind of activity and communication to happen and to create the conditions that would allow it to have an impact.

The second challenge confronting planning strategically from the middle of an organization is that many departments and units in complex organizations

Mantere's 7 Factors for Active Middle Management Participation	Narration
	Contextualization
	Resource Allocation
	Respect
	Trust
	Inclusion
	Refereeing

Figure 3.4 Mantere's 7 Factors for Active Middle-Management Participation

have only limited control of their budgets and consequently little access to the resources that may be needed to achieve specific goals. In higher education, budget issues are even more complex and less transparent than in most institutions of similar sizes. Regardless of whether a university or college generally uses a centralized or decentralized budgeting process, not infrequently departments and subunits are not actually involved in the budgeting process or only in a very perfunctory fashion. A department or subunit may be asked to submit a budget request, but even that, frequently, is more of a pro forma activity. Furthermore, budgets often do not change much from year to year (Gibson 2009). At the most basic level, budgets and budgeting represent the matching of revenue sources and expenditures. In many cases, specific departments do not have any connection to specific revenue sources. Departments and units receive an allocation based on a budgeting process that takes place at several levels removed from the actual operational activity, particularly teaching in the classroom or elsewhere. An allocation represents the actual assignment of a specific amount of money for use by a particular department (Massy 1996). Overall, the process looks like this. The revenue side of the ledger may include tuition, money from the state government (if a public institution), endowment revenue, income from the athletic department, and money generated by ongoing services such as dormitories, dining, the book store, student activities and so on. The expenditure side represents the money spent to keep the school's doors open, so to speak. The largest expense in virtually all colleges and universities is instruction and research, but obviously there is a wide range of ongoing annual operating expenses.

A significant aspect of an institution-wide strategic planning process is to align the institutional resources, including budgetary resources, with the vision, objectives and goal of the university. For example, the George Washington University's Vision 2012 Strategic Plan calls on the school to focus on innovation based on cross-disciplinary collaboration, to embrace globalization and to capitalize on its location in Washington, D.C., to enhance its engagement with government and policy issues, among other themes. Then, as is standard in a university strategic plan, the themes are subdivided into a series of objectives and actions. For example, one objective is to design graduate and undergraduate programs and experiences to provide a global education and promote cross-cultural competency. Another objective is to create and foster cross-disciplinary research institutes that bring together faculty and students from different departments to address complex, multifaceted questions. These objectives are supported by several concrete actions. In this example, the action is to identify four to eight potential interdisciplinary institutes and identify potential faculty and start-up funding for them. As a part of the plan, the university has also laid out strategies to provide the resources needed to take the action that will achieve the goal and fulfill the plan. In total, the school estimated that it would cost between $126 million and $243 million over a decade to implement the actions described in the plan. The plan is expected to be financed through the reallocation of internal funds, philanthropy and research grants, among other sources. Clearly, not only is the strategic plan ambitious, but it necessarily allows a lot of room for flexibility and adjustment. The difference between $126 million and $243 million is like saying, to borrow from comedian Jon Stewart, a person is between 4 feet and 8 feet tall. That is a wide range. The question is not just what happens as GWU works to implement the plan, but assuming an interdisciplinary research institute is successfully established, what comes next? Presumably, such an institute would receive an allocation from the university and begin operation. Though this may not be the case in this specific example, in many settings the institute would not have control of its own income but would instead have to operate within the allocation provided to it by the university. This allocation may offer very little flexibility and very little discretion to the administrators actually managing the institute.

The same kind of constraints and limitations may apply to the units or departments responsible for driving the growth of online education at an institution. Once an allocation for a Center of Online Education, for example, is established, in many routine circumstances, the Center will have to live within the confines of that allocation, regardless of the changes in the operation. Allocations frequently don't change that radically from year to year. Given these circumstances, if a department or institute were to create a formal strategic plan, one of the major challenges in the plan would be to identify the resources needed to execute the plan. In contrast, since planning strategically can be applied in a more focused manner, identifying and securing resources is addressed very early in the planning process and presents itself as one obstacle that has to be overcome. If that obstacle can't be overcome, there is no failure, as the planning team moves on to the next idea.

In summary, planning from the middle improves the possibility of achieving strategic goals. But it is not easy. Planning strategically from the middle works only when those doing the planning can, in some way, capture the attention of the appropriate senior stakeholders for any specific goal or objective. At the same time, planning strategically from the middle reflects the weaker organizational position of those doing the planning. Done correctly, it minimizes the risk of failure for those doing the planning. It reduces the chances that a lot of time will be devoted to developing a plan that will be shelved and never have the intended impact. And planning strategically helps identify the goals and objectives that can realistically be achieved.

Overall Organizational Structure

The first step in establishing a framework to plan strategically from the middle is to determine where the responsibility for online education lies within the overall university's organizational structure and which teams, groups, departments, committees or units have the authority, as well as the motivation, to propose, initiate and implement plans. That task is easier said than done. In the corporate world, the term the "middle" implies "middle management," which in many cases is easy to identify. Not uncommonly, corporations have a hierarchical and rigid organizational structure. In contrast, most traditional, private and public colleges and universities adhere to the principle of shared governance, or the concept that faculty, administrators and staff all participate in both planning and decision-making activities and all have some administrative accountability for the successful execution of those decisions (Olson 2009). As Olson notes, however, the term "shared governance" is not well understood. From the perspective of many administrators, many faculty members believe that shared governance implies that the faculty should make all the major decisions guiding the direction of the university, and they believe it is the role of the administrators to facilitate those decisions, manage the non-academic aspects of the university and support the faculty. People in the middle of a traditional business organization would never assume that kind of authority. Faculty members may view themselves as the "heart" of the university, as teaching, learning and in some cases research are central to institutions of higher education; however, in practice, faculty are not the final arbiter of major decisions. In most cases, final decision-making authority and governance lies with boards of trustees or overseers and, in the case of public universities for certain issues, with state legislatures. Typically the governing board delegates its management authority to the president of the institution, who, in turn, empowers other officials, committees and local "governing" bodies such as the academic senate or alumni council.

Despite the hierarchical structure of most institutions of higher education, since the 1960s governance has widely been seen as a collaborative process. In 1966, the American Association of University Professors, the American Council on Education, and the Association of Governing Boards of Universities and Colleges (respectively, the primary organization representing faculty nationally, a major organization charged with preparing academic administrators, and the association charged with promoting best practices in college and university governing boards) issued a joint statement that said, in part:

> The variety and complexity of the tasks performed by institutions of higher education produce an inescapable interdependence among governing board, administration, faculty, students, and others. The relationship calls for adequate communication among these components, and full opportunity for appropriate joint planning and effort.
>
> Statement on Government (AAUP 1966)

While the statement continues on to assign priorities to different stakeholders for different tasks—the faculty, for example, have the primary responsibility for developing a curriculum that achieves the institution's educational objectives—the net result is that, in many areas, colleges and universities are governed by committees made up of representatives of the different stakeholders (faculty, administrators, staff, alumni, the community, the legislature and students), depending on the specific issue at hand and the specific nature of the particular college or university. As unwieldy as governance by committee may seem on the surface, the complications are exacerbated by several other factors. First, although governance may largely take place by committee, typically colleges and universities are made up of what can be thought of as organizational silos. Most of the responsibility for teaching and learning will fall into the domain of the academic affairs unit, which is generally headed by the provost or the vice president of academic affairs. The dean of students may direct the operations that relate to student life such as the dorms and extracurricular activities. A vice president for enrollment management and marketing has responsibility for recruiting students, and the vice president for finance will manage the budget, and so on. And while shared governance implies that stakeholders from different constituencies will convene in appropriate committees to make major decisions, the lines of communication between the organizational silos typically are weak or non-existent.

The challenges posed by having a tradition of shared governance overlaid on an organizational structure made up of rigid operational siloes are multiplied because most universities have many different schools. So while the provost or chief academic officer may be nominally primarily responsible for the academic program, the deans of the different schools have various amounts of influence, depending on the history, traditions and development of each institution. The various schools are allies in competition for resources with other divisions in the university and competitors with each other for other resources. Moreover, certain services may be centralized at the university level or distributed to different schools. For online educational programs, where information technology services are situated can be particularly salient, as they play such a vital role. In some institutions, technology services are centralized at the university level; and in other cases, not. But the provision of other student services ranging from library services and counseling to disability services and career development will also play a role in planning strategically for online education. A further complication for the shared governance model that has been predominant in higher education for the past 50 years is that, given the pressures on higher education, many critics believe that the organizational model is inefficient and not flexible enough to meet the contemporary challenges colleges and universities face from many different directions. Trustees, government officials and others argue that shared governance limits institutional agility, nimbleness, responsiveness and flexibility. They contend that shared governance processes are sluggish and primarily present obstacles to change. In the face of such criticisms, defenders of the traditional governance mechanisms believe that the pressure to abandon them reflects a further corporatization of higher education. Shared governance, in this view, leads to better decisions based on deliberative and intentional processes that have preserved traditional academic values as the center of the university. Bypassing those processes can lead to colleges and universities inappropriately bowing to financial, political or social pressure at the expense of quality and fidelity to the educational mission (Gayle et al. 2003).

The struggle to manage the growth of online education has helped to pull into the foreground many of the organizational and governance battles being waged in higher education. For example, in 2012, Theresa Sullivan, the president of the University of Virginia, was fired by the university's Board of Visitors because board members felt that the university was not moving fast enough to capitalize on the opportunities presented by Massive Open Online Courses (MOOCs) and online education generally (Jaschick 2012). And in 2013, the Florida legislature authorized the creation of the University of Florida Online, with a mandate to be up and running within seven months (Straumshein 2013). Both of those efforts represented top-down efforts to jump-start online education at major state universities. Neither worked out as anticipated. A campus-wide protest that included both faculty and students led to the reinstatement of Theresa Sullivan as president. And the University of Florida Online did not come close to meeting its enrollment projections, leading it to cancel a massive 11-year contract worth as much as $186 million it had with Pearson to build and manage its online programs (Jaschick 2015). But that is not the end of the story. At the University of Virginia, in the wake of the flap created by Sullivan's dismissal, a faculty task force determined it was already offering nearly 200 online courses, including 11 degree-granting graduate programs. About half of the online courses were directed toward undergraduate students. But, the task force found, online education was being offered in an ad hoc and uncoordinated fashion (Seal 2012). In other words, there was no strategic plan driving online education. At the time, the University of Virginia was engaged in a strategic planning process, but the strategic plan for the academic division published in December 2013 focused on the use of educational technology to enhance the residential educational experience (The Cornerstone Plan 2013), nothing about robust online education, reflecting the caution expressed in a strategic assessment document circulated earlier that year, which specifically stated: "You have to be careful to avoid going too aggressively with online education and other things that would take the university off on a tangent away from its core mission and strength" (The Cornerstone Plan 2013). Nevertheless, the School of Continuing and Professional Studies at the University of Virginia offers a bachelor's degree in Professional Studies in Health Science Management and a range of graduate and undergraduate certificate programs online. The University of Virginia's College at Wise, a public, four-year residential liberal arts college located in the lush mountains of Southwest Virginia, also offers a significant number of online courses, as does its Darden

School of Business. And the university runs several MOOCs through the MOOC provider Coursera. Online education remains an under-the-radar effort at the University of Virginia, at least under the radar as far as it pertains to the university's strategic plan.

The story at the University of Florida took a different turn. After it jettisoned its venture with Pearson, the university did not abandon its effort to set up a totally online campus. Instead, the university hired a new director, scaled back its ambitious enrollment goals, focused on serving students from Florida (the initial business plan was based on attracting a significant number of out-of-state students) and developed an optional package allowing online access to campus amenities such as recreation centers and shuttles. Online students received a discount on tickets to athletic events. In short, the goal was to more fully incorporate the University of Florida Online as an option for both non-traditional and traditional students primarily in Florida. It is being governed and managed accordingly (Straumshein 2016).

Situating Online Education Within the Organization

Where online education is situated within the university has a significant impact on its operation. In fact, Howell, Williams and Lindsay asserted that the success or failure of online educational programs could be attributed, to a large degree, to where they are situated within the university (2003). Minimally, the organizational location of the online education will define a program's reporting structure: to whom the administrators of online education are answerable; what resources are directly available to online education; and, what new lines of communication may need to be established. At base, both strategic planning and planning strategically are, in their essence, communication processes (figure 3.5).

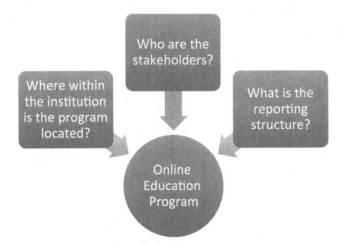

Figure 3.5 Planning Strategically for Online Programs

Consequently, having a clear understanding of the stakeholders to whom the plans must be presented, negotiated and communicated is essential. Moreover, in many ways, where online educational programs are lodged in the overall organizational chart of a university provides a clear message about the importance of the overall project at any given time (Shelton and Saltsman 2005).

Identifying the organizational context for online education for any specific institution presents three immediate conundrums. First, online education has largely developed in an ad hoc fashion, driven by unique local factors with roots in many different areas of the university (King and Alperstein 2015). For example, a study of online education at six universities and university systems, by the consulting group PwC in conjunction with the Educause Center for Applied Research, found at least three distinct modules as state university systems began to build out their online educational programs in earnest more than a decade ago (Lozier et al. 2002). For example, the State University of New York established the SUNY Learning Network (SLN), which provides online registration, access to library resources, student orientation for online courses, technical support and an online catalog that lists all the online courses offered throughout the 60-plus-campus network. Advanced Learning and Information Services in the system's office of the provost governs the SLN. An advisory board comprised of a subset of campus presidents and vice presidents also oversees operations. But the SLN is not a separate degree-granting institution. Each campus individually decides what courses and programs to offer through the SLN and provides actual registration and other student services. When the SLN was established, SUNY had already since the 1970s been operating Empire State College, a "campus" geared toward the needs of adult learners that made extensive use of distance education.

In contrast to the SUNY initiative, the Pennsylvania State University, which has 24 campuses and 17 colleges, launched its World Campus in the late 1990s specifically to cater to off-campus students. It is administered by the vice president for outreach and extension and has an extensive staff for marketing, finance, technical support and instructional design. As a cost center, the World Campus identifies the programs it wishes to offer and is required to cover all of its own development and operating costs. The Penn State World Campus is not charged with providing support for online education on the residential campuses. Finally, at the time of the study, the University System of Georgia relied on what it called the Advanced Learning Technologies (ALT) unit to provide online learning opportunities for its 34 institutions ranging from research universities to community colleges. ALT was led by an assistant vice chancellor for Advanced Learning Technologies and housed in the system's academic and financial affairs division. It had a staff of 18 and a budget of $3 million. At the time the study was conducted, three major state university systems had engaged in online education in three different ways. At the system level, SUNY had established what could best be called a clearinghouse or portal.

Penn State established what in essence was a freestanding virtual campus. The driving force for online education at the system level for the University System of Georgia was primarily a technical support unit that could provide services to the individual campuses. The organization location and governing structure for each of those initiatives constrained and defined the kinds of planning they could reasonably do to develop online education in their respective settings.

The roots of online education and the primary responsibility for online education are just as varied from campus to campus. An informal survey of online educational programs demonstrated that online education started from at least six different organizational locations on different campuses. In some cases, online education was an outgrowth of a continuing education initiative or division. In others, the information technology unit had a mandate to try to foster the general use of educational technology, and online education emerged from those activities. In other settings, individual academic departments launched the first online programs. Sometimes the deans of specific schools within a university had the vision to build out online educational programs. And sometimes pressure to create online programs came from the office of the provost or other senior administrators. Not infrequently, the drive for online education comes from interdisciplinary centers for teaching and learning (figure 3.6).

Given the variations in the ways in which online education programs are started, so too are the organizational structures just as varied. From a high-level perspective, online education can have one of three different relationships to the overall structure of a university. In many cases, it is still completely independent and autonomous from the primary academic project. In some cases and to some extent, online education has been completely integrated into the regular operation of a specific campus that also offers more traditional educational programs, although this has not frequently emerged in practice. And, in most cases, online education is no longer completely isolated, nor is it completely integrated.

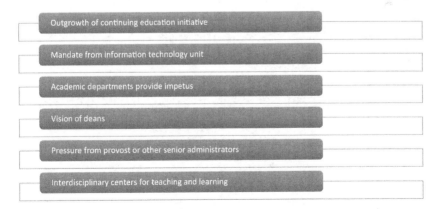

Figure 3.6 Origin of Online Programs Within University

Each of these relationships poses strategic challenges (Hill n.d.). The second difficulty in assessing the institutional context for online education is that in many cases, since online education touches on many different aspects of the university, the management of online programs cuts across institutional lines in ways that other university operations do not. For example, at the Northern Illinois University, the office for online program development and support is a joint venture between the office of the vice president for outreach, engagement and regional development, and the provost's office. At the Florida Institute of Technology, there is a vice president for online learning, but that person reports not to the vice president for academic affairs but directly to the university's chief operating officer. Moreover, the responsibility for academic technology lies with the vice president for information technology, and the instructional design group is under the direction of the vice president for institutional effectiveness. In other words, the resources needed to move online programs forward has been dispersed among four different organizational divisions, which may or may not have the appropriate lateral lines of communication established to work in concert.

As the pressure on senior administrators from boards of trustees and state legislatures to launch online educational programs has grown, new kinds of structures such as centers for innovation have been developed (figure 3.7). The relationship between those new centers and other lines of authority in the various institutions is not always entirely settled. Indeed, as Gilmore, Hirschorn and Kelly have pointed out, colleges and universities have seen a proliferation of subunits, which, although loosely coupled, are also what they called pervasively loosely coupled. The subunits can be comprised of directors, administrators, faculty members and support personnel from many different sectors of the university. Consequently, the path to move initiatives forward is not clear (Gilmore et al. 1999).

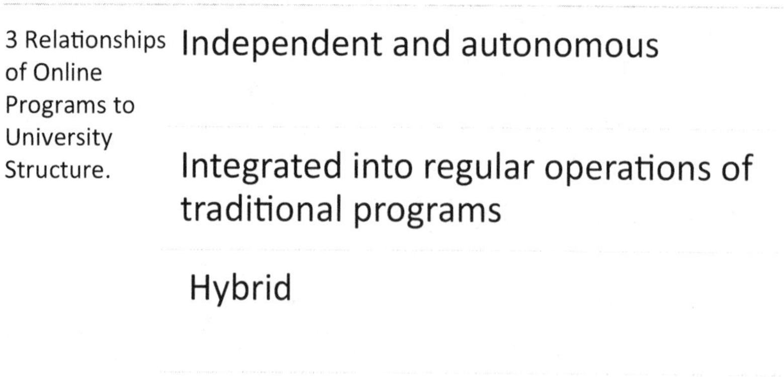

3 Relationships of Online Programs to University Structure.

Independent and autonomous

Integrated into regular operations of traditional programs

Hybrid

Figure 3.7 3 Relationships of Online Programs to University Structure

The third difficulty in identifying the organizational context for online education is that as online education expands in any specific setting, responsibility for creating, administering and managing online programs often shifts as well. For example, at one public institution in the Midwest, responsibility for distance learning and online education moved from the director of information technology to an assistant provost and then back to the director of information technology within the space of just a couple of years. Complicating matters, there were three provosts in five years, making it hard to establish a steady relationship between online education and academic affairs. At another university, the responsibility for online education was originally located in the office of technology services. (Since technology services offices generally are responsible for the implementation and administration of a university's learning management system, in many cases that is where administrators turn first when they initiate online learning efforts.) As interest in online education grew among senior administrators, the provost's office took the lead in exploring options, and online education was added as a specific responsibility in an associate provost's portfolio. After a year, the deans at the various schools in the university became more (or less) active in promoting the growth of online education. And while online education was still at a nascent stage overall, information technology, the provost's office and the various deans were all active in some aspect of the organization and governance of the programs. Examples like these are commonplace. Forty percent of the participants in a 2009 survey about managing online education revealed that online operations had reorganized within the past two years and 59 percent expected to reorganize within the next two years. Even more revealing, 30 percent who had undergone reorganization within two years expected to reorganize again within the next two years. The main catalysts for the reorganization were budgetary, challenges in leadership at either the institutional or the program levels, and an overall effort to make the administration of online education more centralized (Green and Wagner 2011). Planning in higher education is always a challenge. But the wide variation for online education within the organizational structure magnifies that challenge. If strategic planning and planning strategically both imply somehow aligning priorities, it is difficult to know who will actually control the resources necessary for a plan to succeed: the appropriate lines of communication to make the case to secure those resources, and the relationship of those responsible for the growth of online education to the other stakeholders in the university. Planning strategically helps to clarify those questions.

Academic Planning Structure

Whenever an institution engages in a planning process, several questions immediately present themselves. First, who specifically should be included in the process? How long should the process take? How binding should the results of the process be on the future activities of the institution? And what incentives should be in place to encourage participation in the process and implementation of the plan (figure 3.8)?

On the university level, assembling the personnel for a strategic planning process follows one of two paths. In some cases, a university may have a permanent strategic planning committee made up of key stakeholders across the university. Alternatively, colleges and universities will convene an ad hoc steering committee to guide the strategic planning process, which will disband once the plan has been created. Both approaches, at the university level, have their strengths and weaknesses. Neither, however, can be an effective model of planning strategically from the middle, although, within certain contexts, they could be modified to be functional for online education.

A permanent strategic planning committee has three primary strengths (Hinton 2012). First, planning is a complicated process, and, by establishing a permanent committee, members can gain expertise in the planning process. Second, since planning cuts across normal divisional lines and, correspondingly, members of the committee will be drawn from disparate corners of the university, a permanent structure enables committee members to get to know each other better and to develop ongoing working relationships. Finally, a permanent committee can help monitor the progress made toward achieving the plan's goals. But a permanent strategic planning committee has several drawbacks as well. As Hinton points out, sometimes a planning committee will expect that every decision and step taken to fulfill the strategic plan must be approved by the committee—at best, setting up bureaucratic obstacles to achieving the plan's goals and, at worse, engaging in power struggles with other governance bodies. At the opposite end of the spectrum, some permanent strategic planning committees do not believe that they are empowered to make any decisions at all, and

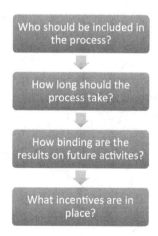

Figure 3.8 Questions Regarding the Planning Process

their plans take the form of suggestions or ideas that are easily ignored. Both of those pitfalls can potentially be circumvented if the strategic planning committee's charge and responsibilities are carefully delineated. The most common reason that permanent committees for strategic planning fail, however, is that they are not embedded tightly into ongoing university decision processes. Strategic planning committees cannot communicate effectively enough or regularly enough to other stakeholders in the university to implement their plans: they are not positioned in a way that would allow them to provide strong leadership; and they cannot collect enough input into the process to ensure their plans are relevant and meaningful (Wirkkula 2007). In short, permanent planning committees often are marginalized, and their recommendations carry little weight with important constituencies across campus.

The alternative approach to campus-wide strategic planning has been developed to address the specific shortcomings and pitfalls of a permanent strategic planning committee. In place of a permanent planning committee, a steering committee with the mandate to guide the strategic process planning is formed with the intention that the committee will disband at the end of the planning process. That committee, in turn, determines the initial framework for the planning process. Typically, the strategic planning steering committee will then establish a series of subcommittees to address different aspects of the strategic plans as well as a series of efforts to solicit the advice of the larger campus community. The strategic planning steering committee then takes the lead role in actually crafting the plan and guiding it through the governance process. The animating spirit behind this approach is the idea that the larger the community involved in the strategic planning process, the greater the likelihood that it will be embraced and have the intended impact over time. But there is little evidence that this approach is more effective than the alternative (Birnbaum 2000). It, too, has several potential shortcomings (Rowley et al. 1997). Not surprisingly, the makeup of the steering committee has a major impact on the development of the plan. By definition the assignment is temporary, and identifying people, particularly faculty members, who are willing to serve and are also in a position to make the time commitment demanded can be problematic. Moreover, major constituencies must be represented on the steering committee without allowing one perspective to be over-represented or under-represented. In many universities, faculty members perceive themselves as being at the center of the university experience; managing faculty representation can be tricky. The first question to address is: what should be the overall percentage of faculty representation on various committees? If the faculty feels that it does not have a significant voice, many members of the faculty might simply ignore the strategic planning process in general and any plan produced. But if faculty representation is too large, other important functions of the university may be slighted or overlooked. In general, many faculty members do not have expertise in planning, and many are more focused on their own work than that of overall governance of the institution. The same kinds of issues that arise in the creation of the committees appear when subcommittees are formed as well. But even the basic premise of creating subcommittees and trying to include as many stakeholders as possible can be questioned. In sum: the greater the number of people who offer input during the planning process, the less likely that individual voices will be heard. In this way, the entire process can be discredited.

Finally, the appropriate relationship of the university president to the strategic planning committees is up for debate. If the president plays too active a role, voices with differing opinions may be silenced or the plan may be too closely associated with the president, inviting opposition. But if the president is not engaged enough, observers may conclude the president is not committed to the outcome (Rowley et al. 1997, 158). Some observers argue that the same models used for campus-wide strategic planning can be used at the unit level such as for online education as well (Rowley et al. 1997, 172). But the same sorts of challenges that bedevil university strategic planning committees are not ameliorated when scaled down to a unit level, and in many ways the problems are exacerbated. An alternative to employing classic strategic planning committees, either permanent or ad hoc, is to attempt to employ ongoing governance or oversight committees for online education in a planning process. Many institutions already have in place an advisory board for online education (or for the interdisciplinary center that has ground-level responsibility for online education). Alternatively, in some institutions, the academic senate has empowered committees to deal with issues around online education and distance learning. In most cases, however, these committees will not be well positioned to chart the future course of online education in an institution, and in many instances such committees can actually serve as a barrier to progress. At one university, for example, under the guise of wanting to ensure quality, the Academic Senate's Distance Learning Committee claimed the authority to approve every proposed online course. Their guidelines were complex; their approval process was slow and lacked transparency. As a result, very few faculty members ever proposed online courses. The process was too fraught with difficulties and delays. Even in situations in which the members of an oversight or advisory committee do not have an active antipathy for online education (although eventually even those who are opposed to online education must be brought into the planning process), many of the members of the ongoing oversight, advisory or governance committees will not have the expertise or commitment necessary to help develop online education and create its future. Since online education is in a period of rapid evolution, effective stewardship and planning requires a significant understanding of the broader trends at work and how they intersect with the particular institution. This takes time and attention, more time and attention than most busy people fulfilling a service obligation are willing to give.

Planning strategically, as opposed to strategic planning, requires a fluid and flexible approach to engaging with other stakeholders. In the place of a strategic planning committee, either permanent or temporary, or permanent governing bodies, at either the university or the faculty level, planning strategically requires the development of a network with whom those responsible for online education can collaborate. The exact participants in any planning process can change, depending on the specific task at hand.

Planning Online Education

Not surprisingly, as colleges and universities have attempted to address the issues raised by the growth of online education, from time to time, the people most responsible for promulgating online efforts on campuses have attempted to create strategic plans. In those situations, planning committees have been assembled, responsibilities assigned, proposals debated, and reports written and published. The exact size, makeup and charge of the committee varies from campus to campus, depending on several variables including the current state of online education at the specific institution and the support for online education from the senior administration. For example, in 2012, a community college in Southern California convened a planning committee to create a distance-learning plan. The college had been engaged in distance learning for more than a decade at that point, but the initiative was haphazard, uneven and floundering. Individual faculty members could propose their own online courses, which would be approved by the curriculum committee of the Academic Senate, or not, often with little explanation. At other times, the faculty member would opt to implement a "course in a box" from a third-party vendor, with little oversight. Complicating matters, as is not uncommon in community colleges, many of the instructors had adjunct or affiliate status. After ten years, nobody knew exactly how many courses were online, but the estimate was that in any given semester, perhaps 5 to 10 percent of the total courses offered were available online. In 2009, a new associate vice president for instructional and information technology services came onboard with an initial goal of transitioning the school from its home-grown learning management system to a more contemporary LMS and to integrate the new LMS with other campus management software systems. As part of that process, the issues of distance learning arose. How could, should and would the new LMS support online education? The answer depended in part on what the nature of the distance learning or online education program at the university would be. To address the question, a task force was convened that was chartered by the college's central planning committee—its highest level of governance—and co-chaired by the associate vice president for instructional and information technology services and a professor of English. The committee had four members—two faculty members, an associate dean for academic service and the system's librarian. The result was a formal ten-page strategic plan. The process at that community college was very different from the steps taken at a prestigious research university in the northeast. In that case, one of the nine schools at the university had an online program that had been largely funded through a grant. In addition, there were other online educational efforts sprinkled throughout the university. As interest in online education grew in the general public and as the university's competitors began to launch Massive Open Online Courses (and reap the accompanying publicity), the chief information officer, who was evaluating several major new information systems, commissioned a white paper to investigate what online education at the university might look like five years into the future, and whether the institutional structures were in place to support it. The white paper, which mandated the creation of a director of online learning for the entire university, came to serve as a guide for the ongoing growth in online education at the university level while many of the operational and tactical decisions about what to do were delegated to the individual schools.

In another example at a regional state university in the south, the president saw a major opportunity to expand the campus's reach and brand recognition through expanding its presence in online education. A strategic planning committee made up of primarily deans and associate deans from the university's various professional schools, representatives of information technology, and members of the instructional design groups was convened. The executive director of the division of eLearning and professional studies chaired the committee. As part of a larger strategic planning exercise at the university, the work of the committee, which had 13 members but only two faculty representatives, was guided by an outside consultant and used a methodology common to academic strategic planning. More than 400 online instructors were surveyed. Key stakeholders were interviewed, and focus groups were consulted. The end product was a formal strategic plan for online education at the university.

In each case, a different process to creating a strategic plan was followed. And none of the approaches failed, in the sense that a plan was actually produced. But despite their differences, each instance had three pivotal elements in common that suggest that none may be a sustainable approach to planning strategically for online education. First, a very small inner core of people did the bulk of the work. Input from other stakeholders was solicited by various methods, while synthesizing that information and packaging it into goals and strategies fell to an inner group most responsible for online education. Second, executing the plans required outreach and evangelism to many parts of the university as the goals and objectives reaching into many different areas of the university. Though in some cases the responsibility for implementing certain goals was assigned, prioritizing those responsibilities would inevitably vary from setting to setting depending on the particular pressures felt by the leadership of those groups. And even in the most expansive process, not every stakeholder was well represented in the inner group that actually crafted a plan. For example, while the planning committee in the most formal process had representatives from the deans' offices of the various schools, there was very little faculty representation, which potentially could set up a contentious dynamic. But the clearest evidence that the committee approach may not be the most efficient for planning strategically is that in many cases in which a strategic plan for online education has been developed and published, there are no plans to replicate the process, even when the timeframe for the plan has expired. While they are useful exercises, particularly to generate conversation about online education, the impact of those plans does not seem to justify the effort in many cases.

The Planning Network

The concept of developing a planning network for planning strategically in lieu of creating either an ad hoc or permanent strategic planning committee or using an established oversight or advisory committee to develop a strategic plan rests on the four key observations and principles based on a review of more than 25 strategic plans for online education developed at colleges and universities ranging from community colleges to Ivy League universities over the past five years. First, in most cases, the bulk of the plans were actually written by two or three key members of the committee—those most committed and interested in online education. (In some cases, consultants drafted the majority of the plan. Those plans face the most daunting challenges in being embraced widely, because nobody from the permanent campus community "owns" the plan or need be fully invested in the plan.) The observation that people most identified with online education should be the heavy lifters when it comes to planning could have been anticipated and in many ways is very efficient. The people most committed to online education will be the people who are also most aware of the national trends and the specific local opportunities and constraints. Those most committed to online education will be the most willing to devote the time needed to plan—should be in the best position to implement the plan and the most capable and interested in measuring its effectiveness. However, although a small team of leaders—perhaps two or three people—can be expected to do the majority of the planning, they cannot work in isolation. As planning takes place, they must be mindful of a concentric set of communities and audiences to whom the plan will ultimately need to be communicated and embraced in some way. Those communities need to be included in the planning process in some way and at some point, depending on the specific objective or goal.

Beyond the core leadership, certain segments of any college or university are implicated in almost every aspect online education. They include the faculty, the information technology group (particularly the instructional technology team), and the library. Finally, most proposals that will emerge from a process in which people are planning strategically will be subjected to some kind of approval or governance process. Depending on where the impetus for online education is located, the senior administrator from the division or organization in which online education is situated has an ongoing interest in the development of online education. With that in mind, an advisory board made up of representatives from the different parts of the university that have an ongoing relationship online education can serve as a sounding board during a planning process. This committee cannot be expected to do the homework needed to create a plan or develop the proposals. But it can be used to understand the obstacles any specific proposal may face and suggest tactics to overcome those obstacles. While an advisory board can serve as a permanent early feedback mechanism, the next component of the planning network will vary from objective to objective or plan to plan. Although the advisory board should have at least one member oriented toward governance, many of the proposals that emerge from a planning process may be subjected to complex approval and governance processes. For example, proposals may need approval from the academic faculty, senior academic administrators, and regulatory bodies; there may be budgetary implications. The precise approval process depends both on the organizational and situational context of online education as well as the specific proposal itself. Different goals touch different parts of the institution in different ways. But the stakeholders and decision-makers that will be impacted by any particular proposal must be identified and consulted with during the planning process. This part of the planning network is opportunistic and ad hoc. The final ring of the planning network consists of representatives to the communities to whom the plan must be embraced if it is to be successful. For example, if a goal is to facilitate the creation of additional online courses, faculty members who have strong lines of communication to their colleagues should be identified. If a goal is to expand the number of online programs, lines communication to the marketing teams must be established. Ideally, this kind of outreach should begin in the planning process and not wait until a proposal has been ratified.

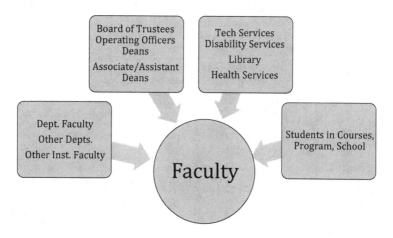

Figure 3.9 Example of Planning Network

Grunig and Hunt (1984) developed what they referred to as a linkage model that is useful in developing a planning network. As can be seen in Figure 3.9, the model separates stakeholders into four groups: enabling stakeholders, like boards of trustees that have authority and control over an organization; functional stakeholders, which might refer to employees or consumers, which in the case of higher education might refer to students; normative stakeholders, which might include other faculty or departments; and diffused stakeholders that arise from time to time, like the library. Freeman identifies stakeholders as those groups or individuals who are affected by an organization or who can affect achieving an organization's objectives (1994). Grunig, however, took an issues orientation to identify stakeholders, suggesting that in the case of higher education, planning networks may be conceptualized as fluid, because stakeholders may come and go as issues arise and become diminished as planning proceeds toward achieving the organization's objectives.

In summary, the concept of a planning network mirrors and informs the concept of planning strategically. The people most committed to online education are at the core. Those are the people who prioritize online education and will devote the time needed to develop good proposals to appropriately develop online education in their specific setting. The network emanates from the core, enveloping those who should or may have an interest in a specific proposal or objective. The less the ongoing interest in online education, the less time demanded from the participants. Creating a planning network as opposed to a planning committee offers several advantages. As planning gets underway, it alerts the key planners to barriers and obstacles any specific idea may ultimately encounter. Second, it helps identify and clarify the needed approval processes, which is essential for establishing a realistic timeframe for implementation. Third, it alerts key stakeholders about new ideas and proposals early, both allowing them to provide feedback, and more importantly, enabling them to lay the groundwork needed to implement the idea, if approved. Finally, it recognizes that for any plan to succeed, it must be effectively communicated to larger constituencies in the university that have varying degrees of interest in online education generally.

Conclusion

The concept of planning strategically represents an effective alternative approach distinct from both formal strategic planning and traditional operational planning. It has been shaped by several fundamental factors and insights. First, while strategic planning has been widely adopted in both the corporate world and higher education, its impact on the direction of those organizations has been mixed at best. In trying to understand why so many strategic plans do not work as expected, one of the variables researchers have identified that can have a significant impact on the success of an institutional-wide strategic plan is the degree in which people in the middle of the organization are involved in the process at every level from information gathering to execution. In fact, some observers believe that in the final analysis, middle-level managers are the ones primarily responsible for the ultimate contours of any strategic plan as it unfolds through the actual experience of the organization. On most campuses, the ongoing responsibility for the day-to-day activities associated with online education is located somewhere in the middle of the organizational structure (or else in a marginal unit such as continuing or professional education). Consequently, those most responsible for shaping the future of online education will be structurally in the middle of the organization as well, and not have either the institutional authority or the resources required by traditional strategic planning. Planning strategically represents a methodology for those in the middle to effectively chart a course to the future within the context of what may be possible at any given time, recognizing the limits of their own influence. Since the approach embodied by planning strategically is not seen as the strictly within the domain of senior management, the general constructs associated with strategic planning are not necessarily needed or even desired. The organizational structure of a university does not lend itself for those in the middle—faculty or directors on the staff level—to convene a committee, either permanent or ad hoc, to manage a planning process. Moreover, the governing or oversight committees commonly in place do not generally have a mandate to create a plan for online education. In most cases, the members of those committees will not have the expertise, interest, time or commitment to craft a comprehensive plan. Nor will they be well positioned to implement, execute and evaluate the plan. The limits of the traditional strategic planning process can be seen through a review of the efforts of campuses that have utilized the plan. In many settings in which a university has undergone a traditional strategic planning process for online education, while a plan has emerged (an indication that the process has not technically failed), the participants did not plan to repeat the process, even when the proposed timeframe for the plan had expired. Therefore, the process was not seen as an ongoing element in the development of online education.

Planning strategically requires a different framework and perspective. Those responsible for online education must first understand where they are situated organizationally in the university: to whom do they report; their champion at the senior administrative levels; and with whom do they have to collaborate to achieve their goals and objectives. Based on that analysis, those driving online education forward can build a planning network to support planning activities. A planning network consists of a concentric series of stakeholders that can be consulted in the planning process based on their involvement in online education; their commitment to online education; and their position in the governance and approval process for any specific initiative. Viewed in this way, anybody associated with online education, even if they do not have the primary responsibility, can effectively plan. In other words, departments that run online programs can effectively plan strategically. Centers for online education, distance learning or teaching effectiveness can use these concepts. Continuing education or remedial education units focused on adult learners or degree completion can plan strategically. Senior administrators can facilitate planning strategically for online education specifically within the groups they manage. In each case, the specific players in the process will be different, but the planning process can still be successful, with success defined as the plans actually being implemented and their effectiveness assessed in an ongoing effort to plan strategically. Despite the difference in approach, particularly the jettisoning of the formal committee structure, planning strategically retains many of the concepts of strategic planning. The units of the university steering the future course for online education need to have a mission and a vision. They need to establish goals and objectives. And they need to propose measures to gauge their success. But in place of a large, formal, comprehensive process, planning strategically is nimble and flexible. It acknowledges from the outset that planning is a communication activity, and, to succeed, a communication strategy must be an integral part of the process. Online education touches on many parts of the university, and most steps forward will require buy-in from stakeholders for whom online education is not a priority, if it is on their agenda at all.

Planning strategically has broad applications and can have a powerful impact in shaping the future. It can be applied to goals and objectives of various sizes, scopes, magnitudes and time frames. Planning strategically can be utilized by units in the university that are deeply involved in online education and those with only specific or limited interest or responsibility. But most importantly, by planning strategically, planning can become a continuous, ongoing process, rather than a batch (to borrow a term from computing), time-bound activity. And that will allow online education to develop at the most expeditious pace possible within any given set of circumstances.

References

179 Creighton Faculty and Staff Complete Online Teaching and Learning Course (n.d.). Center for Academic Innovation. Retrieved from: www.creighton.edu/center-for-academic-innovation/news-and-events

AAUP (1966). Statement on Government of Colleges and Universities. Retrieved from: https://www.aaup.org/report/statement-government-colleges-and-universities

Birnbaum, R. (2000). *Management Fads in Higher Education: Where They Came From, What They Do, Why They Fail.* San Francisco, CA: Jossey-Bass, p. 195.

Bracke, A. (2004). Strategy and the Middle Manager. *Training: The Magazine of Human Resource Development.* Retrieved from: http://kepner-tregoe.de/linkservid/54F02F00-AB8F-4BBB-9CAA4B7731F70478/showMeta/0/

Collins, J. C. (1995). Building Companies to Last. Inc. Special Issue: *The State of Small Business.* Retrieved from: www.jimcollins.com/article_topics/articles/building-companies.html

Collins, J. C. (2001). *Good to Great: Why Some Companies Make the Leap . . . and Others Don't.* New York: HarperBusiness.

Collins, J. C. and Porras, J. (1994). *Built to Last: Successful Habits of Visionary Companies* New York: HarperBusiness, p. 9.

Cornerstone Plan, The (2013). Retrieved from: http://planning.virginia.edu/current-strategic-plan

Elliott, G. (n.d.). The Role of Middle Managers in Strategy. *Performance and Strategy.* Retrieved from: www.performanceandstrategy.com/articles-of-interest/middle-managers

Floyd, S. and Wooldridge, B. (2000). *Building Strategy From the Middle: Reconceptualizing the Strategy Process*. Thousand Oaks, CA: Sage Publications, pp. 38–39.

Freeman, R. E. (1994). The Politics of Stakeholder Theory: Some Future Directions. *Business Ethics Quarterly*, 4:4, pp. 409–421.

Gayle, D., Tewarie, B. and Wright Jr., A. Q. (2003). *Governance in the Twenty-First-Century University: Approaches to Effective Leadership and Strategic Management*. ASHE-ERIC Higher Education Report, Eric Clearinghouse on Higher Education, Washington, DC, pp. XI–XII.

Gibson, A. (2009). *Budgeting in Higher Education, Education Department of the General Conference of Seventh-Day Adventists*, Silver Spring, MD. Retrieved from: http://education.gc.adventist. org/documents/Budgeting%20in%20Higher%20Education.pdf

Gibson, A. (n.d.). Resource Allocation in Higher Education: Budgetary Concepts and Terms, Allocation Concepts and Terms, Achieving Normative Consensus, Conclusion. *Stateuniversity.com*. Retrieved from: http://education.stateuniversity.com/pages/2368/Resource-Allocation-in-Higher-Education.html

Gilmore, T., Hirschhorn, L. and Kelly, M. (1999). Challenges of Leading and Planning in Higher Education. *CFAR*, p. 4. Retrieved from: www.cfar.com/sites/default/files/resources/Leading_Planning_Ed.pdf

Ginzberg, M. (1978). Steps Towards More Effective Implementation of MS and MIS. *Interfaces*, 8, pp. 57–63.

Green, K. and Wagner, E. (2011, January/February). Online Education: Where Is It Going? What Should Boards Know. *Trusteeship Magazine*, Association of Governing Boards of Universities and Colleges. Retrieved from: http://agb.org/trusteeship/2011/januaryfebruary/online-education-where-is-it-going-what-should-boards-know

Grunig, J. and Hunt, T. (1994). *Managing Public Relations*. Boston, MA: Centage Learning.

Henrickson, D. (2015, October 8). *Message to Campus*. Creighton University. Retrieved from: www. creighton.edu/office-president/messages-campus/october-8-2015.

Hill, C. (n.d.). *Integrating Distance Learning Programs Into the Institution. Distance Learning Administration and Policy: Strategies for Achieving Excellence*. Magna Publications, p. 23. Retrieved from: www.facultyfocus.com

Hinton, K. (2012). *A Practical Guide to Strategic Planning in Higher Education Society for College and University Planning*, pp. 14–16. Retrieved from: www.scup.org

History of Technology at Creighton University (n.d.). Retrieved from: https://blueline.instructure. com/courses/1076543/pages/history-of-technology-at-creighton-university?module_item_id=9727408

Howell, S., Williams, P. and Lindsay, N. (2003, Fall). Thirty-Two Trends Affecting Distance Education: An Informed Foundation for Strategic Planning. *Online Journal of Distance Education Administration*, 6:3. Retrieved from: http://www.westga.edu/~distance/ojdla/fall63/howell63. html

Jaschick, S. (2012, June 20). The Email Trails at UVa. *Inside Higher Ed*. Retrieved from: www.inside-highered.com/news/2012/06/20/e-mails-show-uva-board-wanted-big-online-push

Jaschick, S. (2015, October 22). U of Florida Cancels Huge Pearson Contract. *Inside Higher Ed*. Retrieved from: www.insidehighered.com/quicktakes/2015/10/22/u-florida-cancels-huge-pearson-contract

King, E. and Alperstein, N. (2015). *Best Practices in Online Program Development*. New York and London: Routledge.

Langley, A. (1989, December). In Search of Rationality: The Purposes Behind the Use of Formal Analysis in Organizations. *Administrative Science Quarterly*, 34:4, pp. 598–631.

Linn, M. (2008). Planning Strategically and Strategic Planning. *The Bottom Line: Managing Library Finances*, 21:1, pp. 20–23.

Mantere, S. (2008, March). Role Expectations and Middle Manager Strategic Agency. *Journal of Management Studies*, 45:2, pp. 294–316.

Massy, W., ed. (1996). *Resource Allocation in Higher Education*. Ann Arbor: University of Michigan Press.

Olson, G. (2009, July 23). What Exactly Is Shared Governance. *Chronicle of Higher Education*. Retrieved from: www.chronicle.com/article/Exactly-What-Is-Shared/47065/

Perry, K. H. (2014, March 5). Creighton Hunts for Jobs to Cut or Share as Part of New Strategic Plan. *Omaha World-Herald*. Retrieved from:www.omaha.com/news/creighton-hunts-for-jobs-to-cut-or-share-as-part/article_487d873e-a57c-5669-a874-8b6be6f0cb96.html

Perry, K. H. (2015, April 7). Creighton Faculty Leaders Say School's Vision Flawed, Issue No-Confidence Vote in Strategic Plan. *Omaha World-Herald*. Retrieved from: www.omaha.com/news/education/creighton-faculty-leaders-say-school-s-vision-flawed-issue-no/article_5bee1320-4db9-560b-96d3-8d2a7accb2e4.html

Rivera, G. (2012, September 11). *Emergent Strategy*. Interaction Institute for Social Change. Retrieved from: http://interactioninstitute.org/emergent-strategy/

Rowley, D., Lujan, H. and Dolence, M. (1997). *Strategic Change in Colleges and Universities*. San Francisco, CA: Jossey-Bass Publishers, pp. 170–175.

Seal, R. (2012, July 12). Faculty Senate Task Force Releases Report on U.Va. Online Learning Initiatives. *UVAToday*. Retrieved from: https://news.virginia.edu/content/faculty-senate-task-force-releases-report-uva-online-learning-initiatives

Shelton, K. and Saltsman, G. (2005). *An Administrator's Guide to Online Education*. Greenwich, CT: Information Age Publishing, p. 37.

Straumshein, C. (2013, October 1). How to Build a University in Several Months. *Inside Higher Ed*. Retrieved from: www.insidehighered.com/news/2013/10/01/u-florida-races-create-online-campus-jan-1-opening-date-approaches

Straumshein, C. (2016, November 15). Florida's New Plan for Online Education. *Inside Higher Ed*. Retrieved from: www.insidehighered.com/news/2016/11/15/u-florida-online-looks-ahead-after-canceling-deal-pearson

Surbhi, S. (2015, May 6). Difference Between Strategy and Planning. *Key Diffences.com*. Retrieved from: http://keydifferences.com/difference-between-planning-and-strategy.html

Wirkkula, L. (2007, September). *Human Perspectives on Strategic Planning: The Lived Experiences of Deans and a Public Research University*. PhD. Thesis, University of Minnesota, pp. 24–27.

4
Vision and Mission

In 1851, Reverend Dr. Paul Cullen, soon to be archbishop of Dublin, Ireland, invited John Henry Newman to serve as the first rector of the Catholic University of Dublin. It was a bold move. Newman was a controversial figure, best known as the leader of the Oxford Movement in England. As the vicar of St. Mary's University Church in Oxford in the 1830s, Newman along with others had authored a series of tracts calling for the reincorporation of some older Catholic traditions into the Anglican theology and liturgy, culminating in what came to be known as Tract 90, which, like many of the other tracts in the series, made the argument that the Anglican Church was ecclesiastically more oriented toward Catholicism than Protestantism. That stance made Newman's position untenable at Oxford. In its wake, in 1845, Newman converted to Catholicism and traveled to Rome, where he was ordained as a priest in 1847 (Kane 1977). Dublin was the home of Trinity College, founded in 1587 and one of the seven "ancient" universities of Britain and Ireland. Trinity College was established in part to consolidate the Tudor monarchy in Ireland and seen as a symbol of the Protestant domination there. In contemporary terms, the Catholic University was being established to compete with Trinity and would provide access to an underserved population.

One of Newman's first activities upon arriving in Dublin was to deliver five public lectures, in which he laid out his vision for a university—not just the university he was organizing, but for university education at large. These lectures eventually formed the basis of his seminal book *The Idea of a University* that was first published later that year. The lectures were timely, he argued, because, after a long period of stagnation, the English university was in a period of great self-reformation (Newman 1952). Newman's vision for a university was a "school of universal learning, in which professors and students interested in knowledge of all kinds and drawn from all parts of the country gathered for the communication and circulation of thought, by means of personal intercourse" (Modern History Sourcebook n.d.). This assertion concerning the nature of a university was not necessarily obvious, even in the 1850s. After all, Newman noted, with printing and publishing as developed as it was at the time, people had easy and ready access to knowledge and information. Why was there a need to gather together at a university to circulate and distribute knowledge? The answer Newman offered was this: "[I]f we wish to become exact and fully furnished in any branch of knowledge which is diversified and complicated, we must consult the living man and listen to his living voice." No matter how complete and detailed, books could not answer every question discerning readers may raise when reading them, echoing a similar complaint Socrates had lodged against reading more than 2,000 years earlier. For that, "we must come to the teachers of wisdom to learn wisdom." According to Newman, it is in that gathering of intellectuals that books have their origins (Modern History Sourcebook n.d.).

The gathering of professors and students representing all areas of knowledge to exchange that information was only one vision of university education that emerged in the second half of the nineteenth century. In 1862, the U.S. Congress passed the Morrill Act, which established what came to be called land grant institutions (because the federal government granted land to the states to sell with the proceeds directed to establishing universities). The universities established through the Morrill Act envisioned teaching agriculture and the mechanical arts, alongside classical and scientific studies. In the 1870s, the Johns Hopkins University was established with research and the creation of new knowledge as its central mandate, and around a decade later Clark University was founded as a university for graduate students only (Newfield 2003). Ironically, however, as Newfield points out, although the new universities of the mid to late nineteenth century offered various visions of their purpose, at the same time they resolutely declined to define their mission in concrete and specific terms. Instead, in some ways perhaps with the intention to keep their options opened, they put forth only the most generic of descriptions. For example, Cornell University was to be an institution in which any person could find instruction in any subject. Its first president, Andrew White, contended that four years of good study in any one area was probably equal to four years of good study in any other area. And Daniel Coit Gilman, the founding president of the University of California, suggested that the university was a collection of agencies geared to advancing the arts and sciences of every sort and train students for the intellectual life in all fields (Newfield 2003, 26). While modern American universities may have been first established with only broad visions of their missions, at least to a great extent that has changed over time.

Mission and Vision Statements in Organizations

Today, the mission statement and vision statement serve essential roles in strategic planning in both the corporate and non-profit worlds. According to the management-consulting firm Bain and Company, since the 1990s mission statements have been ranked as one of the top-ten management tools in the corporate world, reaching as high as second in the year 2000 and seventh in 2014. Though the use of mission statements in corporate America has dipped in recent years, the satisfaction rate for those who continue to invest the time and effort in developing and refining mission statements remains high (Rigby 2015). And in a landmark study published in 2002, Mullane reported that the senior executives he interviewed overwhelming believed that mission statements helped to both unify organizations and establish internal clarity and direction (2002).

It is not surprising that as colleges and universities have moved toward deploying more contemporary corporate management techniques, devoting resources to crafting specific, at times detailed, mission and vision statements, which are periodically renewed or updated during the strategic planning process. In the best-case scenarios, the mission statement and the vision statement serve as the rudders that guide the choices of the remainder of strategic planning both in the corporate world and in higher education. Choices must be made and defended according to their support of the mission and vision both in the planning process and in the implementation of the plan. Unfortunately, as with many other corporate management techniques generally, and strategic planning generally, the model used for mission statements in the private and the non-profit sectors has not fit comfortably within the organizational structure of the university. Nevertheless, crafting mission statements has become commonplace in the academic world generally, and mission statements have become more frequent at the departmental and administrative unit level.

Understanding the concept and role of mission and vision statements is significant for planning strategically from the middle of the organization for three reasons (figure 4.1). First, given the loosely coupled nature of colleges

3 Reasons for Mission Statements in Planning Strategically	Planning at the unit level has to be justified within the overall university strategic plan
	Planning is part of ongoing development
	Essential tools for assessment

Figure 4.1 3 Reasons for Mission Statements in Planning Strategically

and universities, any planning that takes place within individual units has to be justified within the context of the university's overall strategic plan. Online education is no different. Colleges and universities launch online educational programs for a variety of reasons but in most cases, those reasons will be justified in some way in the strategic plan. And on those campuses in which online education is a low priority, finding those aspects of the overall strategic plan that can be used to justify online education can be the difference between success and failure in new plans and initiatives. Planning strategically from the middle including for online education is premised on the notion that part of the planning process is geared toward gathering the appropriate resources to achieve the desired objectives. Lodging those objectives within the context of the overall strategic plan is critical. Consequently, planning strategically requires an appropriate understanding of the overall mission and vision of the institution as a way to ensure buy-in and support from important decision-makers. Second, a mission and vision are essential components for the ongoing online education's ongoing development. Done right, the mission and vision statements orient planners toward agreed upon goals. And as Lewis Carroll once remarked, "If you don't know where you are going, any road will get you there." Without intentional choices, the end of the road may not at all be what is desired. Settling on a mission and vision is no trivial task. It has to reflect the interests and goals of those responsible for moving online education forward in a given setting, while, at the same time, winning support from those who influence the allocation of resources needed to achieve those goals, even when online education may not be a significant priority for them. Moreover, the mission statement may have to be used to defend online education from its detractors. Finally, mission statements at the program and department level are essential tools for assessment. The struggle to develop online education is ongoing. To compete for resources, leaders of online education must demonstrate that some goal is being achieved and the investments are being well used. A clear mission statement is essential to that process.

This chapter will define the difference between a mission statement and a vision statement and then explore the role that mission and vision statements have come to play in the planning process. It will explore the nuances of developing a mission statement first by examining their use in the corporate and non-profit sector and then by examining how they have been modified in their application in higher education. The chapter will then present a strategy for developing effective mission and vision statements for online education, regardless of the specific circumstances on a given campus. This section on crafting a mission statement for online education has three components. First, it will examine a set of existing university strategic plans and suggest ways in which online education can be justified within the context of the plan. Then, the chapter will detail several specific processes that can be followed to develop a mission statement and a vision statement for online education. Finally, it will propose strategies to assess the strengths and weaknesses or departmental and program mission statements.

In reviewing the experience at John Jay College of Criminal Justice, a part of the City University of New York, in starting John Jay Online, Bruce Rosenbloom observed that while it is very difficult to launch an online program with the support of the senior administration, it is almost impossible to do so without that support. He observed that in the five years that John Jay Online was in development, mid-level administrators and some far-sighted faculty members on other CUNY campuses tried to initiate online offerings, but those efforts rarely had satisfying outcomes and often generated acrimony. It is impossible, he wrote, to develop a vision and implement a vision for online education without every stakeholder being onboard (Rosenbloom 2014). A well-crafted mission statement and vision statement developed within the parameters established by the university's strategic plan are tools to help engineer the consent and more toward the consensus needed to nurture online education. As important, the mission and the vision statement in the corporate world is the cornerstone for the entire planning process.

Mission Statement vs. Vision Statement

In the corporate world (and in other organizations that have adopted strategic planning management techniques), the terms "mission" and "vision" are often confused (Sufi and Lyons 2002). As management consultant Jennell Evans reported, often organizations will develop mission statements that are, in actuality, vision statements and vice versa. Sometimes an agency will develop one but not the other. However, as a guide to planning at the institutional level, both mission statement and the vision statement are important (Evans 2010).

Figure 4.2 3 Considerations When Crafting Mission Statements

In the most basic formulation, the mission statement concisely answers three questions: what an organization does; how it does it; and for whom it does it (figure 4.2). Within that framework, a mission statement for an academic program in a university might read, for example: "The Mission of the Biology B.S. degree program is to prepare students for employment in various biology-related areas and/or for the pursuit of advanced degrees in biology or health-related professional schools by educating them in the fundamental concepts, knowledge, and laboratory/field techniques and skills of the life sciences" (Assessment Department, University of Connecticut n.d.). But that may not be enough. In his very popular TED Talk, which had been seen by nearly 30 million viewers by early 2017, the author and consultant Simon Sinek addressed the question of why some people and organizations inspire great actions and some don't. He argued that all the great leaders and organizations share something in common—what he called the golden circle, which actually consists of three concentric circles (figure 4.3).

The outer ring consists of what Sinek called "what." Most people and organizations in the world know what they do every day, he asserted. Sinek called the second ring "how." The "how" describes the way people go about doing what they do. For companies, he said, this ring may consist of their unique selling proposition or what differentiates them from their competitors. At the center, however, according to Sinek is "why," what is the organization's reason for existence and why should anybody care about the organization (Sinek 2009). An effective mission statement should address all three rings of Sinek's golden circle. Being able to answer the question "why" a company, organization, administrative unit or other element exists is important in harnessing the emotion energy of those involved. It helps foster commitment and belief in the

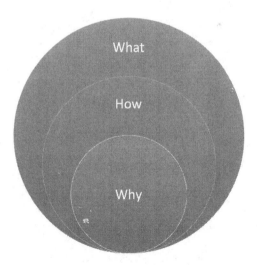

Figure 4.3 Sinek's Golden Circle

tasks at hand. It motivates people, provides a general frame to guide actions and serves as a baseline for decision-making (Horwath 2005).

Consequently, according to Horwath, the mission statement should actually have four components (2005). The first is the definition of the function of the organization. And while it would seem that companies and organizations know what they do (at least Sinek assumes they do), that is not always the case. In a seminal article in 1960, Ted Levitt argued that too many companies focused on the product they were selling rather than the customer needs they fulfilled, so they didn't really understand the role they played in their customers' lives. In doing so, they missed opportunities and were vulnerable to changes in the arenas in which they competed (1960). He called this "marketing myopia," and in its formulation, as automobiles became the dominant mode of transportation in the first part of the twentieth century, companies that provided the bridles and whips for horses and carriages should have redefined themselves as providing leather products to the transportation industry and as suppliers to the new automotive industry instead of failing as carriage manufacturers collapsed. The danger of not really understanding what the function or purpose a company or organization serves is captured in two cautionary cases of corporate shortsightedness. In the late 1970s, Thomas Murphy, the chief executive officer of General Motors, is purported to have remarked that General Motors was not in the business of making cars; it was in the business of making money. Unfortunately, that view led General Motors to continue to build large cars with high profit margins but low quality, long after the oil shocks of the 1970s and the large-scale entry of Japanese automakers in the United States had fundamentally reshaped the auto market. Throughout the 1980s, GM lost market share and often lost money, culminating in the need for a bailout in 2009 by the federal government. Along the same lines, Kenneth Olson, the chairman of the Digital Equipment Corporation, the second-largest computing company in America in the 1970s and 1980s, once opined that he saw no reason that anybody would ever need a personal computer. In 1998, Compaq Computer, a manufacturer of personal computers, purchased Digital Equipment. Clearly, not fully understanding the function an organization performs can have devastating results. Unfortunately too many companies run on their past successes and inertia.

The second element of a mission statement is how a company or organization functions and the tasks it performs. Companies and organizations go about doing their business in various ways, some intentional and some not. While in many industries, organizations perform the same tasks, they go about doing them using different approaches, techniques and tools. This certainly is the case in higher education generally and in online education specifically. The function of all four-year undergraduate colleges and universities is to provide an education that results in a bachelor's level degree. But the way Swarthmore College, with an enrollment of about 1,600 students, goes about providing that education is qualitatively different than the Ohio State University with an enrollment of nearly 50,000 undergraduates in the 2015–2016 academic year. And the way the philosophy department educates its students may or may not differ from the way the chemistry department goes about teaching its students.

The third question a mission statement should answer is for whom the company performs its function. For private enterprise, this part of the mission statement primarily serves to define the market and market segments that it addresses. But in addition to their customers or clients, many companies also recognize their relationships and responsibilities to other stakeholders such as their employees, their shareholders or owners, the communities in which they are located, and even the global community. In short, this part of the mission statement often acknowledges that companies and organizations operate within a complex web of relationships, and that they have obligations to multiple parties beyond their primary customers or clients.

The final aspect of the mission statement, according to Horwath, is the element that addresses Sinek's "why." The goal behind this part of the mission statement is to place the organization within a larger framework and provide emotional ballast for the organization. In many ways, according to Sinek, this final component is the most significant. Another way to conceptualize a mission statement is that it consists of two primary statements. The first is a statement of purpose that lays out what the organization hopes to accomplish and why. The second is a business statement that expresses how the organization goes about accomplishing its purpose and for whom (Meshkano n.d.). To a large degree, those two statements answer the same questions addressed earlier.

The Vision Statement

Although they are often confused with each other and often conflated into a single unit, a vision statement differs from a mission statement in several key respects. Most importantly, a vision statement is aspirational—it describes the future that will emerge from the successful pursuit of the mission. The importance of a compelling vision statement was captured by a famous quote generally attributed inaccurately to Walt Disney: "If you can dream it; you can do it" (Novak 2015). The vision statement is the dream. The organizational vision is what links the present to the future, energizing people and giving meaning to their work (Brecken 2004).

According to Burt Nanus, author of *Visionary Leadership*, a vision statement should be based on eight elements (figure 4.4). First, it should be oriented to the future but grounded in the present. It has to be linked coherently to the organization's history and traditions and reflect its values. An effective vision statement must be consistent with the mission statement and the purpose of the organization, clarifying its purpose and direction. It must be inspirational and set a future to which people can relate and embrace. It must have a positive

8 Elements of a Vision Statement	Oriented toward the future
	Linked to organization's history
	Reflect the organization's values
	Set standards of excellence
	Clarify the organization's purpose
	Inspire enthusiasm
	Be unique
	Be ambitious

Figure 4.4 8 Elements of a Vision Statement (Nanus 1992)

impact on the stakeholders, generating enthusiasm and commitment. It should be ambitious. And, perhaps most significantly, it should be unique, or at least distinct (Nanus 1992).

Crafting powerful vision statements is a complex process. Ironically, one of the most widely touted vision statements came from Microsoft founder Bill Gates in the mid-1970s, who said the company's vision was "to put a personal computer on every desk and in every home" (Alter 2000). Perhaps audacious at the time when the popular image of a computer was that of huge machines powered by punch cards that could not be "bent, folded, spindled or mutilated," the vision proved to be not ambitious enough. By the mid-to-late 2000s, the personal computer was commonplace, and Microsoft began to flounder. In 2013, then CEO Steve Ballmer began to promote a new vision for Microsoft, presenting a vision statement that read, "At Microsoft, our mission and values are to help people and businesses throughout the world realize their full potential." That didn't really help the company's performance or direction, and the new CEO Satya Nadella modified the vision again in 2015. The vision statement for his watch has been: "Empower every person and every organization on the planet to achieve more."

The evolution at Microsoft demonstrates the strengths and weaknesses of vision statements as well as the challenges involved in crafting them. In the 1970s, it was very hard to imagine a computer on every desktop and every home. It was not clear what anybody would actually do with a personal computer—indeed the concept of a "personal" computer had not yet emerged. So Gates, who saw the possibilities, was truly visionary at that moment. But 25 years later, when personal computers were commonplace and dynamic new technologies such as the Internet and more sophisticated cell phones such as Blackberries began to capture the public imagination, Microsoft lost its way. And the vision statements that were to come from both Steve Ballmer and later Satya Nadella could just as easily have come from a self-help guru as much as a technology-focused company.

Mission and Vision in the Corporation

The concept of a mission and a vision is deeply grounded in both religious and military organizations. In both those contexts, the differences in the terms are easy to determine. For example, at its most basic, early Christians were exhorted by Jesus to travel to the far corners of the earth to convert people. Conversion was their mission. The vision was to create God's kingdom on earth. In the military, each operation represents a specific mission—to capture or defend territory perhaps. The vision, of course, is maintaining or restoring peace under the specific terms sought by the government.

As with the concept of strategy itself, the use of mission and vision statements began to migrate to the corporate world in the mid-twentieth century, reflecting a profound shift in the understanding of the nature of the corporation that emerged at that time. Peter Drucker was perhaps the most influential voice in placing the definition of a corporate mission and vision on the agenda for senior management. Drucker, a professor and management consultant, is widely seen as the "father" of modern management (Denning 2014). In 1946, Drucker published his landmark book, *Concept of the Corporation*, based on a two-year study of General Motors. It is considered the first systematic internal study of the way a complex, multifaceted entity like General Motors actually operated. For two years, Drucker examined the way people at General Motors went about conducting business: how the company was structured organizationally; how decisions were made; how power was exercised; and how relationships among different constituencies involved with the corporation were managed. Drucker saw a corporation not as a series of inputs and outputs but as a human and social organization that produced different kinds of value for different stakeholders. In line with that perspective, in the 1970s, Drucker posed the question, "What is a corporation?" which he answered in his 1973 book *Management: Tasks, Responsibilities, and Management*. He wrote: "A business is not defined by its name, statutes or articles of incorporation. It is defined by the business mission. Only a clear definition of the mission and purpose of the organization makes possible clear and realistic business objectives" (David 1990).

In parallel with the growth of the strategic planning as a widespread management technique, in the 1980s many companies began to craft vision and mission statements Coupled with concerns about the specific content that should be included in the mission statement, debates erupted about the overall value a mission and or vision statement could or should provide. A review of the literature in 2008 revealed that theoretically at least, mission and/or vision statements—the distinctions between the two not always being clear—could help companies assert their market leadership (at times by defining the market in which they led). Mission and vision statements were important tools for employee communication, uniting employees in a common purpose and directing them to achieving the corporate goals. Mission statements were seen as effective public relations devices that could generate enthusiasm for the company. They could serve as the rationale for allocating resources and a guide for making critical decisions. In summary, as they become more commonplace in the corporate world, mission and vision statements came to be seen as important and powerful tools that could play a measureable role in improving corporate performance (Stallworth Williams 2008). If one of the keys to a successful business is for managers to keep their eyes on the proverbial "ball," the mission statement and the vision statement helped define the "ball" for all the stakeholders involved (Stallworth 2008).

But well-conceived and executed mission statements could potentially serve a greater role in shaping the direction of an organization and contributing to its overall success. A study in the late 1990s found that the mission statements of innovative companies had demonstrably different content and characteristics than those of what the researchers described as "non-innovative" companies. In innovative companies, the researchers observed, the mission statements often more clearly identified their competitive strategy, giving better definition and focus to their business activities. The mission statements for innovative companies were also more focused on employee behavior and standards as well as financial goals than those of non-innovative companies. Finally, innovative companies had a clearer vision and a better sense of future needs. The study buttressed a growing understanding that mission statements vary considerably among different kinds of organizations and the contexts in which they have been developed (Bart 1998).

As could be expected, the mission statements that companies craft vary greatly in quality. For example, in a frequently praised mission statement, Amazon.com states, "Its goal is to be the earth's most customer-centric company, where customers can find and discover anything they want online." Google's original mission statement was "to organize the world's information and make it universally accessible," which was pared with the mantra "don't be evil." Both the Amazon and Google statements are succinct and powerful descriptions of the companies' core businesses. But both demonstrate the limit of mission statements. Amazon's does not include its growing business in Web services, for example, or its investment in original video content. As for Google, in 2014, Larry Page, the company's CEO, acknowledged that the original mission statement was no longer sufficient but that the top management had not yet determined the new direction or overarching vision for the company—which had already plunged into an array of new businesses from virtual reality to autonomous driving vehicles to spacecraft (Gibbs 2014). The recognition that

Google had moved beyond its original mission statement led in part to the restructuring into two divisions—Google, which was charged with operating the core search business (whose mission was reflected in the original mission statement), Youtube.com and the Android operating system for mobile phones; and another division that encompassed everything else, including its research labs, life sciences division and venture capital arm. The eclectic nature of the array of businesses in which Google had become involved was reflected in the name for the new company, Alphabet. The new company, Alphabet, did not have a formal mission statement when it was launched. Rather, its vision was for the other companies in the portfolio to operate relatively independently (Hof 2015).

For better or worse, over the past 30 years, many of the world's top companies have developed succinct mission statements. For better, the mission of the British Broadcasting Company is: "To enrich people's lives with programmes and services that inform, educate and entertain." And the furniture company Ikea's vision is to "to create a better everyday life for the many people. Our business idea supports this vision by offering a wide range of well-designed, functional home furnishing products at prices so low that as many people as possible will be able to afford them." Other companies have not been as successful in crafting effective mission statements. For example, Albertson's mission statement says: "To create a shopping experience that pleases our customers; a workplace that creates opportunities and a great working environment for our associates; and a business that achieves financial success." Critics noted that the mission statement fails to mention that Albertson's is primarily a supermarket chain. And MGM Resorts mission statement asserts that "MGM Resorts International is the leader in entertainment & hospitality—a diverse collection of extraordinary people, distinctive brands and best in class destinations," which is a flattering description of the company but does not state what the company actually does for whom and for what reasons (Zetlin 2013). Even successful companies can have mission statements that are vague and generally not useful. For example, Starbucks is one of the great entrepreneurial successes of the past generation. Starbucks has to great extent reinvented drinking coffee, turning it into a lifestyle experience and a personal expression. It also pioneered the concept of creating a "third space" between work and home. But its mission statement—"To inspire and nurture the human spirit—one person, one cup and one neighborhood at a time"—only alludes to coffee when it says "one cup," and could be ascribed to a wide range of organizations.

Given its widespread use, the uneven quality and the uncertainty of its overall impact, exactly how much time, effort and concern companies should invest in developing and revising mission statements has generated some controversy too. In a 1997 survey, only 8 percent of the respondents felt that their firms' mission statements were clear to all their employees (Mullane 2002). And in a 1997 editorial, Pamela Goett, the editor and publisher of the *Journal of Business*

Strategy, slammed mission statements as formal, stilted, vague statements of the obvious, primarily extolling generic values with which no one could disagree and declared them as basically useless (Goett 1997). Despite the disagreement about their value, however, mission statements are widely seen as remaining as a permanent management tool and the starting point for strategic planning. Along the same lines, planning strategically, as opposed to formal strategic planning, requires a clear vision and mission statement as well.

Mission and Vision in Higher Education

As early as the 1930s, some colleges and universities began to publish "statements of purpose" in their catalogs (Scott 2006). And in the 1960s, as state colleges and universities systems grew in scope and reach, the different campuses that comprised the systems began to differentiate themselves in an effort to rationalize the allocation of resources among them. But it was not until the 1980s, when the concepts of corporate strategic planning began to be embraced in higher education, that many individual institutions, private and public, small and large, began to create specific mission statements. By the 1990s, based on a survey of more than 100 colleges and universities in the southeast United States, Walter Newsom estimated that approximately 60 percent of colleges and universities at the time had mission statements that resulted from a formal process (Newsom and Hayes 1991). But in the same way that corporate strategic planning processes did not fit easily into organizational settings, crafting effective mission statements in higher education also presented particular and peculiar problems. First, by the 1980s, when the mission statement came to be seen as cornerstone of strategic planning, generally most college and universities had been operating for decades if not centuries without a formal statement of mission. To develop a mission statement in higher education was not an exercise in which senior leadership engaged in order to define the purpose of the organization, which was largely set in the minds of many stakeholders, but more an effort to understand what the institution was already doing. And since colleges and universities have a complex set of stakeholders and power centers, and as such are diffused organizationally, mission statements in higher education have had to reflect a broader set of concerns than corporate mission statements.

Second, the role and mission within the diffused organizational structure of a university is defined socially and culturally within individual divisions that make up the university. Universities are seen as having broadly defined social and political obligations, along with their obligations to the students and alumni. To that end, Scott argued that as the world has moved from pre-nation-state structures to globalization, the social mission of universities has evolved as well. While in the pre-nation state, the focus of the university was on teaching and learning (with reason being subordinate to Biblical truth); over time the university's role was expanded to include the training of the government elite, the creation of new knowledge through research, preparing an informed citizenry needed for democracy, fostering a commitment to public service to their communities, countries, and the world, and the preparation of professionals to advance the economy (Scott 2006). But as each new socially defined mission for colleges and universities emerged, the older legacy missions did not recede. Generally speaking, teaching and learning, the original social mission for higher education, continues to be central for virtually all colleges and universities. As a result, mission statements for many universities and colleges often reflect not their unique, or even distinct, purpose but what they have in common with each other—primarily teaching, research and service (Lang and Lopers-Sweetman 1991). In fact, an earlier study showed that most university mission statements were vague with generic goals such as the pursuit of excellence. As problematic, a 1997 study found a significant mismatch between what many colleges and universities assert in their mission statements and what they offer in their curricula. Specifically, the researchers found that although in the prior 20 years many colleges and universities had reoriented their programs toward professional education, their mission statements still privileged a liberal arts education (Delucchi 1997). There is some irony in the fact that many mission statements focus on what the institutions have in common rather than what makes them unique, because virtually every college and university has its own particular history and course of development. Some started as faith-based institutions; others reflected the vision of a grand benefactor. Many were chartered by states. The land-grant institutions founded in the mid to late 1800s each had a specific rationale. Many schools saw their primary mission to teach the liberal arts. Others were more oriented from their inception toward research. Some support undergraduate, graduate and professional school education. Others started as teacher-training institutions. Others restrict themselves to undergraduate education only. Many of the most elite undergraduate liberal arts colleges have fewer than 2,000 students, while large state universities support tens of thousands of students on a single campus. And colleges' and universities' engagement with online education varies just as widely.

The diversity of the college and university experience was captured in the Carnegie Classification of Higher Education for American colleges and universities, which was first established in the early 1970s to support Carnegie's research and policy analysis programs. Carnegie devised a system based largely on the highest degree an institution granted, ranging from associate degrees to doctoral degrees. Then each group was subdivided according to criteria specific to the group. For example, the doctoral classification was subdivided according to the degree of research activity. Colleges that primarily award associate degrees are subdivided according to their disciplinary focus and the type of student (traditional or non-traditional) they serve (Indiana University Center for Postsecondary Research n.d.).

Presumably, at least in a general way, the mission statements from colleges and universities in different Carnegie classifications should reflect their different purposes. A college geared to providing an associate degree in a technical field to a non-traditional student would seem to have a very different mission than a university with high research activity aimed at producing scholars and researchers. But the similarities among the mission statements among colleges and universities that were clearly distinct from each other and the inclusion in the mission statement of elements that no longer seemed central to the university or college raised a fundamental question. Perhaps mission statements in higher education were not actually meant to express a particular university's unique purpose or as a guide and anchor of planning and decision-making. Perhaps, crafting and promoting mission statements in the academic world reflected more simply normative behavior—senior administrators invested in creating mission statements because it was expected. The mission statement fundamentally reflects that, yes, the particular college or university was, in fact, a college and university and followed the standard practices of colleges and universities. Having a mission statement fundamentally represented organizational window dressing.

In a 2006 study that addressed those specific questions, Morphew and Hartley tentatively reported a complex and nuanced answer. On the one hand, differences in the rhetoric used in mission statements was not driven as much by Carnegie classifications as it was by whether the institution was private or public. Public universities included different elements in their mission statements than comparable private institutions. Moreover, even though the language used in many mission statements is often similar and mission statements frequently contain many common elements, the language and elements are often constructed in different ways that may have meaning to specific academic communities. On the other hand, Morphew and Hartley observed, most mission statements are not overtly aspirational. And even those mission statements that were aspirational—making a claim to the leading institution in an area, for example—did not provide a foundation for strategic planning or a specific direction or vision for the college or university. The authors concluded that mission statements play a different role in higher education than they do in the corporate world. Rather than expressing a college or university's unique identity and value proposition, mission statements in higher education are complex signaling mechanisms that express to a range of stakeholders, which differs from institution to institution, that the university operates in harmony with the expectations and values of those stakeholders. Mission statements in higher education are not used so much for planning purposes as they are to assure the complex network of stakeholders within which the university operates that the institution understands what those stakeholder want and that it will be able to provide it (Morphew and Hartley 2006).

The idea that the mission statements for many colleges and universities do not actually function in the same way that corporate mission statements do raises several issues for planning strategically from the middle in the academic world, particularly for planning online educational programs. First, because the mission statements are designed to appeal to a diverse set of stakeholders, they generally are longer than corporate mission statements. Not uncommonly, mission statements in higher education run for several paragraphs and include statements of history and often review the values of the institution. For example, the University of Wisconsin's mission statement is more than 400 words long and begins with: "The University of Wisconsin–Madison is the original University of Wisconsin, created at the same time Wisconsin achieved statehood in 1848" (University of Wisconsin Mission Statement n.d.). Having longer mission statements is not necessarily bad. But the longer the statement, the less likely that the campus community and other stakeholders will have actually read the mission statement or, more importantly, that it can actually serve as a useful platform for planning. After all, mission statements that have something for everybody in them may not offer effective guidelines for making difficult choices, which is what planning involves (Kiley 2011). Brevity in a mission statement, on the other hand, is not necessarily the solution. The mission statement for the University of Rochester is ten words: "Learn, Discover, Heal, Create—and Make the World Ever Better" (University of Rochester Mission Statement n.d.). Admittedly that is very pithy, but it also does not provide a very clear roadmap for decisions.

The second challenge posed by the peculiar nature of a university's mission statement is that even though a school's mission may not distinctly capture what the university does, this does not mean that a sense of mission does not exist. Instead, based on their origins, history, development and current conditions, the mission may be expressed in more diffuse ways than being captured succinctly in a mission statement, but the statement still may hold a powerful sway on the direction and decisions of a particularly institution. For example, the mission statements for many universities in the Jesuit tradition such as Georgetown University and Boston College acknowledge that the university is a "Catholic and Jesuit" university or follows the Catholic and Jesuit traditions. The Georgetown University mission statement bluntly states that it is a Catholic and Jesuit university in the first sentence and reiterates that it operates in the Jesuit tradition in the fourth paragraph (Georgetown University Mission Statement n.d.). At Boston College, the acknowledgement of its Catholic and Jesuit identity does not come until the second paragraph (which follows a long first paragraph), and then it is referred to primarily in passing as the sentence reads: "As a Catholic and Jesuit . . ." (Boston College Mission Statement n.d.). To an outsider, in reading their mission statements, the reference to the institutions' Catholic and Jesuit traditions is a normative signaling to two of its major stakeholders, the Catholic Church and the Society of Jesus. The emphasis in the remainder of both mission statements are those elements that are in common with most university mission statements—teaching, research and service to the community. But concern for the how the Catholic and Jesuit tradition is expressed still has a significant impact on decision-making on those campuses (Bonewits Feldner 2006). For example, in the effort to launch the first online program at Loyola University Maryland, also a Jesuit school, as part of the approval process for the program, the founders drafted a paper demonstrating how online education was compatible with Jesuit educational traditions. Clearly, at least in some settings, the conceptions of a university's mission may play an important role in a decision that is not fully captured in the mission statement.

In most cases, however, the overall mission statement will not offer a firm enough foundation to justify online education. While most mission statements are general enough to accommodate a move into online education, most are not specific enough to provide enough support to prioritize online education in the competition for university resources. Rather than solely trying to justify online education through reference to the mission statement, the mission for online education has to be developed within the context of a college or university's current strategic plan. Of course, strategic plans are also grounded, at least ideally, in the mission statement. With that in mind, the bottom line is that it is necessary for the mission and plan for online education on any campus to be compatible with the overall university mission, however that may be expressed. But that is not sufficient to support the development of online education. To prosper and grow, online education must also be clearly embedded in specific elements of the university's strategic plan (if it has one) and overtly attached to the appropriate goals and objectives of the plan.

Creating a Mission Statement for Online Education

Despite, or perhaps due to, the general nature of most university mission statements, to be able to effectively chart the future of online education in any specific context, a mission statement, though perhaps not a vision statement in many cases, can be a useful tool. A vision statement is not appropriate in some instances because planning for online education often does not occur organizationally where an expansive vision can be developed. Online education plays a role in the overall life of the university but the people managing online education frequently are not empowered to set the long-term vision for online education, nor can they project the overall outcome on the institution as a whole. Leaders of online education on any given campus can, however, define their own mission for online education—its purpose or the function of online education; how it will go about achieving its purpose; for whom the function exists; and, finally, the "why," or why developing online education is significant.

In some respects, the methodology for creating a mission statement for online education resembles to a large degree the methodology that will be

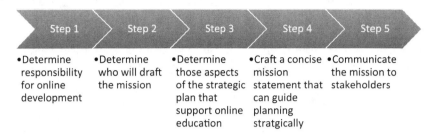

Step 1	Step 2	Step 3	Step 4	Step 5
•Determine responsibility for online development	•Determine who will draft the mission	•Determine those aspects of the strategic plan that support online education	•Craft a concise mission statement that can guide planning stratgically	•Communicate the mission to stakeholders

Figure 4.5 5 Steps in Planning Strategically for Online Programs

outlined in Chapter 6 for planning strategically generally. It consists of five steps (figure 4.5). First, determine where those responsible for the development of online education are lodged organizationally in the institution. Second, determine who will draft the mission. Third, identify those aspects of the university's strategic plan that can be used to support online education. Fourth, craft a concise mission statement that captures the essential elements in a way that it can be used as a touchstone and guide for planning strategically. Fifth, communicate the mission to the relevant stakeholders.

The first step in drafting a mission statement is one of self-reflection—who are those responsible and where are they located organizationally? As noted in Chapter 3, online education has entered into many colleges and universities through a wide array of portals. To provide a more detailed look at how complicated the roll out of online education has become, consider in depth the situation at the University of Virginia. An audit of online education at the UVA conducted in 2012 demonstrated the many paths that online education followed to arrive on campus. The audit was conducted after the University of Virginia's Board of Visitors complained that the university was not moving into online education aggressively enough. A Task Force on Online Education empowered by the faculty senate found that UVA offered undergraduate, graduate and professional development and continuing education courses online. It offered fully online courses and hybrid courses. Some of the courses were part of predominately traditional programs conducted generally in face-to-face classes, but the school also supported 11 online-only graduate degree-granting programs and 14 online-only certificate-granting programs. Around 8 percent of its online courses were aimed at the general public. At the time of the audit, no centralized agency at the university level was charged with monitoring, much less managing, online educational programs, and even within the individual college, there were no specific offices that cataloged, coordinated, supported or promoted online education. At the same time, virtually all UVA students engaged with online educational material via the centralized learning management system. And though the central Information Technology Services office maintained many of the technology-enhanced classrooms, the availability and use of instructional technology was not cataloged or uniform across the campus (Guilford 2012). Clearly, at that moment, many different communities of people were engaged in planning and delivering online education program and planning potentially could take place at any level. Departments offering online courses or running online degree programs could fruitfully engage in planning strategically. Individual colleges within the university could benefit from planning strategically. The Information Technology Services office could benefit from planning strategically. If UVA ever established a central administrative office for online education, it would have to plan strategically. In fact, at an institution like UVA, planning strategically for online education could take place in all those places as well as in a center for teaching innovation or distance learning.

A mission statement itself for online education would look very different coming from each of those bodies within the institution, because they hold different organizational positions, can control different resources and have different roles in the university. Some might focus on course development and the integration of online courses into a larger educational program. Others might look at the growth of new programs or the transitions of existing programs to an online format. Others might be geared toward faculty training. Still others might be involved in the development of an entire division with the university, such as professional development and continuing education or even an entire new college such as the World Campus of Pennsylvania State University. But the process to develop the mission statement would be the same.

The second step in creating a mission statement is establishing the process and procedures by which it will be drafted and vetted. In some cases, a mission statement for a unit or subunit in a university may have to be approved through formal governance (if a new division or college is being established, for example), but in many cases creating a mission statement for a subunit is primarily an internal process. The question is—who is responsible for defining the mission? In the corporate world, the answer to that question is fairly clear—the founder of the company or senior management in consultation with the board of directors sets the mission and the vision for the company. The strategic planning process supports the pre-determined mission. In higher education, at the institutional level, that process has been modified to reflect the more collaborative nature of the organization. For example, Rowley et al. suggest that a mission statement should not be developed for a university until after the strategic planning process is well underway and that institution has a clear understanding of it external and internal environment (Rowley et al. 1997). Commonly, in higher education, developing a mission statement, or at least a tentative, working draft of the mission statement, is one of the first steps in the overall strategic planning process. For example, the University of Tennessee–Chattanooga promoted its working version of its mission statement concurrently with a campus-wide planning process. The working draft of the mission statement was,

The University of Tennessee at Chattanooga is an engaged metropolitan university.

We aspire for and will achieve excellence by:

- Driving student success with quality teaching,
- Initiating connections and collaboration between the classroom and the community that enhance the learning experience, and
- Unleashing the energy of educated and engaged citizens, committed to service, solutions and sustainability.

The working draft of the mission statement was first circulated about 40 percent of the way through the overall planning process but then was subjected to extensive public comments through interviews, surveys and other outreach techniques (University of Tennessee, Chattanooga n.d.). Ultimately, the strategic plan at the university level was to be ratified by the board of trustees, the ultimate governing body, when that body accepted the finalized strategic plan. The process utilized by the University of Tennessee–Chattanooga is the opposite of the process in the corporate world, where determining the mission comes first. In most cases, the final mission statement differs little from the working draft, regardless of the extent of the feedback process. In fact, in many cases, the more extensive the feedback, the less likely the draft will change.

Based on interviews with the leaders of more than two dozen online educational programs, the process for crafting a mission statement at a program or unit level, at least for online education, as with planning strategically in general, differs from writing a mission statement at the institutional level in higher education. Rather than being a collaborative process, mission statement development at the program or department level can be thought of as a consultative effort. The leaders of the unit involved do the majority of the drafting and revising of the program and will often decide on the final outcome. In the process, however, it may be appropriate to consult on various drafts with other stakeholders. For an online academic program at the department level, the faculty should be consulted. If the aim is to develop online educational programs at one college within the context of a bigger university, feedback from department chairs should be solicited and taken into account. If an advisory board or governing board has been established for online education, that body should have an opportunity to share its views during the drafting process. But the driving force in conceptualizing and crafting the mission statement must be those persons most invested in the implementation of online education regardless of the academic setting.

At a minimum, program- and department-based mission statements need to consider these primary questions (University of Connecticut n.d.): What is the purpose of the program or department? How does one go about achieving that pursuit? Who are the beneficiaries of the program or department?

Questions to Consider When Developing a Program-Level Mission Statement

What is the purpose of the program?

How does it go about achieving its purpose?

Who are the benficiaries of the program?

Why is the program needed?

Figure 4.6 Questions to Consider When Developing a Program-Level Mission Statement

And, perhaps the most important, why is the program or department needed (figure 4.6)? In addition to those standard components, program and department mission statements also have to be tailored to conform to the strategic plan of the university. Ensuring that the mission statement for online education is in harmony with the university strategic plan has two implications. First, it recognizes that in many cases, the university's mission statement does not provide a distinct enough foundation to support the innovation that online education represents, as the growth of online education represents a major new dimension in higher education. To compete for resources, the mission for online education is grounded in and justified by the university's plan to develop online education within the timeframe envisioned in the strategic plan, which represents the main blueprint for the allocation of resources for the duration of the plan. Second, the mission statement for online education may, and most likely will, change over time. In any case, when the university undergoes a strategic planning process, the online education mission statements should be reviewed as well. In fact, as departments and programs incorporate the discipline of planning strategically, a review of the mission statement could be appropriately placed on the agenda at any time.

Internal and External Consideration

Developing a powerful and effective mission statement requires both internal, reflective analysis and an outward-looking external analysis. An internal analysis requires outlining a clear understanding of what the program and or department is and what it wants to be. One common approach to gaining that kind of insight and understanding is by conducting what is called a "seven questions" exercise (Scheye n.d.) (figure 4.7). This sort of exercise is often

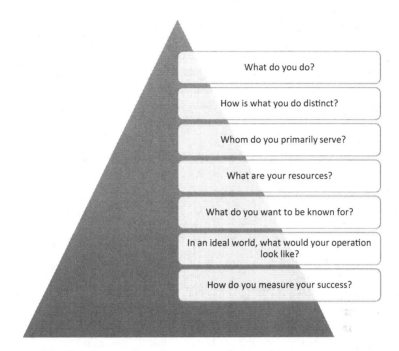

What do you do?

How is what you do distinct?

Whom do you primarily serve?

What are your resources?

What do you want to be known for?

In an ideal world, what would your operation look like?

How do you measure your success?

Figure 4.7 Scheye's 7 Questions for Strategic Planning

used either to kick off a strategic planning process or to evaluate the plan that emerges from a strategic plan. With that in mind, it can also be useful to define the mission for an academic program or an administrative unit such as online education. The specific questions used in the exercise can be modified, depending on the specific circumstances but should generally elicit the same kind of responses.

These questions can be discussed among the leadership of the program or the administrative unit charged with steering the development of online education. Feedback can also be solicited from different stakeholders. The objective of the exercise is to be able to craft realistic and well-grounded answers for the first four elements of any mission statement—why, what, how and for whom.

An alternative approach to clarifying the four main components of the mission statement is to craft a series of additional statements that support each element (Alter 2000). A problem statement defines the problem to be solved. It answers the "why" question. A client statement describes who will be served. A statement of purpose answers the question regarding what is to be accomplished. A business statement details how the purpose will be achieved. While the outcome is the same—a clarification of the main elements of the mission statement—conceptualizing individual statements can potentially lead to a more creativity and a wider scope of activity.

The external analysis involves aligning online education with the goals and objectives of the university as expressed in the strategic plan. For planning from the middle of an organization to succeed, it must take place within the context of the overall institutional strategy. The converse is also true. For an overall organizational plan to succeed, it must be embraced throughout the organization, particularly at the operational levels (Brache 2004). This dynamic provides an opportunity for leaders of online education, if they can position the growth of online education, to contribute to the perceived success of the institutional strategic plan. Planning from the middle of the organization will not likely succeed if it is not seen as consistent with the overall strategic plan, and a strategic plan cannot succeed unless it is embraced and executed at the operational levels of the institution. Since online education has historically often been marginalized at many campuses and faces stiff opposition from faculty members at others, anchoring online education to specific elements of a strategic plan can help overcome those headwinds, at least when it comes to soliciting senior administrators support for resources. From another angle, tethering online education to the strategic plan provides reassurance to senior administrators that the mandates laid down in the strategic plan are understood throughout the organization, which is critical for success (O'Brien and Sharkey 2009).

As noted earlier, the mission statements for most colleges and universities do not provide a firm enough foundation to support the mission for online education. For example, the mission statement for Arcadia University's 2013–2018 Strategic Plan states, "Arcadia University provides a distinctly integrative, global and personalized learning experience for intellectually curious undergraduate and graduate students in preparation for a life of scholarship, service and professional contribution"(Arcadia University 2013–2018 Strategic Plan). The mission statement makes no overt reference to online education. And, in fact, the strategic plan itself does not directly address online education. However, there are elements in the plan that could be used to ground new online initiatives within the strategic plan. For example, the first theme of the plan is "enhancing academic excellence." And the first objective for that theme calls on the university to "[s]trengthen assessment of and professional development for effective teaching/learning practices and environments in both traditional and newly emerging modalities." Online education falls into that category of "newly emerging modalities." Objective 5 in that theme calls for a faculty development program, which could be the rationale for a Center for Online Learning. And an objective in another theme in the plan calls for improvements in the "learning and technological infrastructure," which could also be used to support investments in online education.

In contrast, Vanderbilt University's 2014 strategic plan included embracing educational technologies as one of its major themes, asserting: "We aspire to embrace new Educational Technologies to foster innovation in learning, teaching, and discovery, serving as a leader in best practices for higher education" (Discovery Vanderbilt Learning 2014). Vanderbilt had been engaged in a spirited discussion about online education for a couple of years prior to the publication of the university strategic plan. In that period, it discovered that many of its colleges had already launched online efforts, but those initiatives had not been coordinated or integrated, and there was very little sharing of what had been learned in each of the efforts. Moreover, there had been a spirited discussion about whether Vanderbilt should sponsor Massive Open Online Courses similar to what other research universities it saw as peers were doing. And there was a debate about when undergraduates should be able to take online classes during the regular semesters, or even in the summer. The embrace of educational technology was not a signal that Vanderbilt would move more aggressively into online education. Indeed, the strategic plan explicitly stated that educational technology should be used to enhance on-campus education. But it allowed that

> '[a]ny time we can expand Vanderbilt's ability to educate people, whether on our campus or on another continent, we must evaluate the opportunity carefully,' and 'we must employ new Educational Technologies that advance our ability to educate the whole student and make lifelong learning a reality for all of our students—current, past, and future.'

Appropriately applied, those kinds of statements could be used as justification for online education at Vanderbilt. Moreover, Vanderbilt's strategic plan called for added support for the Vanderbilt Institute for Digital Learning (VIDL), which it established in the same period as well as its Center of Teaching, both of which support faculty in creating online classes. VIDL's mission includes encouraging and overseeing world and local community service by Vanderbilt that involves digital learning, including production and management of Vanderbilt's Massive Open Online Courses (MOOCs) and promoting the sharing of resources (knowledge, human, infrastructure, best practices) on digital learning. It also plays an advisory role in online degree programs, as well as supporting online education for on-campus courses. Those crafting the mission for the VIDL must understand its role in the strategic plan. Others involved in launching online programs, must determine their relationship to the overall plan and to the VIDL. In summary, crafting a dynamic and useful mission statement requires both internal and external reflection. The leaders of online education must clearly understand what they want to do. They must also recognize where online education fits into the larger institutional picture.

Crafting the Statement

Once the answers to the key questions have been answered regarding where the program or administrative unit fits into the overall plan for the university, the actual mission statement itself must be crafted. As stated before, at the institutional level, mission statements vary in length. Some mission statements include a statement relating to corporate values as well, but for the purposes of planning from the middle of the organization, a values statement component is probably unnecessary. Online education should incorporate the values of the organization generally. A well-crafted mission statement should be simple, concise and easy to remember. While the mission statement functions at the program or administrative unit level differently than at the institutional level, it still serves as a mechanism to ensure that everybody understands their roles as well as serving as the grounding point for planning (Hofstrand 2016).

A good mission statement will exhibit certain characteristics—for example, they should be active and audience-centric: missions are all about doing something. They should be consistent with the values of the organization and reasonable given the capability and reach of the organization. For example, if one of the missions of a center for online learning is to train faculty in a large state institution in which there is a considerable faculty resistance to online learning, it may not be appropriate to train "all" faculty. In the same way, an administrative unit that supports online education but is not housed in academic affairs may not want to have moving x number of classes online as a part of its mission. Except in unusual cases, a smaller or regional school may not want to aspire to be a world leader in its mission statement for online education if it is not a world leader in any other part of its academic program. The mission statement must be believable and credible, particularly to those who are charged with executing it. At the same time, mission statements should not be too generic or loaded with jargon. They should be distinct and reflect the personality of the administrative unit or program. The mission statement should inspire people and be specific (Team Infusion 2015).

The length of a mission statement is the subject of ongoing debate. Kevin Starr, director of the Mulago Foundation, an organization that funds scalable solutions to big problems, encourages the agencies it works with to have mission statements that are fewer than eight words, and he suggests the mission should consist basically of a target population, a verb and a measurable outcome. He argues that the brevity forces clarity while still allowing for the mission to be specific. And he eschews terms like "capacity-building" and "empowerment" that he believes are too vague to truly assess (Starr 2012).

While capturing every element in eight words might be too ambitious, mission statements should probably be no more than 150 words in length and are much better if they are less than 100 words. Tightly edited, a mission statement could be fewer than 50 words. As important as the overall length is to crafting a mission statement, so too are the specific word choices. Many mission statements seemed to be loaded with commonplace and overused words. But a 2015 study of the mission statements of the top-100 U.S.-based corporations as measured by market capitalization found that while there was a large overlap in the use of words in corporate value statements, it was not the case in mission statements. The most commonly shared words, the study found, were "improve," "innovate," "best," "quality" and "value" and derivatives of those words (Anderson and Jamison 2015). Other commonly used words were "service," "leader," "growth," "quality" and "customers" (Trout 2006).

In the final analysis, the best mission statements use vivid language to communicate something distinct about the program or the administrative unit. An effective way to think about a mission statement for online education is to conceptualize it as a 30-second elevator pitch commonly used in the entrepreneurial world of startups and venture capital. An elevator pitch is a brief persuasive speech to spark interest in what you are doing. The term came from the idea that if an entrepreneur seeking funding happened to run into a venture capitalist in an elevator, the person should be prepared to say something to intrigue the potential funder within the timeframe of the elevator ride (Hanks n.d.). A good mission statement flows directly into a good elevator pitch. Imagine running into the president of the university, or president of the board of trustees, or a senior faculty member who asks, "What are we doing in terms of online education?" The mission statement should succinctly and persuasively answer that question.

Assessing and Revising Mission Statements

While the burden of crafting a mission statement for online education is best carried out by the people who are most invested in its success, for the mission statement to serve its purpose, it must resonate with the other stakeholders involved. So to some degree, mission statements will not reflect the view of only one or two people. Moreover, a mission statement, particularly for online education, cannot be set in stone. Minimally, when the university undergoes a strategic planning process, the mission statement for those subunits engaged with online education should be reexamined and assessed. More importantly, as planning strategically becomes an integral process in the management of online education, the mission statement can come up for review at any time if it appears that a revision could help advance the program.

Examining the mission statements from a handful of strategic plans for online education across the country reflects a range of possibilities. For example, the mission statement for the strategic plan for online education at Truman State University, a selective public liberal arts and sciences university in Missouri, reads, "Truman State University seeks to provide students expanded opportunities for learning in online environments, where appropriate to the curriculum and student needs, with improved student services, enhanced faculty development, rigorous assessment, and a commitment to best practices in teaching and learning" (Truman State Strategic Plan for Online Learning 2014). This relatively modest mission—primarily to expand access to high quality online education where appropriate—reflects a campus that was historically averse to online education but over the past five years has seen some academic departments begin to more fully embrace it. The administrators spearheading the online effort there have been able to use the plan to expand the number of online offerings during the summer, for example. And it has positioned online education to play a role in degree-completion efforts and new graduate programs. At the same time, according to Kevin Minch, associate provost of undergraduate curricula and outreach at Truman State and one of the primary authors of the statement, his team steered away from intimating how large a role online education might ultimately hold. Moreover, the mission statement did not look to cajole departments that were suspicious of online education to try to move in that direction. Interestingly, the mission statement for Truman State's 2016–2020 strategic plan calls on the university to implement its mission by "expanding its reach to students who aspire to complete a Truman education, yet arrive through non-traditional paths" (Truman State University Strategic Plan 2016). Clearly that opens the door to expanding online education, at least as a degree-completion mechanism and a vehicle to reach non-traditional students.

The University of Alabama–Birmingham (UAB), on the other hand, crafted a more ambitious statement for online education. After the University of Alabama System Board of Trustees established the Division of E-learning and Professional Studies, the division published a strategic plan with the following mission.

"Online learning is a strategic asset for UAB that has a unique capacity to help the university expand its reach, capitalize on promising opportunities and ultimately fulfill its mission" (UAB Online Strategic Plan 2013). As envisioned, UAB Online can:

- quickly expand the reach of the UAB brand on a global scale
- improve undergraduate student retention and 6-year graduation rates by improving student flexibility and access to required courses
- create new revenue streams by helping schools partner with the corporate community to provide online workplace education
- align and integrate individual school efforts to establish a baseline quality standard for online education at UAB

Obviously, this is an ambitious, multifaceted mission that envisions establishing UAB as a global brand.

Which mission statement is more effective? Leslie Collins, senior director for institutional planning at the Texas Tech University Health Sciences Center, proposes the following checklist to evaluate a proposed mission statement (Collins n.d.).

1. Is the statement clear and concise?
2. Is it distinct and memorable?
3. Does it clearly state the purpose of the program or department?

4. Does it indicate the primary function or activities of the program or the department?
5. Does it indicate who the stakeholders are?
6. Does it support the mission of the department, school and university?
7. Does it reflect the program's priorities and values?

This checklist is effective for evaluating the specific content of the mission statement. But Erica Olson, author of the book *Strategic Planning for Dummies*, notes that mission statements have to be assessed from another perspective as well—are they appropriate for the organization and the context within which it is operating (Olsen 2015)? Among the questions she proposes to assess if a mission statement is appropriate are:

1. Is it realistic?
2. Is it based on the organization's core competencies?
3. Does it fit the market environment?
4. Does it state what the organization wants to be remembered for?

Shaping an effective mission statement can be complex, but the process should not be laborious or take an inordinate amount of time. Even within the context of institutional strategic planning, the mission statement does not necessarily reflect a consensus among the stakeholders but is primarily a reiteration of what the organization is all about. It is a tool for the leadership to communicate its perspective to other stakeholders and to rally support for the perspective. Within the context of planning strategically, particularly planning strategically for online education, the mission statement can be even more fluid and open to revision. Since responsiveness to the external environment is one of the fundamental premises of planning strategically, revising the mission statement as circumstances change.

The environment for online education is changing rapidly. The *New York Times* famously declared 2012 as the Year of the MOOC (Papano 2012). That led to a bevy of major research institutions scrambling to experiment in this new area to try to determine the impact of MOOCs on traditional higher education. Within five years, however, while MOOCs had established themselves as an interesting alternative channel for advanced education, the hysteria that MOOCs were about to devour all of academia had subsided. If a department or college had crafted a mission statement for online during the MOOC frenzy, five years later it would definitely be appropriate to revisit it and perhaps rework it.

Conclusion

The mission statement plays a crucial role in planning strategically. When used by programs and subunits of the organization, they often serve primarily as an internal document, keeping the employees of that unit focused on their function and responsibility. They also help to keep the unit oriented within the larger context of the college and university. Written correctly, they serve to focus people's attention on the most important issues confronting them. Mission statements also serve an important external function. Given the loosely coupled and siloed nature of many colleges and universities, where many departments simply have no idea what other departments are doing, mission statements are important short descriptions to succinctly communicate to others within the university what a program or administrative unit is doing. One of the most curious features regarding the spread of online education in the academic world has been that, in many settings, many departments have launched initiatives without anybody else really knowing that those efforts are going on. These ad hoc efforts have taken place at all levels of the university from individual courses to entire colleges within a university. Indeed, it has not been unusual for one academic department to have no idea that another department has embraced online education. Mission statements help programs and departments communicate with others exactly what they are doing.

But most importantly, mission statements serve as the steady guide for planning strategically. Planning strategically is a flexible, nimble, scalable and ongoing process. The key question to ask as different aspects of the online education program move onto the agenda is how whatever it is that needs to be addressed fits within the mission. The mission provides direction and a foundation for all planning activities.

References

Alter, S. (2000). *Managing the Double Bottom Line: A Business Planning Reference Guide for Social Enterprises*. Retrieved from: http://www.setoolbelt.org/resources/96

Anderson, S. and Jamison, B. (2015, May). Do the Top U.S. Corporations Often Use the Same Words in Their Vision, Mission and Value Statements? *Journal of Marketing and Management*, 6:1, pp. 1–15.

Arcadia University 2013–2018 Strategic Plan (n.d.). Retrieved from: www.arcadia.edu/system/files/Public%20-%20accessible%20to%20all%20site%20users/2782/StrategicPlan2013-18.pdf

Assessment Department, University of Connecticut. (n.d.). *How to Write a Mission Statement*. Retrieved from: http://web2.uconn.edu/assessment/docs/HowToWriteMission.pdf

Bart, C. K. (1998). A Comparison of Mission Statements and Their Rationales in Innovative and Non-Innovative Firms. *Journal of Technology Management*, 16:1/2/3, pp. 64–77.

Bonewits Feldner, S. (2006, March). Living Our Mission: A Study of University Mission Building. *Communication Studies*, 57:1, pp. 67–85.

Boston College Mission Statement (n.d.). Retrieved from: www.bc.edu/offices/bylaws/mission.html

Brache, A. (2004). Strategy and the Middle Manager. *Training: The Magazine of Human Resource Development*. Retrieved from: http://kepner-tregoe.de/linkservid/54F02F00-AB8F-4BBB-9CAA4B7731F70478/showMeta/0/

Brecken, D. (2004, Winter). *Leadership Vision and Strategic Direction*. The Quality Management Forum. Retrieved from: http://asq1001.org/papers/Leadership%20Vision%20and%20Strategic%20Direction.pdf

Collins, L. (n.d.). *Writing an Effective Mission Statement: Four Questions to Answer*. Texas Tech University Health Sciences Center. Retrieved from: www.ttuhsc.edu/oiea/presentations/mission_statement/How_to_Write_an_Effective_Mission_Statement.pdf

David, F. (1990). The Company Mission: Its Nature and Purpose. In Campbell, A. and Tawady, L. (Eds.), *Mission and Business Philosophy*. Oxford: Butterworth-Heinmann, p. 288.

Delucchi, M. (1997, July–August). Liberal Arts Colleges and the Myth of Uniqueness. *Journal of Higher Education*, 68:4, p. 414.

Denning, S. (2014, July 29). The Best of Peter Drucker. *Forbes*. Retrieved from: www.forbes.com/sites/stevedenning/2014/07/29/the-best-of-peter-drucker/#7c5419b07ec9

Discovery Vanderbilt Learning: An Academic Strategic Plan in Service to Humanity (2014). Retrieved from: www.vanderbilt.edu/strategicplan/Academic-Strategic-Plan-for-Vanderbilt-University.pdf

Evans, J. (2010, April 24). Vision and Mission—What's the Difference and Why Does It Matter? *Psychology Today*. Retrieved from: www.psychologytoday.com/blog/smartwork/201004/vision-and-mission-whats-the-difference-and-why-does-it-matter

Georgetown University Mission Statement (n.d.). Retrieved from: https://governance.georgetown.edu/mission-statement

Gibbs, S. (2014, November 3). Google Has 'Outgrown' Its 14-Year Old Mission Statement, Says Larry Page. *The Guardian*. Retrieved from: www.theguardian.com/technology/2014/nov/03/larry-page-google-dont-be-evil-sergey-brin

Goett, P. (1997). Mission Impossible. *Journal of Business Strategy*, 18:1, p. 2.

Guilford, W. (2012, July 17). *Overview of Significant Online Education at the University of Virginia*. Retrieved from: http://faculty.virginia.edu/guilford/overview_report.pdf

Hanks, G. (n.d.). The Real Meaning of an Elevator Pitch. *Chron.com*. Retrieved from: http://smallbusiness.chron.com/real-meaning-elevator-pitch-64181.html

Hof, R. (2015, August 10). The Real Reasons Google Will Become Alphabet. *Forbes*. Retrieved from: www.forbes.com/sites/roberthof/2015/08/10/the-real-reasons-google-will-become-alphabet/2/#5ecaf84c3255

Hofstrand, D. (2016, August). Mission and Vision Statements: A Roadmap of Where You Want to Go and How to Get There. *Ag Decision Maker, Iowa State University Extension and Outreach*. Retrieved from: www.extension.iastate.edu/AgDM/wholefarm/html/c5-09.html

Horwath, R. (2005). *Discovering Purpose: Discover Mission, Vision and Values Strategic Thinking Institute*. Retrieved from: www.strategyskills.com/Articles/Documents/Discovering_Purpose-STI.pdf

Indiana University Center for Postsecondary Research (n.d.). *The Carnegie Classification of Institutions of Higher Education*, 2015 edition. Bloomington, IN. Retrieved from: http://carnegieclassifications.iu.edu/classification_descriptions/basic.php

Kane, E. (1977, Summer/Autumn). John Henry Newman's Catholic University Church in Dublin. *Studies: An Irish Quarterly Review*, 66:262/263, pp. 105–120.

Kiley, K. (2011, June 20). Saying More With Less. *Inside Higher Ed.* Retrieved from: www.insidehighered.com/news/2011/06/20/colleges_pare_down_mission_statements_to_stand_out

Lang, D. and Lopers-Sweetman, R. (1991). The Role of Statements in Institutional Purpose. *Research in Higher Education*, 32:6, pp. 599–624.

Levitt, T. (1960, July/August). Marketing Myopia. *Harvard Business Review*, 38:4, pp. 45–56.

Meshkano, R. (n.d.). What Should a Mission Statement Say. *The Idealist*. Retrieved from: www.idealist.org/info/Nonprofits/Gov1

Modern History Sourcebook: John Henry Newman: The Idea of A University,1854 (n.d.). Retrieved from: https://sourcebooks.fordham.edu/mod/newman/newman-university.html

Morphew, C. and Hartley, M. (2006, May/June). Mission Statements: A Thematic Analysis of Rhetoric Across Institutional Type. *The Journal of Higher Education*, 77:3, pp. 456–471

Mullane, J. (2002). The Mission Statement Is a Strategic Tool: When Used Properly. *Management Decision*, 40:5, pp. 448–455. Retrieved from: http://dx.doi.org/10.1108/00251740210430461

Nanus, B. (1992). *Visionary leadership: Creating a Compelling Sense of Direction for Your Organization*. San Francisco: Jossey-Bass.

Newfield, C. (2003). *Ivy and Industry: Business and the Making of the American University 1880–1980*. Durham, NC: Duke University Press, pp. 26–28.

Newman, J. H. (1952). *The Idea of a University*. The National Institution for Newman Studies, p. 1. Retrieved from: www.newmanreader.org/works/idea/discourse1.html

Newsom, W. and Hayes, R. (1990–1991). Are Mission Statements Worthwhile? *Planning for Higher Education*, 19:2, pp. 28–30.

Novak, M. (2015, March 19). 8 Walt Disney Quotes That Are Actually Fake. *Gizmodo*. Retrieved from: http://gizmodo.com/8-walt-disney-quotes-that-are-actually-fake-1692355588

O'Brien, D. and Sharkey, S. (2009, September). *The Role of the Middle Manager in the Strategy Development Process of the Multinational Subsidiary: British Academy of Management Conference,*

Brighton. Retrieved from: http://arrow.dit.ie/cgi/viewcontent.cgi?article=1005&context=bu schmancon

Olsen, E. (2015, October 3). Assessing Your Mission Statement. *Training Course Materials.com.* Retrieved from: www.trainingcoursematerial.com/free-training-articles/strategic-planning-and-thinking/assessing-your-mission-statement

Papano, L. (2012, November 2). The Year of the MOOC. *The New York Times.* Retrieved from: www.nytimes.com/2012/11/04/education/edlife/massive-open-online-courses-are-multiplying-at-a-rapid-pace.html

Rigby, D. (2015). *Management Tools 2015: An Executive's Guide. Bain and Company.* Retrieved from: www.bain.com/management_tools/baintoptentools/default.asp

Rosenbloom, B. (2014, December 30). Strategic Planning and Policy for Online Programs and Instructional Technology. *Envision Online Learning.* Retrieved from: https://onlinelearning.commons.gc.cuny.edu/2014/12/23/lessons-learned-from-john-jay-online-part-1/

Rowley, D., Lujan, H. and Dolence, M. (1997). *Strategic Change in Colleges and Universities.* San Francisco: Jossey-Bass Publishers, pp. 153–155.

Scheye, T. (n.d.). *Culture Eats Strategy for Breakfast.* Unpublished working paper, privately circulated.

Scott, J. (2006, January–February). The Mission of the University: Medieval to Postmodern Transformations. *Journal of Higher Education,* 77:1, pp. 1–39.

Sinek, S. (2009). How Great Leaders Inspire Action. *TEDx Puget Sound.* Retrieved from: www.ted.com/talks/simon_sinek_how_great_leaders_inspire_action#t-207063

Stallworth, L. (2008, April). The Mission Statement: A Corporate Reporting Tool With a Past, Present, and Future. *Journal of Business Communication,* 45:2, pp. 94–119.

Starr, K. (2012, September 18). The Eight Word Mission Statement. *Stanford Social Innovation Review.* Retrieved from: https://ssir.org/articles/entry/the_eight_word_mission_statement

Sufi, T. and Lyons, H. (2002). Mission Statements Exposed. *International Journal of Contemporary Hospitality Management,* 15:5, pp. 255–262.

Sutia, K. (n.d.). *The Mission, Vision, Objectives and Business Description. A Business Planning Reference Guide for Social Enterprises.* Retrieved from: www.virtueventures.com/files/mdbl-chapter2.pdf

Team Infusion Principle (2015, April 23). Powerful Mission Statements Avoid These Five Traps. Retrieved from: http://infusionprinciple.com/powerful-mission-statements-avoid-these-5-traps/

Trout, J. (2006, August 21). Mission Statement' Words. *Forbes.* Retrieved from: www.forbes.com/2006/08/18/jack-trout-on-marketing-cx_jt_0821mission.html

Truman State University Strategic Plan 2016–2020 (2016, October 21). Retrieved from: www.truman.edu/about/mission-vision/strategic-plan/

Truman State University Strategic Plan for Online Learning (2014). Retrieved from: http://online.truman.edu/files/2014/12/Online-Strategic-Planning-Document-final.pdf

UAB Online Strategic Plan (2013, October). Retrieved from: www.uab.edu/elearning/images/documents/strategic-plan-summary-report.pdf

University of Connecticut (n.d.), How to Write a Mission Statement. Retrieved from: http://assessment.uconn.edu/wp-content/uploads/sites/1804/2016/06/HowToWriteMission.pdf

University of Tennessee Chattanooga Strategic Planning Process. (n.d.). Retrieved from: www.utc.edu/strategic-plan/process/calendar.php

Zetlin, M. (2013, November 15). The 9 Worst Mission Statements of All Time. *Inc.* Retrieved from: www.inc.com/minda-zetlin/9-worst-mission-statements-all-time.html

5

Scanning the External Environment

On October 21, 1967, the board of trustees at Vassar College ended a two-day meeting during which the most pressing item on the agenda was a report developed by Vassar's president, Alan Simpson, in conjunction with the president of Yale University, Kingman Brewer, that had the potential to radically change the student population between the two schools. There was also a proposal from a consulting organization with alternatives to the Simpson-Brewer proposal. Both of these had been in the works for almost a year. At the time, Vassar accepted only women, and Yale was an all-male school. At the close of the meeting, the board announced that no decision about the proposals had been made, but it promised to meet as frequently as necessary to reach a conclusion (*New York Times*, October 22, 1967).

Vassar had been founded in 1861 by British-born brewer and businessman Matthew Vassar with a mandate to set the standard for women's higher education, which it had done for more than 100 years. It was the first women's college with a chapter of Phi Beta Kappa, considered by many to be the most prestigious academic honor society (Vassar.edu n.d.). An affiliation with Yale, the subject of the proposals, would mark a major change in Vassar's character and turning point in its history. But Vassar was not alone among prestigious women's colleges contemplating aligning themselves with suitable men's colleges or going co-ed on their own. In fact, in June 1967, Sarah Lawrence College announced that after three months of exploratory talks, it had decided not to merge with Princeton University. The talks apparently had been sparked by news of Vassar's potential alliance with Yale (*New York Times* June 3, 1967).

By the late 1960s both men's- and women's-only colleges, both secular and faith-based, across the country were actively contemplating their futures as single-sex institutions. In 1967, male-only Kenyon College in Ohio indicated that it expected to be co-ed within two years, as did Colgate University in upstate New York. In Los Angeles, Loyola University merged with Marymount College. And the all-male University of Notre Dame was deepening it ties with its neighboring institution, the women's-only St Mary's College (Time May 5, 1967).

Several familiar factors were fueling the drive toward co-education. One cluster revolved around economics. As the cost of higher education rose, many smaller colleges wanted to expand their enrollments, and it was easier to attract students to co-educational institutions. Moreover, a broader student base expanded fundraising opportunities. Finally, institutions that were already located close to each other could share facilities such as libraries and laboratories and offer a broader array of courses to their students while eliminating duplication at the same. Another set of factors driving the move toward co-education went beyond functional aspects of higher education, like libraries and classrooms. Educational leaders argued that more diversity would lead to a richer educational experience; having women and men in classes would provide for a better educational experience for both. And the intermingling of the sexes on campuses provided a better foundation socially for their futures as well (Time May 5, 1967).

But perhaps the most important force propelling the move to co-education was a fundamental shift in the role of higher education in society. Prior to World War II, higher education was available to a narrow demographic slice of American society. In 1937, only 15 percent of Americans between the ages of 18 and 20 attended college or university, and those where overwhelmingly, though not exclusively, white males from middle- and upper-middle-class backgrounds. With the passage of the G.I. Bill toward the end of World War II, enrollments at institutions of higher learning soared. And as returning soldiers generally performed well in their academic performance, the need for access to a university education for people from all social strata became a part of the public agenda (Hunt 2006). The demand for access to a college education continued to accelerate during the 1960s. California, for example, crafted ambitious plans for multi-tiered systems of higher education (Los Angeles Times April 27, 1960). And in 1965, the federal government passed the Higher Education Act that provided for the first time to the general public needs-based financial aid to attend college. In the wake of the act's passage, federal support for higher education jumped from $655 million in 1956 to $3.5 billion in 1966 (Brock 2010). As millions of first-generation college students streamed toward campus, same-sex education seemed anachronistic and out of step with the times. Why shouldn't women have access to the most prestigious universities in the country? And if top women students suddenly had many more options open to them, how would the elite women's colleges compete?

Of course, the transition to co-education was complicated. For one, the transition required the construction of dorms to accommodate the other sex. New policies had to be put in place. For example, a series of court cases in the 1960s compelled colleges and university to stop acting in loco parentis, loosening their control over student behavior (Lee 2011). And there were those who opposed same-sex education on principle: they argued that women would be intimidated by men in the classroom and that men would be distracted by women. Furthermore, the critics of co-education observed, college curricula in general were geared toward male vocational interests and opined that if women were exposed to the classroom competition found in mens' colleges, they would not be satisfied with being wives and mothers upon graduation. Finally, single-sex schools were both more relaxed and created environments that allowed students to focus more on their studies and less on social distractions (Time May 5, 1967). Not all single-sex schools opted to go co-educational. Smith College, Wellesley, Mt. Holyoke and others continued as women's-only institutions (In June 2016, there were only two non-religiously affiliated standalone men's colleges without "sister institutions"—Wabash College and Hampton-Sydney College, which was founded in 1775.) But the decision to eschew the co-education wave of the 1960s was risky. In 1960, there were approximately 233 standalone women's colleges in the United States. By 1986, there were 90 (Harwarth et al. 1997). By the mid-2010s, there were less than 50, and the numbers continue to shrink. The largest, St. Catherine University, a Roman Catholic university in Minnesota, had only around 4,500 undergraduates (and accepted men in associate, graduate and adult bachelor's programs). In retrospect, women's colleges in the 1960s faced many substantial issues, but the quality of the education they delivered was, in general, not one of them. The most serious challenges they faced were external and included a new social role for the universities, opening access to universities to broader communities of people, new economic considerations and, over time, changing expectations for women in the workforce. How each college responded to those factors shaped its history over the next 50 years.

Online education emerged during a similar period of intense change in higher education. Once again the role of the university in society is being debated, with a renewed focus on the idea that the primary responsibility of colleges and universities is to prepare students for the workforce, calling into question the traditional role of liberal arts education. Access to higher education is on the public agenda, particularly the responsibility individual colleges and universities have to diversify their student bodies in order to support people from lower income communities. The overall cost of higher education is climbing, while government support for higher education at both the state and federal is declining. Finally, even the basic quality of the education students receive is being questioned. In one form or another, the growth of online education has come to be seen as associated with each of those major issues—either as a potential solution or has the potential to exacerbate the problem (Green and Wagner 2011).

Analysis in Planning Strategically

One of the essential steps in both strategic planning and planning strategically is to carefully assess both the internal and external environments and other contexts in which the organization operates. In traditional strategic planning processes, this phase entails doing what is called a SWOT analysis, in which an organization's strengths and weaknesses, opportunities and threats are closely examined. This integrated analysis ultimately helps shape and guide the planning process by matching the new possibilities and challenges that emerge from a careful examination of the external environment with a clear-eyed assessment of an organization's competencies and deficiencies. In short, the SWOT analysis combines an environmental and competitive analysis with a comprehensive audit of an organization's capacities and capabilities (What Is a SWOT Analysis 2016).

The importance of performing a SWOT analysis prior to engaging in a planning process would seem obvious. But as with other elements of strategic planning, the particular organizational characteristics of colleges and universities in general and online education specifically pose unique challenges in conducting a meaningful SWOT analysis. First, SWOT analysis's usefulness relies first and foremost on the quality of the data collected. Simply instituting an effective data collection system that generates meaningful and actionable data can present a huge barrier both institutionally for colleges and universities and for distance learning in particular (Ronco and Cahill 2005). Almost by definition, a SWOT analysis assesses factors that are more easily quantified or clearly defined. But the most significant data, particularly data relating to competitive threats from other institutions, is often not readily available. As a result, Jeffry Buller argues, SWOT data too frequently represents little more than guessing, which is not a firm foundation for successful planning (Buller 2015). Second, colleges and universities are comprised of multiple constituencies that often do not share a common vision of an institution's strengths or weaknesses and have deeply divided opinions regarding potential opportunities. Competing priorities of the different constituencies may be reflected subjectively regarding what is a strength and what is a weakness. Indeed, even when useful, a SWOT analysis may not result in determining strategic priorities and potentially may simply produce a series of lists, with no analysis of which items on the list are more significant than others (Symes n.d.). Third, many institutions simply are not set up to take an honest look at themselves. For example, many colleges and universities believe that their faculties are among their strongest assets—in particular, the faculty itself usually has that perspective. It is very hard institutionally for one set of stakeholders to point a finger at another to identify weaknesses. A cursory review of publically available SWOT analyses conducted by colleges and universities reveals that almost inevitably, those writing the report believe that their faculty expertise and commitment are strategic strengths. (This same sort of self-congratulation occurs in the private sector as well, in which companies routinely claim that their employees are their greatest asset.)

Despite these clear limitations, planning cannot take place in a vacuum. To have any chance of success, strategic plans must be developed taking into account the internal and external environments within which the organization operates. This chapter will review the basic components of a SWOT analysis. It will then briefly examine several of the trends that have an impact on the macro environment for online education. The significance of these trends primarily is that they may shape the institutional receptivity to online education and new online initiatives.

Following the analysis of the major factors shaping the overall environment for online education, the chapter will explore using SWOT-like approaches to planning strategically for online education. The exploration has two components. The first component was a survey of the competitive contours of online education. The second aspect looks at ways to assess institutional readiness for online education. Institutional readiness is a critical concept as it turns a critical eye on what a college or university actually has the capacity to do. The chapter concludes by laying out the role the SWOT analysis plays in planning strategically. Although those responsible for charting the future of online education at any specific campus must always be alert and aware to the larger context within which they operate, in most routine situations and in their day-to-day activities, they may not have the institutional authority or resources to respond to the macro environment, either by taking advantage of a perceived opportunity or by responding to a perceived threat. Consequently, for planning from the middle, the more micro-level analysis of institutional and departmental strengths and weakness, particularly those associated with a targeted objective or goal, represents the more useful application of a SWOT analysis. The targeted analysis can help focus planning on goals that potentially can actually be achieved.

Basic SWOT Components

A SWOT analysis is a fundamental element of the strategic planning process. The analytic process is rooted in research funded throughout the 1960s by a group of Fortune 500 companies and conducted by the Stanford Research Institute (SRI). The companies involved felt that their long-ranging planning processes were not effective, and they wanted to know why. During a decade of research involving more than 1,000 companies and 5,000 executives, the SRI investigators concluded that most businesses could be divided into two parts—what they called the base business and what they termed the development business, or new opportunities. The development business changed every five to seven years, which underscored the need for better planning and management of change. The research suggested that the need for better planning and change management could be addressed by answering two questions. The first was, "what is good and bad about the operation?" And the second was, "what is good and bad about the present and the future?" The SRI team coined the acronym SOFT—Satisfactory (good in the present), Opportunity (good in the future), Fault (bad in the present), Threat (bad in the future)—to summarize their framework. The next step in the SRI formula was to apply those questions to six operational areas—product, process, customers, distribution, finance and administration. By 1974, the researchers had codified their ideas into a planning template that was ultimately modified to use the SWOT categories (Humphrey 2005). At its best, SWOT represents an objective organizational balance sheet (Osita et al. 2014). As the name implies, the process entails tallying both the positive and the negative factors both internally and externally that will have an impact on the organization's ability to achieve its objectives. In theory, the analysis drives the planning process, leading to the selection of the key strategic issues the institution or organization faces, the evaluation of potential options, the selection of strategy and, ultimately, the implementation of the strategy. Strategy, within this framework, is driven by connecting the organization's ongoing actual capacity to the changing external environment (Campbell et al. 1999). Some observers argue that the fundamental difference between strategic planning, which seeks to identify opportunities, and traditional operational planning, which focuses more on specific goals (such as increased profitability or lower financial aid), is that strategic planning starts with an outward focus. The goal of strategic planning, in this formulation, is to align the organization or institution with its external environment (Rowley et al. 1997).

Given that the purpose of the analysis is to determine what comes next, in most cases, the SWOT takes place early in the planning process, generally right after the process is initiated (figure 5.1). In some cases, the SWOT analysis may even precede the formulation of the mission statement and the vision statement for a given strategic plan (Pisel 2008). The standard schematic for a SWOT process follows a series of standard steps. It starts on two tracks, an internal analysis that leads to an assessment of organization strengths and weaknesses and an external analysis to identify the external opportunities and threats. Depending on the scope and granularity of the analysis, the results are often presented as a two-by-two matrix with strengths and weaknesses across the top two boxes and opportunities and strength across the bottom two boxes.

Figure 5.1 SWOT Analysis

In most descriptions of the SWOT analysis and in the presentation of the results, each quadrant is given the appearance of having equal weight. In other words, identifying organizational weaknesses is as significant as identifying the external threats. And the internal and external assessments take place in parallel, often by the same team of people (Webster n.d.).

A Shift in Orientation

The initial framework proposed by the SRI group implied that priority should be given the internal analysis with the question that probed what is good and bad about the operation being investigated first. In the mid-2000s, Michael Watkins, then an associate professor at Harvard Business School and an expert in leadership and change, argued that the sequence should be reversed. Discussion of internal strengths and weaknesses often became abstract and unmoored to anything concrete. Instead, he contended, external analysis should be completed first and inform the internal assessment. In place of SWOT, he proposed using the acronym TOWS for threats, opportunities, strengths and weaknesses. In this way, the organization's strengths and weaknesses could be evaluated in terms of the potential opportunities. But the question remains: does a specific weakness make the organization more vulnerable to a perceived threat? Alternatively, are certain opportunities more attractive to pursue because of an organization's strengths? The goal of strategy is to blunt the most significant threats and pursue the opportunities with the most potential (Watkins 2013).

The TOWS orientation seems particularly appropriate given that institutions of higher learning have proven to be extremely resilient institutions, with hundreds of institutions in operation from more than 100 years. But periodically, external factors emerge that reshape the fundamental nature of higher education as well as the character of individual institutions. Co-education and the demand for wider access along with the new public policies that accompanied those changes were an example of external factors that reshaped higher education. Online education is another, and the way that colleges and universities, as well as specific online initiatives, respond to those changes will shape their characters and operations for the foreseeable future.

Conducting an External Analysis

The first step in a TOWS approach is the external analysis of the environment. While, generally speaking, the environmental scanning can be conceptualized as an onion with two layers, from the perspective of planning from the middle of the organization, the onion should be seen as having four layers (Campbell et al. 1999, 99). As strategic planning has matured as a management discipline, environmental scanning traditionally has been grouped into two broad areas—the macro level, which includes social, political and economic trends within which an organization operates, and a competitive analysis of the other enterprises operating within the same market space. These two areas are sometimes labeled the general environment and the task environment. However, when planning from the middle and particularly for online education, to some degree the institution itself represents an external environment of sorts within which the department or unit operates. In the same way that macro trends have an impact on the general operation of enterprise, the overall environment of the university has a profound influence on what the advocates of online education can achieve at any moment in time. For example, the financial health of the institution and its willingness to invest in new ventures will have an impact on the growth of online education. As well, the interests, focus and inclinations of the senior academic leadership must be taken into account.

The final layer of environmental scanning for online education looks at the internal capacities of the institution (as opposed to the unit specifically responsible for online education) to support online initiatives. The growth of online education touches on virtually every aspect of the university. But many of the other university stakeholders are not focused on online education, which, in fact, may not be on their agenda at all. The results of assessing other units—such as admissions, advising, records, among others—must be taken into consideration during any planning process in which online programs may touch on those areas.

The scan of the macro trends in the general business environment have come to be called a PEST or PESTLE environment. The acronym stands for political, economic, social and technical. The final letters in the PESTLE approach are legal and environmental. Other conceptualizations of similar activity have also been called STEP and STEEPLE, as some observers felt the acronym PEST had negative connotations, although none of the formulations imply a preference for one category of information over another (Morrison 2012).

The concept of a PEST or PESTLE analysis emerged from the doctoral dissertation of Francis Aguilar, which was published as *Scanning the Business Environment* in 1967 (Aguilar 1967). Aguilar, who went on to teach at the Harvard Business School for more than 30 years, examined how companies acquired and utilized information about external events and trends to aid in strategic planning. He focused on the methods senior management used to obtain strategic, as opposed to operational, information to guide their companies' futures. In the study, Aguilar explored the sources of information utilized by the managers, and he grouped the information they were seeking into a four-part taxonomy: economic, political, technical and social (Kottler 1967).

In a review of the literature on environmental scanning, Chun Wei Choo of the University of Toronto found that three primary factors influence the degree to which organizations engage in environmental scanning (Choo 1999) (figure 5.2). The first factor was situational. The more uncertainty managers perceived in their environment, the more frequently they engaged in environmental

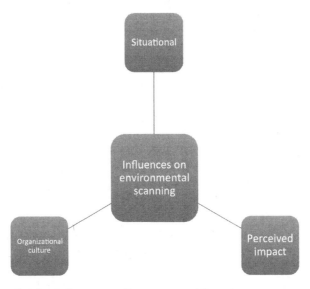

Figure 5.2 Choo's 3 Influences on Environmental Scanning

scanning. The intensity and scope of the scanning also increased. The second factor that influences environmental scanning is the organizational culture itself. If an enterprise is intentionally committed to a specific strategy, it is more likely to scan the environment to ensure that the strategy is intact and working. Ongoing scanning also allows organizations to modify their plans and even their strategies if a shift in the environment demands modification. Finally, scanning is directed toward acquiring information that managers perceive as having the greatest potential for impacting the business. The most common targets for environmental scanning are customers, competitors and suppliers, which are generally the prime sources of data for competitive analysis, which in this analysis represents the second layer of scanning. But changing regulations, demographics and other factors can also have a significant impact.

All three factors are complex and nuanced. For example, environmental uncertainty can be understood in many different ways, and the term "environmental uncertainty" can have several different dimensions. The term "environmental uncertainty" can refer to at least three different conditions (Milliken 1987). First, by appending the word "environmental," the implication is that the uncertainty comes from an external factor. With that in mind, Milliken argued, there can be what he calls "state uncertainty," which is when managers or administrators determine that the external environment or a component of the external environment is unpredictable. In other words, it is hard to predict how certain critical elements of the external world within which the institution operates will change, making it impossible to determine how to respond to those changes. For example, as when a new administration assumes control of the federal government, at the outset it may be impossible to predict how the regulatory environment for higher education or online education may change. The second dimension of uncertainty is the inability to foresee how specific changes in the environment will directly impact the organization. This dimension can be thought of as "effect uncertainty." In this instance, even when new regulations are proposed and passed by a new administration, it may be hard to determine their specific impact on the university in general or the any particular online educational program. For example, one of the drivers for co-education in the 1960s was the new availability of federal financial support for students. It was not clear when the aid became available, however, that it would contribute to the demise of single-sex women's education. But that was one of its effects. The final kind of uncertainty Milliken described is what he called "response uncertainty." This kind of uncertainty acknowledges the difficulty in foreseeing the exact consequences of any particular course of action. Response uncertainty is most acute when institutions feel compelled to react to a change in the external environment for a myriad of external reasons. The pressure on large research universities to launch MOOCs in the mid-2010s primarily because their perceived competitors were getting a lot of public attention for doing so could fall into the category of response uncertainty. The impact of the MOOCs on ongoing operations was difficult to project.

Understanding the kinds of uncertainty an organization faces is significant because the perceived uncertainty shapes the environmental scanning process. Fundamentally, these kinds of uncertainty determine what information about the environment managers feel they need. For example, state uncertainty demands a sustained look outward toward the external environment to determine the critical trends and factors that will shape the future of the institution. Effect uncertainty, on the other hand, necessitates assessing and correlating the potential impact of environmental factors on the internal operations. The external environment may be well understood but the direct impact of the environment on the organization may not. Response uncertainty may call for reaching out to potential stakeholders to assess the possible reactions to different courses of action, or it may involve conducting research to determine an additional array of choices and options. Understanding the factors driving the environmental scan is critical to gathering relevant and appropriate data for planning. Moreover, whether an environment is considered to be in flux or stable has an impact on the characteristics of the scanning. Complicating matters, people who are planning from the middle often do not have the time, resources and often the background to conduct sophisticated scans of the external environment, particularly when those efforts may be directed toward factors that only indirectly influence ongoing operations. That said, a good awareness of the general external environment is essential to planning at all levels. Overall, scanning behavior follows two paths, which are not mutually exclusive. Managers can conduct ongoing surveillance, which involves being generally aware and up to date with current developments in the field. Or they can actively seek information to gain a better understanding of a particularly salient issue (Nishi et al. 1982). Surveillance, in turn, can be divided into two approaches, as can more directed information seeking. Undirected viewing involves staying engaged with the information about the external environment with no particular end goal in mind. Conditional viewing narrows and directs the scanning activities to a smaller subset of topics. More active information seeking can be both informal and formal, with formal scanning being the most intentional and focused (Choo 1999).

There can be no argument that both higher education in general and online education in particular are being shaped by the factors captured in the PESTLE analysis. To a large degree, an institution's senior leadership will shape the responses to those factors. But the development of online education at any particular college or university will be shaped in part both by larger environmental factors and how the senior leadership chooses to respond to them. In many ways, planners for online education must be prepared to educate senior leadership, when possible, about the key trends that have implications for the growth of online education and its potential impact on the institution generally.

Analyzing the Task Environment

The second layer of external analysis in a TOWS process is the examination of what is called the task environment or the microenvironment. The task environment includes those factors that have a direct impact on an organization attaining its goals. The key aspects of the task environment include the industry in which an enterprise operates, its customers, suppliers, distributors, strategic partners and, perhaps most importantly, its competitors. In higher education there are corresponding linkages, including boards of trustees, deans, faculty and students, among others. The task environment is analogous to the competitive environment and in many ways the analysis of the task environment is similar to conducting the major elements of a competitive analysis. The first step in conducting an analysis of the task environment is to distinguish between an industry and a market. Although they are often used interchangeably, for the purposes of planning and strategic analysis, the differences between an industry and a market can be critical. An industry, argued John Kay, a leading British economist and former columnist for the *Financial Times*, is defined by the capabilities of the firms that are competing in a specific arena coupled in ways that support one another. An industry is defined by what companies can do: their skills and competencies. In contrast, according to Kay, a market is defined by customer needs and wants for which companies create products and services to satisfy those needs and wants. To use an imprecise analogy, an industry analysis focuses on the supply side of the equation. What do companies that are roughly classified together make? A market analysis focuses on the demand side—in other words, what do customers want (Kay 1995)? Kay illustrated the distinction by taking issue with Theodore Levitt's seminal article about marketing myopia. Levitt asserted that too many companies do not realize what "business" they are actually in and, consequently, often suffer in the wake of innovation. In Levitt's analysis, railroads, for example, should not see themselves just as railroads, which saw a decline of business as trucks became more popular for shipping goods, but view themselves as transportation companies. Kay noted that in the 1970s, big oil companies heeded Levitt's advice and reinvented themselves as energy companies. They bought coal companies and diversified into other energy markets. The results were generally disastrous, and most oil companies still earn most of their profits by selling oil. Both coal companies and oil companies operated in the energy market, but they were in distinct industries.

The distinctions can be more complex in higher education, which can be seen, in this analysis, as both an industry and a marketplace. As an industry, colleges and universities may define higher education by the way they go about doing their business. The market is characterized by the needs of people who want or need post-secondary credentialed education. Colleges and universities do not have a monopoly on the post-secondary education, which is a market that is rapidly changing. At the same time, the higher-education industry—the way colleges and universities go about doing their business—is under pressure to reform itself as well. And to muddy the waters further, many colleges and universities currently serve multiple markets.

Both industries and markets have competitive dynamics that are in many ways inextricably intertwined. In 1979, Harvard Business School professor Michael Porter published a seminal article in which he asserted that too often enterprises defined too narrowly the competitive forces they face. Competition in an industry is rooted in five forces, he argued, and it is the interplay of those forces that ultimately determines the intensity of the competition. It is through the analysis of these forces that enterprises can determine their own strengths and weakness (the last two steps in a TOWS approach) and craft an appropriate strategy (Porter 1979) (figure 5.3).

According to Porter, the forces that shape market and industry dynamics are the threat of new entrants into the market, the bargaining power of customers, the bargaining power of suppliers, the threat of substitute products and services, and finally, and perhaps most significantly, the tactics and strategies of the current market participants. The interaction and interplay of these forces determines the competitive nature of the industry and marketplace as well as the potential success of the individual participants. The goal of strategy is to defend the companies against the threats posed by those forces and to position the enterprise to capitalize on the opportunities the changing dynamics of those forces may open. Seen through Porter's lens, it becomes clear why higher education in general represents such a stable marketplace with so many

Porter's 5 Forces That Shape Market & Industry Dynamics	Threat of new entrants
	Bargaining power of customers
	Bargaining power of suppliers
	Threat of substitute products and services
	Tactics and strategies of current marketplace participants

Figure 5.3 Porter's 5 Forces That Shape Market and Industry Dynamics

resilient market participants. The cost of entry to establish a new four-year undergraduate degree-granting university is substantial. Porter laid out six determinants of the cost of entry into a marketplace—scale, capital requirements, product differentiation, costs advantages or disadvantages, access, and government regulations—each representing a major hurdle. The last, government regulation, may be one of the most difficult, as it can take years for a start-up institution to be accredited, and accreditation is critically important to most potential students. Consequently, it is no surprise that since the 1950s and 1960s, when state university systems aggressively expanded to meet the demand for greater access to higher education, few traditional, non-profit colleges and universities have been opened. In the traditional, non-profit college and university industry, institutions that are 50 years old are still considered to be relatively new entrants (Jacobs 2015).

Other major forces also tend to bring relative stability to both the higher education industry (i.e., the actual participants) and the higher education market (i.e., the demand for post-secondary education). The demand for the product—the degrees and certificates offered—remains high. Product differentiation, at least as far as the curriculum is concerned, is relatively low. There are no powerful suppliers that can shape the direction of the industry or the market. The customers have very little bargaining power. And the industry is so diffuse and diverse, with so many potential options for students, only in very specific instances are colleges and universities actually competing head-to-head with another specific school. Harvard versus Yale might be seen by some as analogous to Coke versus Pepsi. And even in that case, the competition might be truly head-to-head in only very limited situations, as many students would be very happy to attend either Harvard or Yale if they were accepted at only one.

And, in any case, both Harvard and Yale have many more applicants to most of their programs than they have positions available, so if Harvard does "lose" a student to Yale it still will be able to fill its classes. More generally, colleges and universities are competing with each other more indirectly as potential students work through the many variables they take into account when choosing a university including size, location, social life and campus, admission requirements, and costs and affordability as well as the reputation of the schools, the academic program and the availability of a major field of study (Morse 2011).

Despite the overall relative stability, large market forces are in play for many colleges and universities. Many colleges and universities are dependent on tuition as their primary source of revenue and must work hard to make sure that their first year classes meet their budgetary projections. With the dramatic rise in the cost of higher education in private colleges and universities as well among public institutions over the past two decades or more, identifying enough students able to afford the experience who also meet the academic profile of the kind of student the college wants to attract has become challenging. Moreover, colleges and universities that primarily draw students from a defined geographic area come under pressure with demographic shifts. In many geographic areas, there simply are fewer college-aged students to fill the seats or the demographic make-up of the applicant pool lacks diversity. Most significantly, while the traditional higher education industry is stable, the higher education market attracts new entrants, most notably the for-profit colleges and universities. Since the late 1980s, for-profit universities have enrolled millions of students. However, by the mid-2010s, the model had come under attack for not truly meeting the needs of their students—the largest for-profit university, the University of Phoenix, saw its enrollment drop from over 400,000 at its peak to less than 200,000 in 2016—the carnage was caused largely because of a crackdown by the U.S. Department of Education under President Barak Obama (Lobosco 2016). The growth of online education has also attracted new players to the post-secondary school market. MOOC platforms and other initiatives are exploring avenues for providing post-secondary credentials, including creating their own sets of credentials and certificates such as micro-master's degrees (Carapezza 2017). Over time, those efforts could gain greater traction, and, if they do, it could have a major impact, particularly on graduate education for many institutions (Friedman 2016).

Competitive Analysis

In Porter's model, the pivotal factor in a market analysis is the active participant in the market. Consequently, assessing the specific competition is an essential element of a TOWS exercise. As with other aspects of this kind of analysis, large-scale factors influence the way individual players in a marketplace conduct themselves. Some of the most significant are the relative strength of the each of the participants, the fixed costs, industry capacity and growth, and the cost of exiting a particular market. Each of those factors can constrain the maneuvering room available to each enterprise. Broadly speaking, competitive analysis entails investigation into multiple factors (Hussey 1999). The first step is to identify who the competitors are. In many industries there are only a handful of competitors. That is not the case with higher education, as there are several approaches to determining an appropriate competitive set. Perhaps the most direct way of identifying competitors is through an analysis of cross applications—what is the set of schools to which students apply? But other approaches can be used as well, including membership in specific academic associations, traditional rivalries, membership in sports leagues, grouping by ratings agencies, and institutional aspirations. Most colleges and universities do not compete with every other college and university in the country, however, identifying the competitive set can be quite complex. Once the competitive set has been established, the analysis consists of examining the competitors from two different perspectives. First, competitors should be examined from the customer's point of view. Second, the enterprise should try to understand their competitors as their competitors see themselves by conducting a strengths and weakness analysis (PESTLE Analysis 2015). Some questions that form the foundation of the analysis are: What does the institution do well, and what does it do poorly? Why do or would students select that institution, and why do or would students not choose to go there? What student needs does the institution supply well, and where do they lack? The second element of the market analysis it to try to understand the competitor as the competitor understands itself by asking the following questions: What is its financial situation? What are its marketing messages? Is there an area in which the institution is obviously investing? What kinds of new initiatives have been launched? Some of the richest sources of competitive information in higher education are the strategic plans for colleges and universities, which are frequently publically posted.

Organizational Impact of TOWS Analysis

The goal of the understanding of the external environment gained by undertaking a PESTLE analysis, a market analysis, and a competitive analysis is to be able to identify the key strategic issues facing an organization as the basis for developing an appropriate course of action. The underlying assumption for a TOWS analysis is that the organization's short-term performance and long-term survival are determined in part by their responses to those external environmental factors. But managers are often bombarded with a steady stream of information from multiple sources. Identifying strategic issues—that is, determining those external factors that actually will have a significant impact on organizational performance—requires categorizing the external information appropriately. The impact of the way the information generated by the external environment scan is categorized can have a significant impact in the responses that are crafted. For a TOWS analysis, the categorization involves determining what elements of the external environment should be considered a "threat" and what should be considered an "opportunity" (Dutton and Jackson 1987). According to Dutton and Jackson, the category "opportunity" is associated with three attributes—positive, gain and controlled. "Threat" is associated with the inverse—negative, loss and uncontrollable. And once an issue has been categorized as an opportunity or threat, the categorization serves as a multifaceted filter to understand related information. Once an issue has been identified and categorized, managers will more likely be alert to related information that confirms the status as well as recall old information that is congruent with the categorization. For example, since rising costs for higher education have been categorized as a threat for many institutions, people are more likely to attend to information about the negative impact of rising costs and remember information that confirms the negative impact. Ironically, in the 1990s, rising tuitions were seen as an opportunity by some universities that found if they aggressively raised their tuition, their perceived value also went up (Shipka 2006). Moreover, if planners are missing information or information is ambiguous, the tendency is to assume that information supports the established categorization of the issue. In addition to the cognitive elements, categorizing an issue as a threat or an opportunity has an affective component, according to Dutton and Jackson. People feel more comfortable associating themselves with opportunities and addressing opportunities often attracts a wider community of willing participants within an organization. The response to threats frequently is managed by a smaller group of people, allowing decision-making to be more controlled. In short, responding to threats may involve making hard choices and many people would prefer to avoid hard choices.

The responses to opportunities and threats can be either directly outward— that is, attempting to change the external environment—or inward, which refers to making internal changes. Interestingly, Dutton and Jackson found that managers more frequently address threats by trying to make internal changes such as reorganizing divisions or departments, while issues that are categorized as opportunities elicit more externally focused responses. Finally, the organization's response to strategic issues can vary in magnitude. Significantly, Dutton and Jackson noted, as the psychologists Amos Tversky and Daniel Kahneman have documented, people are more eager to avoid loss than to pursue gain (Tversky and Kahneman 1981). As a result, issues that are categorized as threats are more likely to invoke greater attention and ultimately action than issues that are seen as opportunities, which may receive lower priority. Conducting a TOWS analysis and gaining a better understanding of the organization's impact of the categorization of issues has significant implications for planners of online education. While planners in the middle of the organization have limited resources to shape institutional level responses to the external environment, they must be aware and alert to that environment. As discussion of the opportunities and threats posed by online education rises and falls on the public agenda, senior administrators, boards of trustees and even state legislators, who do have the authority to shape the overall direction of an institution, react and respond, often in an ad hoc manner. The leaders of online educational initiatives must be prepared to engage with the senior administration when the opportunities present themselves. The development of online education on any particular campus rests in part on the ability of the managers to present the online education as a viable response to an external environment that is consistent and congruent with the picture of the external environment held by the decision-makers in the university. In other words, the managers of online education must understand the external environment in which they are operating in a way that is compatible with the view of the senior administration. Moreover, the leaders of online educational efforts should carefully frame the issues they identify. Generally speaking, one of the foundational theories of behavioral economics suggests that issues framed as threats will invoke a stronger and more comprehensive response than issues that are framed as opportunities. The danger, however, in framing issues as threats is that it could lead to a smaller group of people being involved in devising and executing the strategy to respond.

Finally, while people actively involved in online education may be acutely aware of the issues involved, many other stakeholders in the university may not scan the environment for online education regularly. Dependent on incomplete sources of information or narrow perspectives, misconceptions about online education abound (Guri-Rosenblit 2009). Given the rate of change in online education, what may have been true three years ago may no longer be the case today. Conducting a threats and opportunities analysis prepares the leaders of online education to educate the other critical stakeholders and decision-makers in the institution. A comprehensive PEST analysis may be beyond the reach of people planning from the middle, like campus leaders of online education; however, a general understanding of the environment is essential.

PESTLE Analysis for Online Education

Even a cursory a review of the political, economic, social, technological, legal and environmental context for online education reveals several major trends and forces at work that shape the perceived threats and opportunities online education represents. Many of these constraints are not new and have been obvious for a decade or more (Howell et al. 2003). Moreover, the growth of online education has to be considered within the overall external environment for higher education in general. Nonetheless, their impact and salience of specific external factors on the growth has shifted considerably over time. And many of the trends influencing the direction of higher education have a specific and targeted impact on online education, particularly in the arena of traditional non-profit colleges and universities.

By definition, a PEST analysis is aimed at assessing large-scale and general factors. The impact of politics on higher education can be felt on multiple levels ranging from the federal government to state legislatures to regional accrediting agencies. Several developments at the federal level in the recent past potentially have impacted online education. Since the mid-2000s, federal support for higher education in general has climbed while funding from state legislatures has fallen. As significant, federal funding for higher education is qualitatively different from state funding. Federal funding generally is provided directly to students (often in the form of Pell Grants for low-income students or federally guaranteed student loans) or to faculty in the form of research grants as opposed to general operating support (Pew Issue Brief 2015). State support traditionally has been directed more toward the institutions themselves to maintain their campuses and to keep the overall cost of tuition down. The shift in the funding balance between the federal and state governments has several implications. Since the federal government funds individual students, it has become deeply involved in trying to improve degree completion rates, to monitor and increase accessibility to higher education, and to assess and ensure quality. The overall aim is to hold institutions of higher education accountable for their student outcomes (Executive Office of the President 2017). Each of those factors has a direct and often complicated effect on online education, which has come under considerable scrutiny. For example, on one hand, online education is seen as a viable option to help students complete their college degrees. A wide range of colleges and universities—spanning from the City University of New York to Immaculata University, a small Catholic university outside of Philadelphia, which has approximately 1,000 full-time undergraduates students—have launched online programs tailored specifically to help people complete their degrees. On the other hand, the research concerning the completion rates for online education itself is mixed. Some studies suggest that, at least in certain circumstances, degree completion rates for online students equals or exceeds those for students in traditional program (Shea and Bidjerano 2014). Other studies indicate that online students' degree completion rates may be marginally lower than traditional students. And the popular perception, shaped in part by the publicity surrounding MOOCs and the abysmal completion rates at for-profit colleges and universities, which were early adaptors of online technology, is that the completion rate for online students is shockingly low (Haynie 2015).

The federal government's increased influence on online education has also led to a debate about the definition of a credit hour, which is a unit upon which the amount of financial support is predicated. With the emergence of asynchronous online classes, "seat time" clearly cannot be used to determine a credit hour. So online programs have to document that the educational experience they provide is the equivalent to the traditional credit hour (U.S. Department of Education 2010). With credit hours potentially untethered from "seat time" and coupled to the direct assessment of learning, in 2014, the U.S. Department of Education launched an experiment that would provide federal loan support for students in competency-based educational programs, and it expanded the experiment the following year. In the competency-based model, students progress toward a degree not through the number of classes they take or the hours that they spend in class but by demonstrating specific competencies. In the expanded program, the Department of Education indicated its willingness to support a subscription model of education in which students could take as many courses and learn as much as they were able to in defined period with no additional charges (Mitchell 2015). The competency-based model holds the potential to bring about major changes in post-secondary education. But perhaps the most significant regulatory change in online education has been the expansion of the State Authorization Reciprocity Agreements, known as SARA. Historically, higher education has been regulated primarily at the state level in conjunction with regional accrediting institutions. As online programs were launched, schools had to get authorization from each state to serve students in that state, a cumbersome, laborious and costly process. SARA is an agreement among the states establishing standards for online education. If any member state approves an online program, that program can be offered in all SARA participant states (NC SARA 2016). By 2017, 47 states were participating in SARA, with California, Florida and Massachusetts the holdouts. In essence, SARA has created a national market for online education, which also reflects a major change in higher education. Clearly, the focus on completion rates, quality, and assessment; the willingness to experiment with competency-based education; and the creation of a national market for online educational programs are hugely important to the leaders of online education on every campus. They are examples of the kind of issues that can be identified through the analysis of the political environment.

Economic and Social Factors

Economics and social factors play an important role in setting the context for planning a strategy for online education, along with politics and regulation. The economic struggles facing many colleges and universities have been identified for a decade or more and actually date to at least the 1970s, if not earlier. Rising tuitions and higher costs have led to huge student debt and economic stress for students as well as the colleges and universities they attend. Institutions that rely heavily on tuition for the bulk of their revenue may find themselves in a struggle to fill their incoming class of students. The question is: what role can online education play to help address those issues? A once obscure school like Southern New Hampshire University, for example, aggressively pursued online strategies that not only stabilized their operations, but also turned them into a financial powerhouse. In ten years, Southern New Hampshire, which has around 3,000 residential students, added more than 30,000 online students.

And it extended its online operations in 2014, when it launched its College for America (CFA) division that utilizes a competency-based subscription education model. At CFA, 120 "competencies" earns an associate's degree, and, in the first cohort, one student finished the program in 100 days (Kahn 2014). In 2014, Southern New Hampshire University projected that its online division would generate more than $200 million in revenue with a double-digit profit margin (Pulley 2014). While eye-catching, the online component of Southern New Hampshire University is only part of the story. The online division there relies almost entirely on part-time instructors who serve more as class monitors than teachers delivering standardized courses. And it employs marketing techniques that resemble those of for-profit universities more than traditional colleges and universities. Even the graduates of its residential campus feel its marketing approach has hurt the value of their degree (Hechinger 2013). However, reviews of the quality of the education provided are mixed at best.

While some colleges and universities have been able to use online education to help stabilize their finances, the overall economics of online education is more complex. The hope that a move to online education would significantly lower the overall cost of higher education has not materialized. Although nearly 90 percent of colleges and universities offer at least some online courses, tuition continue to rise. And while most colleges and universities charge the same tuition for online and residential courses, around 30 percent actually charge more for online classes, often in the form of a technology surcharge (Casement 2013). The extra cost for online courses, at least in the start-up phase, is not unreasonable or arbitrary. Using the technology costing method created by WCET, the Western Interstate Commission's Cooperative for Educational Technologies, Russ Poulin, the organization's director of research and policy, observed that the primary expense for any specific course is the cost of instruction and that cost does not disappear for online education. On the contrary, many of the functions commonly assumed by traditional instructors such as course design, the creation of course materials such as PowerPoint slides, and assessment might entail additional expenses in the online environment. Online courses can require additional technology and student support along with other factors, like demands on the library. If a school starts with the same basic cost— the cost of the instructor—and must pay for other functions and services, the overall price tag must go up, Poulin concluded (2012). While other studies have shown that the cost of an online course can be reduced, the approach primarily relies on reducing the cost of instruction by relying on automation or employing lower-paid adjunct faculty. Both of those raise questions about the overall quality of the courses (Casement 2013, 17).

Course development is part of the equation; as online education is relatively new, launching new programs has considerable start-up costs and relatively long lead times. Given the competition for resources on all campuses, identifying the source of the investment funds for online programs may be daunting. That is one reason some campuses have opted to outsource the infrastructure, marketing and technical support for online education to third-party providers in exchange for a portion of the revenue generated. While these kinds of partnerships provide a lower-cost, less risky way for colleges and universities to move into online education, the overall results have been mixed at best. Not infrequently, faculty members will express discomfort working with a third-party provider, and there have been concerns that the outside vendor would not have the appropriate commitment an institution's mission and values or understanding of the campus culture. For the economics to work for the vendor, classes need to be of a certain size and sometimes class scheduling has to be revised. Over time, many campuses that initially worked with outside vendors struck out on their own with new programs or severed their ties with third-party providers completely. In other cases, however, the vendors and the campuses have been able to maintain fruitful, mutually beneficial relationships (Finkel 2013).

The long-term economic trends for higher education are firmly in place, but the impact on online education varies from campus to campus. Along the same lines, several major social factors are important in shaping the external environment for online education. Perhaps most critical are the changing demographics of the undergraduate student population, which has been well documented. According to the Lumina Foundation, in 2016, 38 percent of the undergraduate student population was more than 25 years old. More than half of those students are working in addition to attending school. More than a quarter of students are raising children. Nearly half are footing their own bills for college. The number of students of color is climbing at a much faster rate than white students (Lumina Foundation 2016). Only about one-third of undergraduates are the traditional 18- to 22-year-olds. And fewer still, less than 15 percent, live on campus (Azziz 2014). But other large-scale social trends that are shaping the contours of online education have received less attention. First, an increasing number of high school students take online courses at some point in their high school careers, so taking online courses is becoming more familiar to them. In fact, the number of K–12 students taking online classes has grown at double-digit rates in the recent past. Helping to fuel the growth, many states require students to take at least some courses online to earn a high school diploma (Sheehy 2012). And students in middle school and high school are becoming very comfortable using mobile devices for learning, particularly for self-directed and collaborative assignments. While those devices are still primarily used within the context of a classroom setting, it is a short step from the use of a mobile device in the classroom to online education (Taylor 2015).

Online education is making even more dramatic in-roads in the post-undergraduate educational environment. In the mid-2010s the use of e-learning in the corporate marketplace was projected to climb 11 percent annually through 2020 (Technavio 2016). Moreover, the top trend in continuing education in the post-college arena is the growth of on-demand courses. Working professionals in need of CEUs for credentialing, maintaining a license, or seeking to broaden their professional skill set, are looking for courses that are flexible and immediately accessible. Online offerings obviously play an important role in meeting that need (Horn et al. 2016). If colleges and universities are going to play the pivotal role in lifelong learning, online education represents a vital mechanism for achieving that goal. Other social trends will also have an impact on online education. For example, higher education is becoming increasingly global, and online education enables schools to compete for international students. The demand for access to education continues to climb, as does the access of different communities to the broadband infrastructure. A systematic assessment of major social trends would reveal a plethora of impact factors on online education.

Technological Forces

The most significant external factor influencing the overall direction of online education—and the factor that promises to create the most opportunities as well as pose the most significant threats—is the development of technology itself. The concept of distance learning was not invented with the advent of the Internet. As far back as the 1880s, the Chautauqua movement popularized the idea of education by correspondence and in 1892, the University of Chicago, then a start-up institution, began offering correspondence classes. Distance learning was widespread enough that in 1915, the National University Extension Association was formed to accredit programs (California Distance Learning Project 2011). Each wave of new communication technologies brings with it new opportunities for distance education. Educational radio was launched in the 1920s and educational television was launched in the 1940s, at the very beginning of the television era. But the rate of technological change with the Internet, particularly with the emergence of Web 2.0 technologies that made content creation and interaction on the World Wide Web commonplace (along with providing the technological foundation for applications like Facebook and Twitter) has had an unprecedented impact on the costs and quality for online education. Low-cost video production, video conferencing and cloud computing, among other technologies, have dramatically changed the essential quality of online education.

The entire technological infrastructure for colleges and universities is in a period of transition, and the way campuses manage that transition will have an important impact on online education on every campus. Perhaps the most significant trend is what has come to be called the digital transformation of learning. Many of the technological tools used to support online learning also had an application in other parts of the educational experience, including face-to-face classroom interaction. The digital transformation of learning is premised on several insights. First, the use of technology can fundamentally change the learning experience. Second, as digital content becomes routinely available, it potentially can be accessed anywhere and at any time. Third, the use of technology can generate new forms of data for assessment and analysis. Fourth, within a digital platform, information about students can be more integrated, better managed and more effectively applied, leading to better student outcomes (Duncan 2010). The digital transformation of learning caused university campuses to scramble to restructure their technological infrastructures.

According to Educause, a leading non-profit association for IT leaders in higher education, the top IT issues on campus are information security, learning how to use data and predictive analytics to improve student success, and providing the campus community, from the administrative leadership to students, with the data and business intelligence tools needed to make data-driven decisions (figure 5.4). Interestingly, while providing scalable and well-resourced e-learning services, facilities, and staff to support increased access to and expansion of online education was a top priority in 2016, supporting the online education infrastructure had fallen out of the top-ten priority list in 2017, presumably subsumed under the heading of the digital transformation of learning (Grajek 2017). Within those broad trends, colleges and universities are rethinking their IT infrastructures in very granular ways. Many are moving to cloud-based applications. The effective use of customer relationship management systems is becoming more critical. And there are an array of new technologies including adaptive learning and collaboration packages making their way onto campus. In total, according to the market research company Gartner, by the mid-2010s, colleges and universities in the United States were investing nearly $40 billion in information technology (Gartner 2016). At any given point in time, many exciting new technologies that could have a significant impact on the quality of online education are always seemingly just around the bend. Technologies like virtual/augmented/mixed reality, artificial

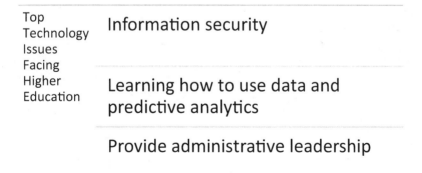

Figure 5.4 Top Technology Issues Facing Higher Education

intelligence, and gaming and simulation, among others, could have a profound impact as they mature (Kelly 2017). In short, online education is the progeny of technological change. Monitoring the technological change is essential to charting the future of online education and for planning an effective strategy.

Competitive Analysis

The PESTLE analysis—an acronym for Political, Economic, Social, Technological, Environmental, and Legal—is the first part of the environmental scan in a TOWS assessment. The second part is a systematic examination of competing institutions. By understanding the strategies of the competition, an institution can effectively position itself to the students it wants to attract and those it can realistically attract (Marketing Teacher n.d.). Traditionally, students use a range of explicit as well as other often-unstated reasons to select a college or university, the most common of which are the academic programs offered, acceptance criteria, overall cost and the availability of financial aid, geographic location, campus size and number of students attending, reputation, and quality of the campus social life, among others. The often-unexamined influences include family and friends, high school guidance counselors, the desire to participate in specific campus activities like sports and co-curricular opportunities (Dockery 2012). At this stage in its development, online education has changed the calculations in selecting an academic experience by lessening the weight of some of those factors and increasing the importance of others. Most significantly, the decision process has placed the focus more squarely on the availability of a specific academic program and cost. While still important, geographic considerations do not have the same place in online education as with campus-based opportunities. SARA has, in essence, for the first time created a national marketplace for higher education and competing on a national level is new for many, if not most, colleges and universities. And even for universities that have been offering online programs for a considerable period of time, the market is very fluid. For example, consider the impact of academic reputation or status of the institution offering an online program. In traditional private and public institutions, academic reputations are relatively fixed and stable. In the new national market for online education the reputations of the different players for online education have not been clearly established. To illustrate this point, one of the best known mechanisms for establishing or reinforcing academic reputations is through outside ratings reported in the media. While U.S. News and other organizations dutifully publish "best of" rankings for online education, the institutions that often rank highly for their online education are not congruent with the institution's traditional reputation. In the 2017 rankings of online undergraduate programs by U.S. News, for example, Temple University in Philadelphia ranked second, and the University of Oklahoma ranked third. At the time, Temple had less than 200 online students, and Oklahoma had around 1,300 (U.S. News & World Report n.d.[a]). In the U.S. News traditional rankings of bachelor's programs, Temple was ranked 118 among national universities—not accounting for all the other categories into which colleges can be placed—and had more than 28,000 undergraduate students, while Oklahoma was number 111 in national universities with around 22,000 students (U.S. News & World Report n.d.[b]). California University of Pennsylvania's online bachelor's degree is ranked number 6, while its traditional campus-based program is judged to be a second-tier regional university in the North. Although it may be ranked second for online undergraduate students, Temple University's online program is hardly competitive with Harvard University's program, which is ranked second among traditional undergraduate programs.

So how do students choose which online program to attend? According to a study by the Learning House, a provider of online educational services, and Aslananian Market Research, tuition and fees represent the single most important factor that students use in selecting an online program. But after tuition and fees, no single element truly seems to be driving the decision. Among the characteristics that students took into account in almost equal weight included overall academic reputation and the profile the university has in the field of study, prospective workload, and whether the program was synchronous or asynchronous. In terms of reputation, the baseline was that students wanted the program to be accredited and recognized by others in the field (Clinefelter and Aslanian 2015). Although the report's data supports the idea that the selection criteria for online programs, and consequently the market positions of colleges and universities offering online programs, is still in flux, it contains several other important insights. While online education operates in a national marketplace, geography still matters. According to the survey, about half of both graduate and undergraduate students selected programs and campuses less than 50 miles away, and less than a quarter enrolled in programs more than 100 miles away from where they reside. Secondly, students generally are looking for a specific program of study and then seek an institution at which it is offered. Finally, and perhaps most important, students often "pre-select" institutions. About one-third of students who choose online programs apply to only one institution, and 70 percent contact three or fewer. By far, the most important criteria for ultimately selecting an institution is that the applicants believe the program was a good fit for the field of study they wanted, followed by cost and reputation. Online education's distinctive market characteristics have critical implications for a competitive analysis. As opposed to the traditional higher education market in which decisions may primarily be based on the school's reputation, when it comes to deciding on an online education, competition is at the program level, rather than at the institutional level. It is important to point out that in the mid-2010s, the majority of online programs were still largely concentrated in business administration, nursing and computer science, which means the market for scores of other academic programs have not been developed. If the online program is attractive, the competition for the students is more narrowly focused, with generally only one or two other rivals in the running. And even though many online students will never set foot on campus, the competitive space for online education may be as local or regional as that of the traditional higher educational market. All of those factors serve to define the competitive context for strategically planning for any particular online program.

Institutional Readiness

The PEST and competitive analysis are the standard starting point for a TOWS analysis. An assessment of the external environment clarifies the threats and opportunities an organization faces. Fashioning a response to those threats and opportunities requires a levelheaded assessment of the organization's internal strengths and weaknesses. Online education modifies that process and requires an additional step. From one perspective, the institution itself can be understood as an external environment within which online education is situated. Before the strengths and weaknesses of the unit responsible for online education can be assessed, the institutional readiness of the college or university itself must be ascertained. The implementation of online education touches almost every part of university operations. Planning must consider the capability and preparedness of those units within the university for whom online education may not be a primary responsibility or priority, but nevertheless will be needed to perform the new tasks that any given plan may require of them. Like the general external environment, institutional readiness can be measured on two levels—the mindset of the organization toward online education and then the effectiveness of specific administrative functions involved. The approach to the use of educational technology illustrates the different planes on which readiness can be ascertained. As Carol A. Twigg, the president and CEO of the National Center for Academic Transformation and former vice president of Educause, has written, many colleges and universities have turned to educational technology with the hope of lowering the cost of instruction without reducing quality, thereby increasing academic productivity. But to do so, the university needs at least two components. Strategically, it has to have an idea regarding how to employ technology to improve outcomes; bland admonishments to incorporate technology where appropriate or providing technology as a general resource for faculty is not sufficient. At the same time, the college or university must have a mature enough IT department to provide support beyond technical assistance for those on the frontlines (Trigg 2000). Such support goes beyond managing the digital learning system (LMS) to include supporting accessibility measures, like closed captioning of videos. The latter is an ancillary task for many IT departments that may not be prepared to take on that charge.

Understanding the campus climate for online education is essential to constructing plans that will support the program's chance of success. Perhaps most troubling, over the past decade or more, a large majority of full-time faculty have been skeptical about the effectiveness of online education, even as many chief academic officers and other senior administrators projected that online education would play a significant role at their institutions. A 2014 study found that only 9 percent overall of full-time faculty believe that online classes could result in the same outcomes as face-to-face classrooms and that only 5 percent of faculty members who had never taught online (which is most professors) believed online education could equal to face-to-face classes (Lederman and Jaschik 2013). Assessing attitudes within the institution toward online educational initiatives is essential to planning, in part, because it helps clarify where opposition to any specific plan may arise and can suggest approaches to addressing resistance and barriers. While the view toward online education has been steadily unfavorable for a significant period of time, those negative attitudes are not completely and irrevocably fixed. In 2016, a team lead by Peter Shea of the University at Albany, State University of New York, replicated the Jaschik and Lederman study but surveyed faculty teaching in the Open SUNY system of online education. In operation for more than a decade, Open SUNY is considered a good model of online program administration and faculty support. The researchers' hypothesis was that a good environment for online education would have a positive impact on faculty and other stakeholders' attitudes. The results confirmed the hypothesis. More than half the SUNY faculty surveyed thought that the outcomes of online classes could match those of face-to-face classes and nearly half strongly ascribed to that belief. The researchers concluded that the condition under which online education is taking place has a dramatic impact on faculty attitudes (Shea and Bidjerano 2016).

In addition to the general campus climate for online education, the specific functional areas needed for successful online programs must be assessed. This assessment can also take place on two levels. Since many of these functions are outside the domain and control of the people primarily planning and implementing online education, it is critical to know if the other units can accommodate any new initiatives or ideas. For example, can the records department technically manage the growth of online enrollments? Or is the campus library able to provide access to materials for online students? Beyond that, since many plans for online education may require change in other areas of the university, an understanding of the decision-making process in those areas is essential, and must be factored into any planning exercise.

The Online Learning Consortium's Quality Scorecard is perhaps the most widely known guideline for assessing the administration of online education (OpenSUNY 2014). The Quality Scorecard lays out nine categories for assessment in five broad areas (figure 5.5). The areas include institutional support, technology support, course development and instructional design, course structure, teaching and learning, social and student engagement, faculty and student support. Within the nine categories, 75 quality indicators have been developed

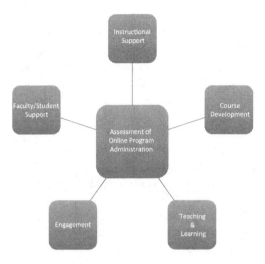

Figure 5.5 OLC's Quality Scorecard

and can be ranked on a scale of zero to three with zero being deficient and three being exemplary. The most heavily weighted areas are course development and structure, which account for 60 total points on the 256-point scale, and student support, which accounts for another 48 points (Online Learning Consortium 2017). The OLC Quality Scorecard can be a useful planning tool by helping to put a focus on weaknesses of specific areas of online programs that may be appropriate targets for planning strategically. For example, in technology support, the Quality Scorecard calls for a documented technology plan that includes electronic security measures such as password protection, encryption, secure online or proctored exams and so on; it requires that the plan be operational in way that ensures a quality level that is consistent with established standards and regulatory requirements. If that kind of policy does not exist, it could become a target for planning strategically. But the Quality Scorecard is not enough to guide planning, because many of the areas of assessment are generally outside the domain of responsibility of those managing online education programs. Consequently, even if an area is judged to be deficient, it is not clear if or how the deficiencies can be rectified. For example, developing a documented policy for electronic security is clearly the responsibility for the information or technology services team not the online education group. If developing a policy is not on the agenda for the information or technology services in a given year, it is difficult to see how that would be rectified.

A second approach to the assessment of institutional readiness for online education focuses more on the way decisions concerning online education are made throughout a specific campus or university system. Called the Generational Model of Online Program Development, this approach, which is based on maturity models deployed in other industries, lays out four decision-making processes that can be broadly applied. In the first generation, decisions are made on an ad hoc basis. When fully mature, decision-making for online education is fully embedded into the ongoing operation of the university (King and Alperstein 2015). In this case, technology for electronic security for online education, the Generational Model can help planners to determine if the issue can be addressed at any specific point, and if so, how the issue should be approached, given an understanding of the way decisions of this sort are made at a specific university. The Generational Model can help planners ascertain, for example how formally engaged the IT team is with online education and ask how issues are placed and ranked on their agenda. The answers to those questions are essential for planning. In essence, the Generational Model can be applied to all of the functional areas describe in the OLC Quality Scorecard.

Core Competencies

The final step in a TOWS analysis is applying the assessment of external opportunities and threats as well as the institutional readiness for online education to the core competencies of the unit most directly involved with developing online educational initiatives and efforts. In doing so, the organization can better understand its organizational strengths and weaknesses. Does the organization, for example, have the internal capabilities to respond to the threats and capitalize on the opportunities? Does it need to cultivate talent or capacity in a specific area to address a weakness, or should it shift its strategic focus in a way that capitalizes on its organizational strengths? Assessing core competencies and organizational strengths is not an easy process. In most cases, people like to believe that their organization is capable and competent. Based on that assumption, Smallwood and Ulrich have proposed assessing organizational capacity across ten dimensions. Among the most significant of the dimensions are the individual talents of the people in the organization, leadership, ability to collaborate, accountability and capacity to learning. Unity of purpose, common identity, speed and engagement with customers are also important considerations. These categories, Smallwood and Ulrich suggest, can form the basis of what they call a capacities audit, or a systematic way to identify strengths and weaknesses of an organization. The goal of a communication audit is not merely to identify weaknesses but to identify those capabilities that will have the biggest impact on achieving the unit's strategic goals (Smallwood and Ulrich 2004).

The first step in conducting a capacity audit for online education is to understand how online education is institutionally situated. Universities are experimenting with a variety of institutional models for online education, ranging from ambitious standalone online universities that are separately accredited and headed by their own president, such as the University of Florida Online, to very modest hybrid programs lodged within existing academic departments that also offer traditional face-to-face programs (UPCEA 2017). The organizational configuration will partly determine what the internal competencies and capabilities of the unit responsible for online education are and should be, and which of those capabilities are most associated with specific strategic goals. In turn, the assessment of the organizational strengths and weakness should define the strategic issues that can and should be defined at any specific time. For example, a program lodged in a department may have very little control over its marketing efforts and, if the program is largely faculty-driven, may have very little expertise in marketing. Consequently, a plan to improve marketing will not succeed. In that case, a strategy to collaborate more closely with those who are responsible for marketing would be more appropriate. If online education is the primary responsibility of a unit of the university, the unit must first understand what it can and can't do given where it is situated in the university's organizational structure; that determination underscores the entire process of planning strategically.

Conclusion

A fundamental premise of both strategic planning and planning strategically is that an organization must understand its external environment if it is to develop effective strategies for charting its course. Traditionally, a SWOT analysis—an assessment of an organization's strengths and weakness, opportunities and threats—has been the primary way to scan the external environment and correlate the scan to the operational profile of the organization. While initially a SWOT analysis first looked internally at strengths and weaknesses, over time the process was reversed. Organizational strengths and weakness can only be understood in relationship to the external environment; as such SWOT became TOWS.

For many reasons, conducting a comprehensive analysis of the external environment is beyond the capacity of many institutions of higher education, and well beyond the ability of those responsible for online education on any specific campus. Nonetheless, the underlying principles and assumptions embodied in a TOWS analysis are a critical element both strategic planning and planning strategically. Rather than being a discrete step in strategic planning, TOWS should be an ongoing activity. Planners for online education should continually monitor both the external environment for online education and the internal campus environment. It is through this surveillance that targets for planning will emerge. Once an issue rises on the agenda, additional research can be conducted.

In addition to guiding the planning process, an ongoing TOWS process is critical to enable the leaders of online education to educate other stakeholders about the opportunities and threats online education poses to the campus. As with the growth of co-education in the 1960s and 1970s, the choices colleges and universities make in response to the growth of online education will shape their institutional character in the decades to come. It is through a TOWS analysis that those responsible for online education can potentially help guide the senior leadership at the institutions to make informed decisions.

References

Aguilar, F. (1967). *Scanning the Business Environment*. New York: MacMillan.

Azziz, R. (2014, April 28). A Looming Challenge in Higher Education: Our Changing Student. *The Huffington Post*. Retrieved from: www.huffingtonpost.com/dr-ricardo-azziz/a-looming-challenge-higher-education_b_4855108.html

Brock, T. (2010, Spring). Young Adults and Higher Education: Barriers and Breakthroughs to Success. *Transition to Adulthood*, 20:1, pp. 109–132. Retrieved from: http://futureofchildren.org/publications/docs/20_01_06.pdf

Buller, J. (2015). *Change Leadership in Higher Education: A Practical Guide to Academic Transformation*. San Francisco, CA: Jossey Bass.

California Distance Learning Project (2011). *History of Distance Learning*. Retrieved from: www.cdlponline.org/index.cfm?fuseaction=whatis&pg=3

Campbell, D., Stonehouse, G. and Houston, B. (1999). *Business Strategy*. Oxford: Butterworth, Heinemann, p. 2.

Carapezza, K. (2017, February 15). These Top Schools Are Offering Big Savings on Master's Degrees, But There's a Catch. *NPR Morning Edition*. Retrieved from: www.npr.org/sections/ed/2017/02/15/504478472/how-to-get-20-000-off-the-price-of-a-masters-degree

Casement, W. (2013, Summer).Will Online Learning Lower the Price of College. *Journal of College Admission*. Retrieved from: http://files.eric.ed.gov/fulltext/EJ1011796.pdf

Choo, C. W. (1999, February/March). The Art of Scanning. *Bulletin of the Association for Information Science and Technology*, 25:3. Retrieved from: http://onlinelibrary.wiley.com/doi/10.1002/bult.117/full

Clinefelter, D. and Aslanian, C. (2015, July). *Online College Students 2015: Comprehensive Data on Demands and Preferences*. Louisville, KY: The Learning House, Inc. Retrieved from: www.learninghouse.com/ocs2015-report/

Dockery, D. (2012, March 23). School Counselors Support for First Generation College Students. *American Counseling Association Conference*, San Francisco, CA. Retrieved from: www.counseling.org/resources/library/VISTAS/vistas12/Article_61.pdf

Duncan, A. (2010, November 9). *The Digital Transformation in Education: U.S. Secretary of Education Arne Duncan's Remarks at the State Educational Technology Directors Association Education Forum*. U.S. Department of Education. Retrieved from: www.ed.gov/news/speeches/digital-transformation-education-us-secretary-education-arne-duncans-remarks-state-edu

Dutton, J. and Jackson, S. (1987). Categorizing Strategic Issues: Links to Organizational Action. *Academy of Management Review*, 12:1, pp. 76–90.

Executive Office of the President of the United States (2017, January). *Using Federal Data to Improve the Performance of U.S. Institutions of Higher Education*. Retrieved from: https://collegescorecard.ed.gov/assets/UsingFederalDataToMeasureAndImprovePerformance.pdf

Finkel, E. (2013, May 29). Colleges Finding Partners for Online Course Development. *University Business*. Retrieved from: www.universitybusiness.com/designingdigital

Friedman, J. (2016, January 22). What Employers Think of Badges, Nanodegrees From Online Programs. *U.S. News & World Report*. Retrieved from: www.usnews.com/education/online-education/articles/2016-01-22/what-employers-think-of-badges-nanodegrees-from-online-programs

Gartner (2016, February 25). Gartner Highlights Top 10 Strategic Technologies for Higher Education in 2016. Retrieved from: www.gartner.com/newsroom/id/3225717

Grajek, S. (2017, January 17). Top 10 IT Issues, 2017: Foundations for Student Success. *Educause*. Retrieved from: http://er.educause.edu/articles/2017/1/top-10-it-issues-2017-foundations-for-student-success

Green, K. and Wagner, E. (2011, January/February). Online Education: Where Is It Going? What Should Boards Know. *Trusteeship Magazine*. Retrieved from: www.agb.org/trusteeship/2011/januaryfebruary/online-education-where-is-it-going-what-should-boards-know

Guri-Rosenblit, S. (2009). Distance Education in the Digital Age: Common Misconceptions and Challenging Tasks. *Journal of Distance Education* (Online), 23:2, pp. 105–122. Retrieved from: http://search.proquest.com/openview/2ba422f03b38a0d311993a2453c3d7a4/1?pq-origsite=gscholar&cbl=446313

Harwarth, I., Maline, M. and DeBra, E. (1997). *Women's Colleges in the United States: History, Issues and Challenges*. Washington, DC: National Institute of Postsecondary Education, Libraries and Lifelong Learning, p. 28.

Haynie, D. (2015, January 30). Experts Debate Graduation Rates for Online Students. *U.S. News & World Report*. Retrieved from: www.usnews.com/education/online-education/articles/2015/01/30/experts-debate-graduation-rates-for-online-students

Hechinger, J. (2013, May 9). Southern New Hampshire, a Little College That Is a Giant Online. *Bloomberg*. Retrieved from: www.bloomberg.com/news/articles/2013-05-09/southern-new-hampshire-a-little-college-thats-a-giant-online

Horn, M., Laxton, A. and Lifshits, Y. (2016, August). *10 Trends Ahead for Continuing Education*. Retrieved from: http://entangled.solutions/docs/10-trends-ahead-for-continuing-education.pdf

Howell, S., Williams, P. and Lindsay, N. (2003, Fall). 32 Trends Affecting Distance Education: An Informed Foundation for Distance Learning. *Online Journal of Distance Learning*, Administration. VI:III. Retrieved from: www.westga.edu/~distance/ojdla/fall63/howell63.html

Humphrey, A. (2005, December). SWOT Analysis for Management Consulting. *SRI Alumni Associate Newsletter*. Retrieved from: www.sri.com/sites/default/files/brochures/dec-05.pdf

Hunt, J. (2006). *Educational Leadership in the 21th Century*. National Center for Public Policy and Higher Education. Retrieved from: www.highereducation.org/reports/hunt_tierney/hunt.shtml

Hussey, D. (1999). *Strategy and Planning and Managers Guide*. New York: John Wiley & Son, pp. 74–80.

Jacobs, P. (2015, April 30). The 7 Best U.S. Universities Founded in the Past 50 Years. *Business Insider*. Retrieved from: www.businessinsider.com/best-universities-in-america-founded-in-the-last-50-years-2015-4

Kahn, G. (2014, January 2). The Amazon of Higher Education. *Slate Magazine*. Retrieved from: www.slate.com/articles/life/education/2014/01/southern_new_hampshire_university_how_paul_leblanc_s_tiny_school_has_become.html

Kay, J. (1995, December 1). Learning to Define the Core Business. *JohnKay*. Retrieved from: www.johnkay.com/1995/12/01/learning-to-define-the-core-business/

Kelly, R. (2017, January 18). 11 Ed Tech Trends to Watch in 2017. *Campus Technology*. Retrieved from: https://campustechnology.com/Articles/2017/01/18/11-Ed-Tech-Trends-to-Watch-in-2017.aspx?Page=1

King, E. and Alperstein, N. (2015). *Best Practices in Online Program Development*. New York: Routledge.

Kottler, P. (1967, October). Review of Scanning the Business Environment. *The Journal of Business*, 40:4, pp. 537–539.

Lederman, D. and Jaschik, S. (2013). Faculty Attitudes on Technology. *Inside Higher Education*. Retrieved from: www.insidehighered.com/news/survey/survey-faculty-attitudes-technology

Lee, P. (2011). The Curious Life of in Loco Parentis in American Universities. *Higher Education in Review*, 8, pp. 65–90. Retrieved from: http://scholar.harvard.edu/files/philip_lee/files/vol8lee.pdf

Lobosco, K. (2016, February 8). University of Phoenix Owner Gets Out as 50,500 Students Flee. *CNN.Money*. Retrieved from: http://money.cnn.com/2016/02/08/pf/college/university-of-phoenix-online-sold/

The Los Angeles Times (1960, April 27). Brown OKs Master Plan for Schools (1923-Current File). Retrieved from: ProQuest Historical Newspapers Los Angeles Times (1881–1986), p. 1.

Lumina Foundation (2016). *Today's Student Statistics*. Retrieved from: www.luminafoundation.org/todays-student-statistics

Marketing Teacher (n.d.). *Positioning in Marketing*. Retrieved from: www.marketingteacher.com/positioning/

Milliken, F. (1987, January). Three Types of Perceived Uncertainty About the Environment: State, Effect and Response Uncertainty. *The Academy of Management Review*, 2:1, pp. 133–143.

Mitchell, T. (2015, November 17). The Competency-Based Education Experiment Expanded to Include More Flexibility for Colleges and Student. *Home Room: The Official Blog of the*

Department of Education. Retrieved from: https://blog.ed.gov/2015/11/the-competency-based-education-experiment-expanded-to-include-more-flexibility-for-colleges-and-students/

Mitchell, M. and Leachman, M. (2016, May). *Undergraduate Enrollment.* The Condition of Education, National Center for Educational Statistics. Retrieved from: http://nces.ed.gov/programs/coe/indicator_cha.asp

Morrison, M. (2012, June 11). History of PEST Analysis. *RapidBI.* Retrieved from: https://rapidbi.com/history-of-pest-analysis/

Morse, R. (2011, January 27). Students Say Rankings Aren't Most Important Factor in College Decision. *U.S. News & World Report.* Retrieved from: www.usnews.com/education/blogs/college-rankings-blog/2011/01/27/students-say-rankings-arent-most-important-factor-in-college-decision

National Council for State Reciprocity Agreements. (2016). *Basic Questions About SARA.* Retrieved from: http://nc-sara.org/content/basic-questions-about-sara

The New York Times (1967, June 3). Sara Lawrence Declines Merger. Retrieved from: http://query.nytimes.com/mem/archive/pdf?res=9C02E0D7123AE63ABC4B53DFB066838C679EDE

The New York Times (1967, October 22). Vassar Still Undecided on Affiliation With Yale. Retrieved from: http://query.nytimes.com/mem/archive/pdf?res=9E05E1DB1131E53ABC4A51DFB6 67838C679EDE

Nishi, K, Schoderbek, C. and Schoderbek, P. (1982). Scanning the Organizational Environment: Some Empirical Results. *Human Systems Management,* 3:4, pp. 233–245.

Online Learning Consortium (n.d.). *OLC Quality Scorecard.* Retrieved from: https://onlinelearningconsortium.org/consult/quality-scorecard/

OpenSUNY. (2014). *Institutional Readiness and Open SUNY.* Retrieved from: http://commons.suny.edu/opensuny/wp-content/blogs.dir/16/files/2014/01/Open-SUNY-Institutional-Readiness-20141015.pdf

Osita, I. C., Idoko, I. O. and Nzekwe, J. (2014). Organization's Stability and Productivity: The Role of SWOT Analysis an Acronym for Strength, Weakness, Opportunities and Threat. *International Journal of Innovative and Applied Research,* 2:9, pp. 23–32. Retrieved from: http://journalijiar.com/uploads/2014-10-02_231409_710.pdf

PESTLE Analysis (2015, May 21). What Is a Market Competitor Analysis and How to Do It. Retrieved from: http://pestleanalysis.com/marketing-competitor-analysis/, downloaded February 10, 2017.

Pew Issue Brief (2015, June 11). *Federal and State Funding of Higher Education: A Changing Landscape.* The Pew Charitable Trusts. Retrieved from: www.pewtrusts.org/en/research-and-analysis/issue-briefs/2015/06/federal-and-state-funding-of-higher-education

Pisel, K. (2008, Summer). A Strategic Planning Process Model for Distance Education. *Online Journal of Distance Learning Administration,* XI:II. Retrieved from: www.westga.edu/~distance/ojdla/summer112/pisel112.html

Porter, M. (1979, March/April). How Competitive Forces Shape Strategy. *Harvard Business Review,* pp. 137–145.

Poulin, R. (2012, March 22). Should Online Courses Charge Less? It Doesn't Just Happen. *WCET.* Retrieved from: https://wcetfrontiers.org/2012/03/22/should-online-courses-charge-less/

Pulley, J. (2014, January 29). The Secret of Southern New Hampshire University's Success. *Campus Technology.* Retrieved from: https://campustechnology.com/articles/2014/01/29/the-secret-of-southern-new-hampshire-universitys-success.aspx

Ronco, S. and Cahill, J. (2005). *Start Your Planning With a SWOT.* Florida Atlantic University. Retrieved from: http://iea.fau.edu/inst/sair05.doc

Rowley, D., Lujan, H. and Dolence, M. (1997). *Strategic Change in Colleges and Universities.* San Francisco, CA: Jossey Bass, p. 37.

Shea, P. and Bidjerano, T. (2014). Does Online Learning Impede Degree Completion? A National Study of Community College Students. *Computers and Education,* 75, pp. 103–111. Retrieved from: www.sunyresearch.net/hplo/wp-content/uploads/2014/03/c-e-paper-2014.pdf

Sheehy, K. (2012, October 24). States, Districts Require Online Ed for High School Graduation. *U.S. News & World Report.* Retrieved from: www.usnews.com/education/blogs/high-school-notes/2012/10/24/states-districts-require-online-ed-for-high-school-graduation

Shipka, T. (2006). The Costs of College and Perceived Value. *WYSU.org.* Retrieved from: http://wysu.org/content/commentary/costs-college-and-perceived-value

Smallwood, N. and Ulrich, D. (2004, June). Capitalizing on Capacities. *Harvard Business Review.* Retrieved from: https://hbr.org/2004/06/capitalizing-on-capabilities

Symes, S. (n.d.). The Disadvantages of Using SWOT Analysis. *Chron.com.* Retrieved from: http://smallbusiness.chron.com/disadvantages-using-swot-analysis-17835.html

Taylor, A. (2015, April 30). Students Report Digital Learning Supports Goals of Self-Directed and Collaborative Education, National Survey Finds. *SpeakUp*. Retrieved from: www.tomorrow.org/speakup/pr/SU14_April_PR.html

Technavio (2016, January 27). Global Corporate E-learning Market 2016–2020. Retrieved from: www.technavio.com/report/global-education-technology-corporate-e-learning-market

Time (1967, May 5). Better Coed Than Dead. 89:18, p. 77.

Trigg, C. (2000, March/April). Institutional Readiness Criteria. *Educause*. Retrieved from: www.thencat.org/Articles/erm0024-1.pdf

Tversky, A. and Kahneman, D. (1981). The Framing of Decisions and the Psychology of Choice. *Science*, 211:30, pp. 453–458.

UPCEA (2017). Hallmarks of Leadership in Online Education. Retrieved from: http://upcea.edu/wp-content/uploads/2017/03/UPCEA-Hallmarks-of-Excellence-in-Online-Leadership.pdf.

U.S. Department of Education (2010, October 29). *Program Integrity Questions and Answers—Credit Hours*. Retrieved from: https://www2.ed.gov/policy/highered/reg/hearulemaking/2009/credit.html

U.S. News & World Report (n.d.[a]). Best College. Retrieved from: http://colleges.usnews.rankingsandreviews.com/best-colleges

U.S. News & World Report (n.d.[b]). Best Online Bachelor's Programs. Retrieved from: www.usnews.com/education/online-education/bachelors/rankings

Vassar.edu (n.d.). A History of Vassar College. Retrieved from: https://info.vassar.edu/about/vassar/history.html

Watkins, M. (2013). *From SWOT to TOWS.The First 90 Days: Proven Strategies for Getting Up to Speed Faster and Smarter*. Boston, MA: Harvard Business Press, pp. 151–152.

Webster, K. (n.d.). How to Use a SWOT Analysis — a Perfect SWOT Analysis Example. *Leadership Thoughts*. Retrieved from: www.leadershipthoughts.com/how-to-use-a-swot-analysis/#effectiveswotanalysis

6
Techniques for Planning Strategically

The Columbus State University story is not unusual. Located about 100 miles southwest of Atlanta, Georgia, it was established as a part of the great revolution in access to higher education that followed World War II. In 1949, the Columbus Chamber of Commerce proposed establishing a junior college in the city, known as one of the last battlegrounds of the Civil War for a clash that took place after Robert E. Lee had already surrendered at the Appomattox Court House and Abraham Lincoln had already been assassinated. Those plans took a major step forward in 1958, when the Georgia State Legislature initiated a plan to open junior colleges throughout the state. After moving to its current location in 1963, the college, a member of the University System of Georgia, which is comprised of 30 institutions of higher education, entered a period of rapid expansion. The Georgia Board of Regents approved its application to become a four-year institution in 1965 and the first B.A. degrees were awarded in 1970. During the period, the school also launched an array for master's degrees and other post-baccalaureate training programs. By the mid-2010s, Columbus State consisted of four colleges, offering approximately 80 undergraduate and graduate degrees ranging from associate's degrees to a doctorate in education (EdD) to more than 8,000 students. With a low in-state tuition of under $8,000 per year for a full-time course load, the university primarily attracts students from Georgia and the southeastern United States.

Since the fiscal crises of 2008, the University System of Georgia, like higher education institutions elsewhere, has been under pressure to cut costs and become more efficient. As of 2011, the system has undergone several rounds of contraction, reducing the number of independent institutions from 35 to 26 (Gwinnett Daily Post 2017). The consolidations were driven by six principles that the system administrators adopted in 2011. Those guidelines include improving access to education, avoiding duplication of educational programs and enabling students to raise education attainment levels (USG.edu 2011). Within that environment, every campus must continually review its position in the overall system, maintain its ability to attract and retain students, and ensure that it meets the standards set for remaining independent. In practice, over the years, schools about the size of Columbus State University have merged into larger institutions. For example, in 2017 Armstrong State University, with about 7,000 students, merged with Georgia Southern University. In 2016 Darnton State College, a two-year college with approximately 6,000 students, merged with Albany State University. And in 2014, Kennesaw State University absorbed Southern Polytechnic State University, which had approximately 6,500 students.

The upheaval that took place in the state university system in Georgia makes the moves taken in 2007 by the Department of Counseling, Foundations and Leadership in the College of Education and Health Professions even more significant than they may have been under normal circumstances. That year, a group of faculty decided to offer its existing program in educational leadership online. The impetus for the program came from two directions. First, the state established criteria to be certified in educational leadership and was offering subsidies for students to become certified. Second, faculty members in the department were interested in online education, according to Gary Shouppe, an associate professor in the department, who also headed a strategic planning committee for online education at Columbus State. At the time, as with most schools, many faculty members across the university were either not interested in online education or opposed it. The faculty senate had a distance learning committee, but meetings were poorly attended. With 12 people on the committee, for most meetings only six would show up. And as nobody was yet teaching online or hybrid courses at Columbus State, it was difficult to get people to focus on online education. To launch their program, the faculty members in the department did not craft a master plan informed by an overarching vision. Instead, according to Shouppe, they locked themselves in a room and determined what needed to be done and then worked it out from there.

And there was a lot of work. For example, standardized course shells needed development. Ownership of the intellectual property developed for the program needed to be determined. Faculty members needed to be recruited and trained to teach in the program. Quality standards needed to be established and state certification requirements met. And, of course, students needed to enroll and to be retained. Each individual problem needed a solution and those problems and solutions were not necessarily linked to each other. Sometimes the solutions Shouppe and his colleagues devised worked as expected. Sometimes they did not. And not infrequently, the solutions created a new set of challenges to be addressed. For example, since no faculty members taught online at the time, teachers had to be recruited and trained. The initial approach taken to meet that challenge was straightforward and, from one perspective, very effective: faculty members were generously paid to move their courses from a face-to-face format to online. Indeed, at first, they were paid $50 per student enrolled in each online course. And since the online courses could enroll 50 to 100 students or more, the monetary incentive to move online was enticing. But the move toward direct compensation also created serious problems. Faculty members from other departments objected vigorously. So the department moved away from the pay-per-student scheme to a system of faculty grants to support specific aspects of online programs such as course development and course review.

Teachers need students and probably the key hurdle for any new educational program is attracting students. To facilitate this process, Columbus State opted to partner with a third party. Since the mid-2000s, many colleges and universities have turned to what has come to be called online program management providers (OPMs) to help jump-start their online programs. In exchange for a percentage of tuition, often around 50 percent or more, the OPM will manage several aspects of an online program, often assuming with varying degrees of responsibility, marketing and enrollment management, technical support, and student advising. Other potential services include course development assistance and they even supply teaching assistants (Zipper 2016). As with the decision to use a third party for almost any service that theoretically could be performed by staff, opting for an OPM involves a series of trade-offs. Online program management providers can enable colleges and universities to launch programs that might not have been started otherwise. OPMs often invest more heavily, aggressively and effectively in marketing than most colleges and universities. Finally, the online program management providers assume most of the risk intrinsic in initiating new programs. But those benefits come with a cost. As online program management providers are paid per student, they want as many students as possible in each program and in each class. Small programs and classes may not generate enough revenue to cover the associated costs; moreover, the need for students can put pressure to lower acceptance standards. Over time, the use of online program management providers could lead to pressure to raise tuition for online programs to enable institutions to reap a larger financial benefit. And there are unusual competitive issues. For instance, one major online program management provider may support similar programs from multiple universities, which might create an incentive to steer students to a more expensive, less competitive program (Newton 2016).

Columbus State's decision to partner with a major OPM led to a series of changes. Class sizes jumped from 18 to 50. To create more entry points into the program, semesters were shortened from 14 weeks to seven weeks. A complicated curricular map had to be developed. The teaching load for faculty became three seven-week courses per semester. The increased course size led to the need for teaching assistants, which the online program manager provided. And to manage the growth in the number of students, additional affiliate faculty members had to be hired. All of these changes led to questions about the overall quality of the program and raised issues about accreditation. As the educational program expanded, the online program manager enrolled students who were not recruited by them. However, as the third-party provider received a significant percentage of revenue for each student it brought in, the Columbus State administration looked for ways to identify those students who found the program on their own so the institution would retain all the tuition in those cases. The move to separate students recruited directly from the program manager from those who found a program on their own led to complex changes in the registration system to identify the path through which each student enrolled in the program, and that determination had a significant impact on revenue.

Many of the challenges that arose were not foreseen when the faculty was first considering moving the educational leadership program online and each problem and challenge had to be solved as it presented itself. In each case, the members of the department would brainstorm until they came to what they felt was a reasonable solution and would then work to implement the solution. And generally, they apparently made sound decisions. The educational leadership program became one of the fastest growing programs at Columbus State and was successfully attracting new students. But even success posed new challenges. Although initially the program continued to be offered in a face-to-face format, over time it moved to be offered online only. The reason—the faculty teaching in the program preferred that format. As the program grew, not surprisingly it caught the attention of the senior administration, which saw it as a potential source of additional revenue at a time when the university in general was facing budget cuts. And, finally, the growth of the program plunged it into the politics of the state university system. As the university system itself was looking for ways to cut down on the duplication of programs among the different campuses, the growth of the educational leadership program at Columbus State had implications for the other campuses in the university system. The question that was raised: Columbus State was attracting students from around the state—should other campuses continue or be allowed to launch their own programs?

The Department of Counseling, Foundations and Leadership's experience with online program development followed a pattern that is not typical. In many cases, rather than following a master plan, online education is first initiated as an entrepreneurial venture, often from a faculty member or department but sometimes at the administrative level. Along with the entrepreneurial vision, program development and success depends on overcoming barriers, obstacles and challenges on an ad hoc basis. Issues are identified and resolved as they arise. The team directly involved with online education can address some of those issues, but some, like determining who should be allowed to offer a specific program in the case of Columbus State, must be decided elsewhere. Pinpointing the most critical steps that need to be taken and key barriers that stand in the way of success is essential for effective planning.

Consider the growth of online education at Florida State University. In Florida, the potential for online education caught the attention of the governor and state legislature in the early 2010s, and in 2013 the legislature approved a business plan for a new entity—the University of Florida Online. The plan envisioned that UF Online would enroll 24,000 students by 2023, with nearly half of them coming from out of state. The state then signed a contact with a third-party online program management provider to facilitate the project's development. By 2015, however, it was clear the plan was not going to work. The contract with the OPM was terminated. And in 2016 the legislature presented a new business plan with significantly more modest goals. It projects around 6,500 students by the year 2020, with in-state students representing around 90 percent of the total (Straumshein 2016b). In this case, the master plan simply did not work as expected. Within the context of the struggles of University of Florida Online, Florida State University has cultivated a robust online education offering in 2017 more than 100 programs with close to 3,000 students, both undergraduate and graduate, taking all of their classes. More than 25 percent of the 41,000 students taking classes at FSU take at least one class online (CollegeFactual.com n.d.). By 2017, several of Florida State's online programs were highly ranked by the U.S. News & World Report, with three graduate programs landing in the top ten in their category (Farnum-Petronis 2016).

The development of online education at Florida State took a very different path than that of University of Florida Online. In 1998, a professor in the school of business decided to move one section of a course online. Later, as course offerings expanded, to attract students, certain fees were waived. Shortly after the initial move to offer online courses, the university received funding from a foundation to more fully explore the opportunities offered by online education. In the years to come, the university was also able to tap into federal funding for innovation in teaching and learning and apply those funds to growing the online educational program. At that point, online education at Florida State was still an uneven, ad hoc operation. The university went through a period of five years in which it had three chief academic officers, and the institutional momentum for online education waned. The key breakthrough came when the state legislature authorized adding a student fee for distance learning on the standard tuition fee. This approach is not unusual. As of 2016, 37 states authorized additional fees for distance learning classes. The fee was split between the faculty members participating in online education, the sponsoring department and the centralized Office for Distance Learning. With the funding model in place, Florida State was able to establish a standard process for establishing online programs and put incentives in place for departments and schools in the university to do so. It was not until online education was well underway and programs coming online in a fairly regular basis that Florida State initiated its first strategic planning process for online education.

While Florida State found a model for online education that has worked, the future for its model rests on factors beyond its control. In 2016, while still ostensibly supporting the growth of online education and particularly for the University of Florida Online, the governor of Florida came out against fees for distance learning. Although Florida State charges less for online classes for students whose entire program is online, for students who take some classes on campus and some online, which represents a large majority of online students, a discount is not offered. The governor's opposition to fees for distance learning stemmed from the idea that distance learning students should pay less for courses than those coming to campus, which was not the case on most campuses in the Florida university system. Other ideas coming from the state capital with the potential to impact the online education infrastructure at Florida State included centralizing services for distance education in what is called Florida Virtual Campus, a Tallahassee-based organization focused on educational change from kindergarten through adult education in Florida (Dunkelberger 2016).

To a large degree, the nature of online education throughout the state of Florida will be shaped by how individual campuses react and respond to the proposals in the state capitol, creating uncertainty and constraining the ability to plan. But that uncertainty does not have to impede the development of online education. As both Columbus State University and Florida State University have demonstrated, the success of their online programs came not from an overall strategic plan but from a series of smaller, targeted decisions, some deliberate and some forced upon them by outside forces. In the experiences at both campuses, it took repeated attempts to resolve problems and overcome obstacles. Identifying the most important next step in the development of online education within a specific context and environment and then crafting a roadmap to take those next steps forward is the essence of planning strategically. As opposed to strategic planning, planning strategically conceptualizes planning as an ongoing, continuous activity. The goal is to determine the following: what needs to be done; what can actually be done next, given the circumstances; selecting what to do, given the options; and then devising a course of action to achieve the goal. While still driven by an overall vision and mission, this approach differs from strategic planning, in which a master plan intended to be in effect for five to ten years coupled with an array of subordinate goals and objectives is developed through a complex, time- and labor-intensive procedure. In its place, in planning strategically, campus leaders for online education determine what needs to be done that would have the most impact at that moment in time and for some foreseeable timeframe.

This chapter describes why the context and environment for online education within institutions of higher learning is more suitable for planning strategically rather than strategic planning. An integrated approach for planning strategically that includes the use of simple rules as strategy, critical success factors analysis, force field analysis, present state/future state gap analysis and scenario planning will be explained. Finally, a case study involving planning strategically will be presented.

Uncertainty and the Strategic Environment

The assumption that lies at the heart of strategic planning is that by applying a specific set of analytical tools with discipline and insight, managers can chart a course through an uncertain environment that will result in a desired outcome. In short, strategy is a mechanism to cope with uncertainty (Courtney et al. 1997). However, according to Hugh Courtney, dean and professor of international business at the D'Amore-Kim School of Business at Northeastern University, the first step in selecting an appropriate approach to developing strategy is to understand the particular type of uncertainty the organization faces. Too often, Courtney argued, decision makers view uncertainty in a binary fashion—either they see the world as relatively predictable or they see the world as basically unpredictable. Those worldviews lead to different strategic choices. Managers who see the world as relatively predicable often make bold moves in a specific direction. In contrast, senior administrators who view the world as entirely unpredictable will often shy away from taking the necessary steps to address the ongoing changes in the environment in which they operate. Both approaches carry with them significant risks. For example, in the late 1990s, Courtney observed, Kodak, the iconic camera and film company that made capturing a "Kodak moment" a part of American culture, made a huge investment into the growth of digital photography. Unfortunately, Kodak misread the market in three fundamental ways. First, its forecasts anticipated that digital imaging would be primarily concentrated at the high end of the market, not within the consumer segment. Second, Kodak was primarily a film processing company, not a camera manufacturer, so instead of building its own camera, it licensed its technology to others. Finally, Kodak did not anticipate that consumer-appropriate digital imaging would be integrated into multifunction devices such as mobile phones. So despite the big investment in a technology whose future seemed certain, in 2012, Kodak was forced into bankruptcy (Crook 2012).

Or consider the $164 billion merger of Time Warner and America Online (AOL) in 2000. At the time it was announced, the deal seemed destined to reshape the media landscape. The Internet boom was in full swing and AOL was the leading provider of online access. Time Warner, of course, was a major producer of media content but had failed to establish a significant online presence. The marriage between the dominant provider of online access and a major producer of content seemed destined to create a media behemoth for the Internet generation. Instead, the multi-billion dollar deal was a disaster. At the moment of the merger, AOL had the dominant position in providing access to the Internet via the telephone network. But that technology was soon to be eclipsed by higher speed broadband services. Only three percent of the United States had broadband access in 2000, but that number soon soared and the AOL business model collapsed (McGrath 2015). Within two years, AOL–Time Warner had to take a $45 billion write down, reflecting the reduced value of

AOL and in 2015 Time Warner sold AOL to Verizon for $4.4 billion. With both Kodak and AOL, the future seemed clear. In both cases, management made bold moves in response to that future. In both cases, management's bold strokes led to the demise of the companies.

On the other hand, Courtney suggested, managers who see the future as completely unpredictable are equally vulnerable to making strategic mistakes. In those cases, managers may opt to simply follow their intuition in making strategic moves. Or, if they don't trust their intuition, they may be unable to respond strategically at all and simply focus on other aspects of managing the business. That approach can also prove risky as managers may miss major trends that can profoundly impact their businesses. For example, throughout the 2000s, although newspaper publishers were fully aware of the growth of the Internet, they were unwilling or unable to respond vigorously enough to the challenges it presented. As a result, in the wake of the fiscal crisis of 2008, the newspaper industry shrank precipitously and experienced massive layoffs. Even the most powerful players in the industry suffered sharp declines. In the final analysis, the leaders in the newspaper industry, while they did not stand still and do nothing at all, were not nearly aggressive enough in responding to the new environment and it cost them dearly (King 2010).

According to Courtney, there are four levels of uncertainty (figure 6.1). At level one, the future is relatively clear. For example, undoubtedly over the next decade online education is going to continue to become more pervasive. And since online education is going to become more widespread, it is clear that more teachers will have to be trained to teach effectively online and that colleges and universities will have to continue to invest in educational technology. Consequently, those issues related to teaching and technology are always going to be on the planning agenda.

The second level of uncertainty in Courtney's framework involves identifying several alternative scenarios that could occur in the future. Governmental regulations represent an example of this level of uncertainty. New regulations may be put into place that will have a material impact on the institution or anticipated regulations will not be put into place. Or a new administration may change those regulations. For example, in 2016, the federal government proposed a series for regulations designed to improve the oversight of distance learning and clarify the standards for providers of online education to receive federal financial aid. Although primarily aimed at for-profit institutions, the rules also applied to traditional, non-profit colleges and universities (Federal Register 2016). But the rules promulgated by one administration can be modified or suspended by a new administration or they just might not be enforced. Often it is impossible to forecast exactly what will happen, but the alternative scenarios and their impact on specific programs can be projected.

How the competition positions itself also often represents level-two uncertainty, according to Courtney. For example, to meet the growing demand for nurses, many colleges and universities have initiated online programs, often aimed at facilitating registered nurses (RNs) earning their bachelor of science or master of science in nursing (BSN or MSN) degree (Smith et al. 2009). By 2015, there were nearly 700 RN and BSN programs, and nearly 400 of those programs were either partially or entirely online. In addition, there were 31 RN and MSN programs in the planning stages, many of which also had an online component or were offered entirely online (Rosseter 2015). As it has a clinical component, nursing education may be the most natural fit for online delivery; however, any college offering a degree program in nursing has to determine what role online education is going to play in this competitive market. Even programs that opt not to offer any online experiences will face the task of clearly explaining that decision in a compelling way. On the other side of the equation, simply offering courses online is no longer sufficient in differentiating a nursing program since so many programs do so already. The ongoing role of online education in nursing training at each program must be strategically planned to meet uncertainty.

The third level of uncertainty involves identifying a range of potential futures. These futures may be driven by a relatively small set of variables but the outcomes could lay anywhere along a continuum. This level of uncertainty often occurs in new and emerging industries. The experimentation in post-baccalaureate education and certifications represents level-three uncertainty. With the growth of online education, many different entities are launching a wide array of new opportunities for post-bachelor's study and certification. For example, in 2015, the Massachusetts Institute of Technology launched what it called the MITx MicroMasters credential, which allows students to take master's-level courses on the edX open online learning platform created by MIT and Harvard. After finishing the courses in the MicroMasters program, students would be able to complete a full master's degree on the MIT campus. The response to the offering was impressive. In the first year, more than 120,000 students from 189 countries enrolled in at least one course, with 7,000 opting for a verified ID credential that would enable them to transfer the credit to the full master's program. Based on that initial success, in 2016, MIT launched an additional 18 MicroMasters programs in collaboration with 13 other universities including Columbia University, the University of Michigan and leading universities in Europe, Australia and around the globe (MIT News 2016).

Each of the MicroMasters programs follows the same format. They consist of four to ten courses offered as Massive Open Online Courses (MOOCs). Students can take the courses for free but must pay a fee if they want to receive a verified credential, which both enables the course to count as credit toward a full master's and be used as an independent credential. Those who opt for verified credential also have their work in the course evaluated by full instructors and not their peers. Upping the stakes, each program in the MicroMasters series comes with a corporate endorsement in MicroMasters. Walmart, for example, has endorsed MIT's supply chain MicroMasters. And edX, the platform provider, is negotiating with companies to enroll their employees in the program (Straumshein 2016a). MicroMasters are not the only new offering in post-B.A. credentials to be launched in parallel with the growth of online education. In 2014, the University of Michigan announced that its accrediting agency had approved a competency-based degree program, a master's of health professions education (MHPE). The program does not have traditional classes. Instead, when students, who are primarily working professionals, from the health-related fields ranging from medicine to pharmacy, enroll in the program, a panel assesses their competencies in a range of areas. To receive the degree, they must demonstrate competencies in 32 of 39 categories and pass a summative assessment based on a learning portfolio (Button 2014).

Other major universities—including the University of Wisconsin, Purdue University and the University of Maryland University College—have joined Michigan in creating competency-based degree programs. And a 2016 survey conducted by Eduventures, a research and advisory service for higher education, revealed that while competency-based education was still in the nascent stage on most campuses, 90 percent of the respondents were intrigued by the opportunities offered by at least some aspect of the competency-based model (Fusch 2016). There are other new models to provide credentials for post-bachelor's education as well, including the use of digital badges to help display skills and accomplishments that are not typically captured by a transcript (Fain 2015).

Given the level of experimentation, it is impossible to foresee what the landscape for post-bachelor's professional education and credentialing will be in five or ten years. Much of the ongoing success of these programs will ultimately depend on whether these alternative credentials win acceptance from employers and other stakeholders and if the students themselves succeed in the marketplace. The threshold question—will employers value these alternatives—is still an open question (Friedman 2016). Consequently, the long-term impact of these approaches cannot be confidently forecast. In fact, James Hilton, vice president for academic innovation at the University of Michigan, noted that his university does not have set goals for its MicroMasters program, and he acknowledges that it is difficult to predict how many students will eventually pay for the courses (Straumshein 2016a). That kind of opacity is often associated with level-three uncertainty in Courtney's framework. Nonetheless, a range of alternative outcomes could be identified, although not as comprehensively or with as much confidence and in scenarios involving level-one and level-two uncertainties.

The final level of uncertainty that Courtney describes is complete ambiguity. In this case, not even a range of potential outcomes can be predicted and at times even the critical variables cannot be determined. Level-four uncertainty is very uncommon and when it does emerge, it usually evolves over time into level-three or level-two uncertainties. Cataclysmic events such as the impact of a major war would fall into level-four uncertainty on a global scale. Within the context of higher education, if a college or university were to expand into an entirely new region in which it had little experience or name recognition, then that could raise uncertainty to level four.

Complicating matters for those responsible for managing the future of online education on a specific campus is that conceptually the university itself can be viewed as an external environment for online educational efforts. Fundamentally, the nature, direction and growth of online education will be shaped at least in part, and often predominately, by the larger trends in place in the university including budgets, university-level strategic initiatives and priorities, the climate for innovation, the overall campus culture and identity, the proclivities of senior administration and campus politics. As with the larger world, the uncertainties embedded in the campus environment can be identified in Courtney's four levels of uncertainty, with certain trends and directions being relatively clear and set and others representing complete ambiguity. A change of leadership in the senior administration to which online educational programs report can pitch online education into level-four uncertainty depending on the agenda, priorities and mandates of the new leaders. Identifying the level of uncertainty about different aspects of the future is critical to planning strategically because it helps identify which issues are appropriate to address and which, perhaps, should receive less attention at any moment in time. Moreover, the concept of uncertainty introduces the need for monitoring the outcome of each strategic choice. Ongoing monitoring to gauge the implementation of the strategy should be based the following: the more uncertain the environment, the greater the need for monitoring.

One of the principles that distinguishes planning strategically from strategic planning is that the former is nimble in the face of shifting circumstances. Planning strategically focuses on specific issues and objectives for which the plans can be successfully implemented. Part of the process in determining which issues to tackle is based on understanding the degree of uncertainty within which the issue is embedded. Clearly, the degree of uncertainty has a

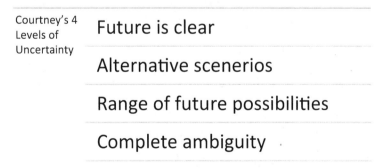

Figure 6.1 Courtney's 4 Levels of Uncertainty

significant impact on the outcome of any given strategy. Not infrequently, a brilliant strategy will fail because the planners misread the future. The key to avoiding strategic failure, according to Michael Raynor, a distinguished fellow at Deloitte Consulting, is to better manage uncertainty by creating strategic flexibility and a range of alternatives and then shifting among those alternatives as the reality of the future unfolds (ERM Initiative Faculty 2007). Planning strategically facilities the creation of strategic alternatives, foregrounds the need for ongoing monitoring and fosters strategic flexibility.

Strategic Intent

Depending on the perceived level of uncertainty, Courtney described three strategic postures organizations can assume regarding the future (2000). An organization can attempt to shape the future, adapt to the future or do what he calls "reserve the right to play." A posture is not a strategy itself but a strategic intent. An organization can choose to try to remake the industry within which it operates by providing leadership, setting standards and introducing novel products or systems. This approach often involves making big bets on new developments or technologies in areas in which the future is very uncertain. The rewards can be great, but the risk of failure is high. Less ambitiously, an organization can opt to adapt to the future—that is, identify the key trends and ensure that the strategic positions the organization takes respond appropriately to those trends. Most conservative strategic planning and planning strategically involves adapting to the future. Finally, an organization may opt to "reserve the right to play." In that scenario, an enterprise invests enough to avoid being eclipsed by a trend without making a complete commitment to the trend or prioritizing the demands needed to fully capitalize on it.

An initial step in planning strategically involves determining the appropriate strategic posture. Four primary factors must be taken into consideration, including the financial impact, the competitive advantages the organization currently enjoys, the rate of change in the environment, and the overall strength of the sector (Abraham 2012) (figure 6.2).

Evaluating those factors can lead to an understanding of how aggressive an organization can be. In terms of online education, without a significant commitment of financial resources, it is unlikely that a university will be able to shape the future on its own. For example, through 2015, the Minerva Project, an innovative experiment in higher education, now affiliated with the Keck Graduate Institute of the Claremont Colleges, that combines online learning with an international orientation to education had raised almost $100 million with funding sources ranging from venture capitalists to Chinese investment firms (Crunchbase n.d.). Minerva aspires to be the first new elite university to be founded since the nineteenth century. But creating the future is expensive.

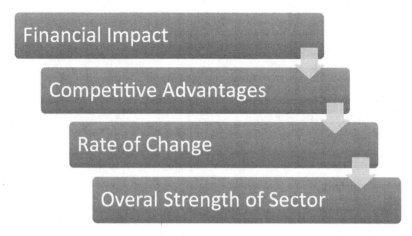

Figure 6.2 4 Factors to Determine Strategic Posture

Only a handful of universities and university systems are in the position to invest hundreds of millions of dollars to pioneer online education.

On the other end of the scale, "reserving the right to play" often involves minor investments. A college can launch one or two online programs or allow students to take a couple of online classes to gain institutional experience. However, this approach carries dangers as well. As Trond Riiber Knudsen, a Norwegian management consultant has observed, reserving the right to play often becomes reserving the right to lose as companies underinvest in important new trends and technologies (Knudsen 2000). While adapting to the future—the midrange strategic posture—is the most common, it too is no guarantee of success. In many ways, "adapting to the future" guarantees that an organization is never the leader in its field and allows its future to always be determined by external forces. The college or university will be able to assert very little agency in determining its future path. The following aphorism gleaned from the retail industry appropriately describes the problem with the adaptation posture: if an organization is always following the trends, it never is setting them.

At different times, each strategic posture may be appropriate. The key, however, is tailoring the strategic posture appropriately, given the external conditions within which the organization competes as well as operational characteristics of the organization itself. Planning strategically enables this sort of analysis throughout the planning process.

Techniques for Planning Strategically

Organizations can plan strategically using several specific approaches. However, in general, the techniques have several characteristics in common. First, planning strategically is intended to be nimble and flexible. Many organizations, particularly departments, units and programs, do not have the time, resources or organizational cultures needed to invest months and years to create a master strategic plan and then successfully execute that plan, as they are too embroiled in conducting their day-to-day operations. Indeed, even when they do engage in large-scale strategic planning, as many colleges and universities do, unfortunately those plans are too often cumbersome, complex and difficult to implement effectively over time. While the objectives and goals outlined in the strategic plan may become priorities for the senior leadership, academic and otherwise, those sectors in the university on which the plan has a direct impact—units, departments and other stakeholders—remain completely untouched by the plans. Techniques for planning strategically are geared to circumvent those challenges and limitations. The time and resources invested in planning should be appropriate to the outcome envisioned. More important, given the rate of change in higher education, academic programs, units and institutions that use the planning strategically approach can build a culture of planning to guide them toward the future. Planning strategically can be incorporated as an ongoing management practice rather than an "event." To borrow terminology from the computing field, with planning strategically, planning is a continuous process, not a batch process.

As important, planning strategically is scalable. The methods and processes used for planning strategically can be applied to issues of varying degrees and dimensions. When applied to online education, planning strategically can be used at every level from the highest institutional layers to individual courses. Planning strategically can applied to developing the overall mission and vision for online education within the institution, determining the appropriate scale, scope and activities of the primary online education unit in a university, developing standard interfaces for online courses, and ensuring that course content meets regulatory mandates, among others. In fact, one of the initial steps in planning strategically and one of its most powerful activities is determining what issues are appropriate to be addressed and at what moment in time should they be addressed. In addition, because planning strategically is scalable, all the stakeholders and participants in online education, both in concert and independent of one other can utilize it effectively. Individuals as well as small teams and larger units can utilize methods associated with planning strategically. The techniques used in planning strategically can be tailored to specific domains of each of the stakeholders and help identify where those domains intersect with other stakeholders' areas of authority. As opposed to strategic planning, planning strategically is not a top-down exercise. From this perspective, even individual faculty members who teach online can use the techniques of planning strategically to improve their courses or identify and address other significant aspects of the online experience. The techniques can be used by the leadership of online academic programs and the academic departments that house those programs and up the organizational ladder to the most senior leadership, including the board of trustees. In the final analysis, every layer of the institution has an impact on the overall success of online education from the most granular (the success of individual courses) to the most global (the institutional vision). Planning strategically is appropriate at every level of the institution.

Within each college and university, specific units and departments may be responsible for the development, growth and nurturing of online education generally; the locus of control for online education varies from institution to institution. Not infrequently, it is lodged in a center for online education, digital pedagogy or academic innovation. Sometimes, online education is housed in a unit that is operationally independent from other divisions within the university, and sometimes the responsibility for online education lies in the office of the dean or the provost. In some colleges, academic departments have the responsibility for building and managing their own online programs. On balance, however, the responsibility for online education can be found somewhere in the middle of the institution's organizational chart. The processes associated with planning strategically are designed are effectively used for planning from the middle.

Planning strategically is designed to be efficient. Individuals working alone can effectively use many of the techniques. In most cases, in this paradigm, planning is the purview of the small team that is directly responsible for specific operations. Depending on the specific issue or concern, planning strategically does not necessarily require significant research, and the research that is required is very targeted. Moreover, in many instances, planning strategically does not require extensive collaboration among all the stakeholders on which a specific issue may have an impact, leading to endless meetings and other kinds of interaction. Instead, the primary stakeholders, those with the most investment in the outcome, are responsible for planning and communicating their proposals to the other stakeholders in their network. Along the same lines, identifying those secondary stakeholders in advance is a central function in planning from the middle. Planning strategically systematically shifts the focus of planning away from process to decision-making. In its most stripped down version, planning consisted of identifying future goals and crafting action statements to achieve those goals. The critical characteristics of strategic planning are similar; however, strategic planning looks to the mid-to-long term and anchoring the plans in an overall assessment of the external environment and internal nature of the organization. Decision-making consists of sifting through feasible goals and choosing among them (iEduNote n.d.). In the typical strategic planning initiative, the vast bulk of the investment is in fashioning the goals and objectives and crafting action plans to achieve them. The focus in planning strategically is on selecting among feasible alternatives. One of the common primary starting questions in planning strategically is the following: among all the possibilities available, what are the issues to which the organization should attend now and why, and what can the organization accomplish now and how?

The actual timeframe can range from the near-term to long-term, but planning strategically starts with a process of prioritization. The prioritization is driven by an assessment of what the organization needs to do and what it is actually in position to be able to accomplish.

Finally, planning strategically is oriented toward making progress in an ongoing process. Managing the implementation of comprehensive strategic plans is cumbersome and unwieldy. Such plans require multiple stakeholders from different levels of the organization to buy into the plan and implement it. That kind of buy-in is difficult to engineer in commercial enterprises and even more complicated in loosely coupled organizations like colleges and universities. As planning strategically is issue-oriented, planning and implementation are tightly tethered and directed at the issues that will have the most impact on the organization. Planning strategically is also geared to identifying, as a part of the planning process, the obstacles and stumbling blocks that may be in the path of achieving a specific goal or objective.

In summary, the methods used for planning strategically are flexible, nimble and scalable. They can be used by anybody involved in online education but are particularly suited for departments and units that are situated in the middle of the organizational chart. They are focused on establishing priorities and achieving appropriate results. Perhaps most importantly, they can help create a culture of planning that can build the foundation for vibrant online education programs in light of the specific context of any individual program.

Planning With Simple Rules

In 1974, the psychologists Amos Tversky and Daniel Kahneman wrote a seminal article called "Judgment Under Uncertainty" in which they explored the way people made decisions when the outcome of the choice cannot be definitively determined (1974). The researchers found that most people develop a set of heuristics, or rules of thumb, to reduce the complex task of assessing probabilities or uncertain values to simpler operations. The problem was, Tversky and Kahneman noted, that while those rules of thumb were often useful, in too many cases, the rules of thumb people used were systematically biased and distorted, leading people to make gross errors. The subjective assessment of probability was, they contended, frequently dependent on data of limited value and, when processed via the common rules of thumb, led to poor outcomes. To improve decision-making, Kahneman argued in a later book, decision-makers should craft a set of objective, measurable criteria and then apply them to the decision at hand. To illustrate this approach, Kahneman cited an experience he had while an officer in the Israeli Army, in which he was asked to improve the methods by which soldiers' fitness was evaluated for officer training. The standard procedure was to subject candidates to an exercise called the "leaderless challenge" in which a group had to work together to solve a problem.

Experienced officers would observe the group and determine which group they felt exhibited the best leadership potential; those candidates would be selected for officer training (Kahneman 2011, 210–212). The problem was that over time it became clear that the process was not effective. As candidates moved through the officer training, the initial assessments did not match their actual performance. Frequently the most promising candidates performed poorly and the most marginal candidates excelled. The predicted outcomes were only a little more accurate than if the candidates' potential had been determined by chance alone. In place of subjective assessments and predications, Kahneman developed a system in which he developed six objective, measureable criteria. Recruits were then scored and selected according to those criteria, in which subjective judgment played only a small role in determining the best candidates. While still far from perfect, the results were significantly improved (Kahneman 2011, 231).

The idea that decisions are be best made based on objective criteria where predetermined rules can be applied in conditions of uncertainty is the foundation of the concept of Simple Rules, an approach to decision-making that has been championed by Kathleen Eisenhardt, the S.W. Ascherman M.D. professor of strategy at the Stanford University School of Engineering, and Donald Sull, a senior lecturer at MIT's Sloan School of Management (Eisenhardt and Sull 2001) (figure 6.3). According to Eisenhardt and Sull, Simple Rules serve as rules of thumb or shortcuts that simplify the way people process information and lead to faster, better decisions. They can be powerful tools to cope with complex situations. And correctly applied, they can make decision-making transparent and easier to communicate to other stakeholders.

The Simple Rules paradigm has several characteristics. First, they are simple and generally speaking are easy to remember. Moreover, for any given situation, only a few rules—Sull and Eisenhardt propose three to seven, and Kahneman preferred six—should be developed. A few easily remembered rules facilitate their use. Second, Simple Rules are unique and context specific; they are not universal, nor are they intended to be applied in all situations. Every organization must develop their own sets of simple rules given idiosyncratic characteristics of their environment. Finally, Simple Rules are applied to specific and defined activities. They are not vague or general such as "provide students with a world-class education."

In a lecture to the Stanford Technologies Venture program, which she co-directs, Eisenhardt illustrated the essence of the application of simple rules. The food writer Michael Pollan, she noted, had proposed three simple rules for eating well. The rules were: people should mainly eat real food that their grandmothers would recognize (that is, very little processed foods); eat mainly plants; and eat in moderation. Those rules could be used to guide healthy food choices and provide a healthy diet for most adults. The members of the Stanford football team, however, Eisenhardt noted, had very different demands on them

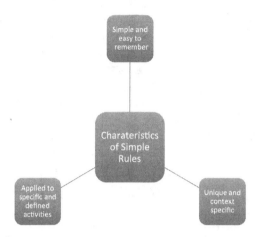

Figure 6.3 3 Simple Rules Paradigm

and lived in a very different environment that did Michael Pollan, a middle-aged college professor. Football players have heavy exercise schedules and often try to bulk up to compete more effectively. The portion control and lack of protein implicit in Pollan's rules would not be effective for them. In their place, the simple rules for eating for the Stanford football team, Eisenhardt observed, were these. First, stay hydrated (when athletes vigorously work out, they also may sweat profusely). Second, eat breakfast. Since college students tend to stay up late at night, this rule was intended to ensure that the players eat throughout the day. Third, eat things that you can pluck, plant or kill (i.e., non-processed foods, including meat, fish and fowl), and eat as much as you want (Eisenhardt 2015). According to Sull and Eisenhardt, simple rules can be developed and applied to five broad categories of decisions. There are "how to" rules that identify the key features in executing a specific process. For example, army field medics have developed simple rules for analyzing causalities on a battlefield and determining who needs immediate attention and who can wait for care. Boundary rules focus on which potential business opportunities should be pursued and which should not. Priority rules can be applied to rank the attractiveness of each opportunity identified through the application of boundary rules. Timing rules help synchronize activities across the organization. And exit rules are used to determine when to terminate a specific activity.

The simple rules approach can be applied to planning strategically, particularly from the middle of the organization. Eisenhardt and Sull argued most approaches to developing strategy focus either the organization's market position or its resources. The primary goal in positioning as a strategy is to identify a defensible position in an attractive market and then fortify that position. The most important strategic question from this perspective is where should the organization be in terms of the competitors and potential competitors in the

5 Broad Categories of Decisions	How-to rules
	Boundary rules
	Priority rules
	Timing rules
	Exit rules

Figure 6.4 5 Broad Categories of Decisions

market? In other words, in which market should the organization compete, with whom and how? By focusing on resources, the strategic goal is to build out the resources needed to execute a strategic vision and then leverage those resources across markets. The summary question in this approach is what should the organization be? That is, what are the resources the organization needs in order to successfully compete in the marketplace?

While both methods of crafting strategy have their advantages, they both work best in well-structured, relatively stable markets, Eisenhardt and Sull argued. But in markets that are rapidly changing and unpredictable, such as higher education generally and online education in particular, it is frequently too difficult to reposition a college or university and too expensive and cumbersome to add resources rapidly enough to capitalize on new opportunities. And since management of online education is generally lodged within the middle of the organization, both of those approaches to strategy may be impossible. In many respects, the positioning of any online educational program will be linked to the market position and reputation of the university itself. As an added complication online education programs must compete with other university stakeholders for resources.

The focus of simple rules as strategy is not specifically or exclusively on either positioning or resources but on key processes. The primary goal, as Eisenhardt and Sull wrote in their 2001 article, is to bridge the gap between strategic intent and action. They proposed a three-step process—three simple rules—for developing strategy (figure 6.5). First, identify a goal, objective or initiative that will "move the needle"—i.e., a process that will have a material impact on the success, development or growth of the organization or program. Second, identify the bottlenecks or obstacles to achieving the goal or objective. Third, craft rules to guide the decision-making to achieve the goals.

This approach provides the organization flexibility to take advantage of opportunities, leads to timely and well-based based decisions even if data is incomplete and the timeframe for the decision is compressed, and it helps decision-makers communicate to other stakeholders the rationale behind the options selected (Sull and Eisenhardt 2015, 215–216). Each of those steps, in turn, leads to a set of simple rules. Identifying what will "move the needle" involves analyzing the changes needed to permanently help the organization achieve its overall vision and goals. For online education, that could mean identifying precisely which students a specific program will serve; what will be the nature of the education offered (such as a degree program, a certificate, remediation as preparation for another program), and how that program can be offered in on a sustained basis, which would look at issues like costs and staffing. Locating the bottlenecks requires understanding the internal and external constraints to determine appropriate action. For online education, internal governance can pose obstacles, as could the need for coordination among different departments, or the requirement for investment. The last step is to determine a course of action, a roadmap that can overcome the bottlenecks and achieve the goals.

For an online program at Loyola University Maryland that the authors direct, the basic Simple Rules approach to planning was applied in this way. The university's first online program, an M.A. degree in Emerging Media, was housed and managed by an academic department, the Department of Communication. After three years, the directors felt that, for the program to become sustainable, it needed more applicants. While the program was exceeding its enrollment projections, it could not be as selective as those running the program felt it should be. Moreover, there was never certainty regarding whether enrollment projections would be met each semester. The uncertainty about enrollment made it difficult to plan teaching assignments and to advocate for more resources. The first strategy to increase the number of applications was to bolster the marketing budget, which had not changed over the first three years

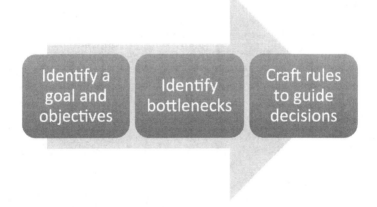

Figure 6.5 5 Simple Rules: 3-Step Process

of the program. But after exploring that option, it became clear that winning approval for a more robust marketing program was an administrative quagmire and had little chance of sustained success. The next idea was to add a specialized certificate programs to the core M.A. offering. As independent programs, the new offerings would receive their own marketing budgets. But since the certificate programs would be integrated into the M.A. program, the additional funds could also be used to promote the overall M.A. program as well. Getting approval for a new program is a time and labor-intensive task that takes about 18 months if it goes smoothly. The strategy to launch a new certificate program raised at least three threshold questions: What should be the topic? Was developing the proposal for a new program worth the investment in time and effort? How likely was it for the proposal to be approved by the university?

Rather than engage in an elaborate research process to investigate the potential of a series of new programs, the M.A. program's leadership developed a set of simple rules. Before developing a proposal, these simple conditions had to be met. First, there had to be a well-defined and healthy job market for the graduates of the program. The M.A. program was geared toward professional development and the certificate program had to fit that framework. Second, could the university offer something distinctive in the marketplace? Under the best scenario, the new program would not have the marketing clout to compete with established programs from other institutions that had higher profiles in the marketplace. The question, why enroll in this program, as opposed to elsewhere, needed clear and compelling answers. Third, could permanent faculty implement the program so as not to add additional costs to the existing M.A. program? In other words, did the permanent faculty have the expertise and the desire to staff the program? If not, the program would not receive the ongoing attention it would need. Fourth, could the program win the support of the appropriate dean and other senior academic leadership? Without senior sponsorship, winning approval for the program would be difficult. Each year, the directors of the M.A. program applied the simple rules and when all four were met, they launched an initiative to create a certificate program, securing extra marketing dollars in the process.

As well as leading to clear, explainable decisions, using the Simple Rules process for planning strategically has several ancillary benefits. First, they are reusable. The simple rules that guided the effort to establish the first certificate program at Loyola can be reused to explore additional programs. Secondly, the rules can be applied at any time when an appropriate opportunity presents itself. Third, they are geared toward making choices and decisions in a timely fashion. They are focused on execution—what the goal is and how can it be achieved. Unfortunately, there is no simple or fixed formula for developing simple rules. They are the result of experience, learning from mistakes and careful reflection. Not infrequently, organizations already make decisions by applying simple rules without being fully aware of them. In those cases, the organizational challenge facing managers is primarily in articulating the simple rules in place and arriving at consensus that those are, indeed, the processes people are using to make decisions.

In many ways, the simple rules approach to planning strategically is radically different than the standard process for strategic planning. Simple Rules is not a recipe or fixed process that organizations follow but a flexible approach to identifying the most important steps that need to be accomplished to advance the vision and mission of the organization, but are also concerned with the barriers that need to be overcome to achieve those goals. As importantly Simple Rules provides a method for prioritizing where to invest time, energy and resources. If a goal faces insurmountable obstacles, it may not be wise to pursue it. Finally, simple rules only have meaning within a specific context and consequently are developed, modified and dropped as the context changes. As a whole, the simple rules approach to planning strategically can be a powerful tool for leaders of online educational programs and initiatives, and other managers who must lead from the middle of the organization, to guide the planning process (Obloj et al. 2010, 98).

The Planning Strategically Toolbox

As noted, the simple rules for planning strategically have three steps: determine what will have an impact on the organization, unit, department or program (i.e., what will move the needle); identify the barriers to accomplishing that goal; and then craft the simple rules to guide decisions to achieve the goal. But while the structure of the approach is straightforward, each step can be complex. In other words, crafting simple rules for planning strategically is not always that simple.

Different, supplemental techniques that focus each part of planning strategically can often help in guiding the process. For example, a planning paradigm that focuses on critical success factors is useful in determining the most important elements that have an impact on an organization achieving its goals. Force field analysis, an important construct developed in the social sciences, can be used to situate the unit in department within its institutional, organizational, cultural and social context, which is essential in shedding light on the bottlenecks or barriers that might stand in the way of achieving critical goals. Finally, present state/future state gap analysis and scenario planning start with an assessment of the potential outcomes that may emerge from different courses of action and works backward to determine the steps needed to achieve the most desired alternative scenario.

Critical Success Factors

The concept of critical success factors first emerged nearly 50 years ago, at a time when the use of computer-based information systems was dramatically expanding throughout the corporate world. At that time, John Rockart, the director of the Center for Information Systems Research at the Sloan School of Management of the Massachusetts Institute of Technology, observed that while the amount of information generated within a corporation was exploding, it was becoming increasingly difficult for senior level managers, particularly chief executive officers, to determine and access the information they actually needed to make the best decisions. Rockart (1979) maintains that the amount of undefined information moving through an organization, based on the increasing data needs of senior executives, makes it difficult to achieve stated objectives. After reviewing the common paths for information to reach senior executives, Rockart described an alternative being explored and applied by researchers at the Sloan School. The idea was based on the concept of "success factors," defined two decades earlier by D. Ronald Daniel, who went on to become the managing director of the consulting organization McKinsey & Company. Daniel contended that there were a limited number of processes that must go right for an organization to flourish. To design effective information systems, the factors that have the most influence on the success of the organization should be explicitly spelled out (Daniels 1961). Rockart and the Sloan team devised a process to help senior managers to uncover those success factors and devise information systems and flows that ensure that senior managers received the critical data they needed for informed decision making without being swamped by the total amount of information available. The approach itself is very straightforward. Rockart proposed that analysts conduct two interviews with senior managers to learn their understanding of the critical success factors for their positions. And while critical success factors vary from organization to organization, they are generally rooted in one of four areas—the structure of a particular industry, the competitive landscape of an industry, general environmental factors and internal, company-specific considerations (Rockart 1979, 86–87). Based on the interviews with managers along with a document review and an understanding of a unit's goals and objectives, information analysts could devise effective management information systems that focus on providing data related directly to the critical success factors (CSFs). Though the initial application of the critical success factors paradigm was geared toward developing management information systems, it was clear that the overarching perspective it embodied could be more generally applied. CSFs can be identified for every organizational level and they can be used for planning purposes (Boynton and Zmud 1984, 19). Determining CSFs has several strengths, particularly for planning strategically and for planning from the middle. First, it is premised on the idea that not everything an organization, unit or program does is of equal importance. Too often, traditional strategic plans lay out five or six top-level goals without indicating their priority or relative importance. Identifying critical success factors keeps the spotlight on what are the most important processes that contribute to the success of the operation.

As the root of CSF planning is a management information systems operation, it is grounded in planning from the middle. In most corporate organizational structures, the information systems unit provides services to the other departments in the organization. It is not a standalone operation and the critical success factors can only be determined through interaction with other stakeholders in the organization. In the same way, at least in some respects, the critical success factors for online education have to be determined in consultation with senior administration and other stakeholders. There is no magic formula for pinpointing critical success factors, as this process requires study, dialogue among stakeholders, and reflection. But an understanding of the critical success factors is essential to planning strategically.

Force Field Analysis

While identifying critical success factors can be a useful perspective for framing "what will move the needle," the first step in Simple Rules for planning strategically is Force Field Analysis, a major theoretical construct for understanding change and change management within complex organizations, which can be helpful in determining the second step—identifying the bottlenecks to change. The psychologist Kurt Lewin in the early and mid-twentieth century developed the foundation for Force Field Analysis. Lewin contended that an array of different social and psychological factors influence both individual and group behavior within any context. Some of those forces lead to desired behaviors while others did the opposite. Engineering change on the organizational level required strengthening the forces that supported the desired outcomes and weakening those factors that impeded the desired outcome (Burnes and Cooke 2013, 409). Although Lewin presented a general theory of psychology, force field theory was embraced in the 1990s for providing insight into resistance to organizational change and a strategy for addressing that resistance. Moreover, Lewin's three-step model of the change process within an organization became a standard management construct. According to Lewin, the first step in facilitating a change process is to strengthen the forces that propel behavior away from the status quo and toward the desired end state, while, at the same time, weakening the forces that support the status quo. That step is called "unfreezing." The next step is to implement the change. The final step is to "freeze" the new array of forces that define the organizational context (Swanson and Creed 2014, 30). Clearly Lewin's three-step model for change management greatly simplifies the underlying processes it describes. Indeed, as Eric Dent and Susan Goldberg, professors at George Washington University argued in a major review of research into organizational change and change management, even the term "resistance to change" may not be useful. Most employees do not resist "change" in the abstract; they may resist specific aspects of change that directly affects them such as a loss of status. Employees may resist added management control, resist the unknown, or they may resist management ideas that they do not believe will work or help them successfully discharge their responsibilities (Dent and Goldberg 2013).

On the other hand, strategic planning and planning strategically is all about change—how does the organization need to change to achieve its goals and objectives. And online education in general potentially represents an ongoing source of major change for colleges and universities for years to come. Approaching change through the lens of Force Field Analysis provides significant benefits for planning from the middle in general and planning for online education specifically. First, Force Field Analysis overtly links the planning process to the organizational context and the need for organizational change. On any specific campus, several factors are driving the move toward more involvement with online education and other factors are impeding its growth. But those forces may line up differently for the different goals and objectives that are developed through critical factor analysis step of the process. For example, faculty resistance to training people how to more effectively use the tools of digital pedagogy, which would ultimately prepare them to teach online, may face less resistance than launching a raft of new online programs. Or nurturing online programs for professional education may be embraced more easily than incorporating online education into undergraduate education. Planning strategically is premised on the idea that managers should try to identify goals that they can actually achieve. Over time, both having a trained faculty and well-established programs are critical for the success of online education. But in planning, attention should be directed to objectives that can be achieved. Most online educational programs operate within successive organizational layers, from the individuals directly involved with online education, to the primary units and departments, the institution itself and the general environment. Bottlenecks and obstacles to change can well up from any of those contexts. Identifying the potential bottlenecks requires a sophisticated understanding of the factors that are driving and inhibiting change.

Present State/Future State Analysis

The final step in the simple rules for planning strategically involve crafting the rules, i.e. how to get where you want to go. A useful tool for executing this step of the process is called present state/future state analysis or gap analysis. In some cases, a gap analysis can be augmented and enriched by scenario planning. Once again, the roots of present state/future state planning come from the information systems arena. The core concept is this: technology is always evolving, but it is not always, or even generally, clear what will be the most efficient investment in technology over time. To be effective, new technology has to meet two criteria: it has to meet specific business needs; and it has to be adopted by the projected end users. Too often, organizations invest in a new technology only to see it ignored by those for whom it is intended. To guide investment, IT managers, for example, often conduct a current state/future state gap analysis, which is considered to be one the simplest tools to guide planning (Kelly 2009). It consists of five steps. First, a specific process or area is selected for analysis. Second, a clear picture of the current state is developed—that is, how is the organization performing now in that area? Third, a desired future state is defined. How does the organization want to be performing in that area in the future? The next step in the process is to assess and measure, if possible, the gap between current state and the desired or future state. And, finally, identify the steps needed to close the gap between the current state and the future state.

The steps needed to close the gap between the current and the future states are sometimes described as a roadmap (Parnitzke 2011) (figure 6.6). A roadmap prioritizes what needs to be done to move from the current state to the future state. Moreover, it should shed light on how each step is linked. Frequently, a person cannot get from point A to point D without going through points B and C first.

The organizational vision and ongoing environmental scanning inform present state and future state analysis. It requires a thorough understanding of the long-term vision for the program, department and organization. But like planning strategically generally, although theoretically it can be used on a global, organizational or institutional level, present state/future state gap analysis differs from traditional strategic planning in several critical ways. Most importantly, the ethos of gap analysis and planning strategically is to focus on carefully targeted objectives that matter that have been designed by people who are planning from the middle of the organization. The goal is to focus on what can have an impact and "move the needle," in some way, and what can be effectively implemented within complex contexts and environments. Moreover, both planning strategically and present state/future state analysis are geared toward clearly laying out the actions need to be taken to achieve the desired future. In many cases, however, those responsible for planning and managing online education are not in control of enough of the factors to truly determine their futures. Many different external forces ranging from regulatory changes by the federal government to a key member of the staff getting a promotion can have

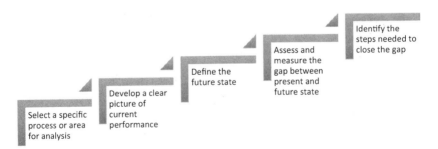

Figure 6.6 Steps in Present State/Future State Gap Analysis

a profound impact on the direction online education program, and an unforeseen change in any external force could have major repercussions. In other words, nobody can ever really know precisely how the future will unfold. And even if the end goal is clear, obvious and unarguable, in most cases the timeline and resources needed to achieve that goal may be more uncertain.

Scenario Planning

To acknowledge that any given desired outcome is variable, planners may engage in scenario planning. As with the other tools, scenario planning starts with a focus on a specific issue or objective. The goal is to then identify the major forces that have shaped the present state and to understand the dynamics of those forces. How do those forces operate and how are they likely to change over time? With that in mind, different scenarios, which can be thought of as little more than possible stories about the future, can be devised, contingent on the how the different forces evolve over time (Wilkinson 1995). The key question in scenario planning involves hypothesizing how the future will differ from the present and how will the constellation of forces shaping the present change over time. According to management consultant and author Dennis Sherwood, to construct scenarios, managers must first develop a keen understanding of the local factors and broader global factors shaping the current environment and rank them in importance and impact. Second, they must determine what he calls levers, or the potential actions and decisions managers can take in response to their particular situation that can influence a desired outcome. Finally, they should assess the effectiveness of those levers as different local and global forces strengthen or weaken (Sherwood n.d.).

Scenario planning may not be needed for every issue that surfaces through the critical factor analysis. But it can be particularly useful for addressing issues such as the size of a particular online program. For example, let's say a program has 50 students, which represents the current state. In scenario planning, the next step is to determine why the program has the number of students it has. What are the most important factors determining enrollments—costs, market size, available faculty, marketing investment, etc.? Third, what levers do the managers of the program have that can impact those factors? Which factors can they influence and which are beyond their control? For example, can the marketing budget be increased? Can they train more faculty? Based on that analysis, managers can create different potential future scenarios given their assessment of how the external factors and forces may change over time. They can also determine what the most desired end state would be and the most promising actions they could take to influence that end state. Scenario planning can play a key role in planning strategically and the need for simple rules for planning in several ways. It places in the foreground the notion that the future is uncertain and many factors that will shape the future are both uncontrollable and unpredictable (Gates 2010, 29). With that clearly in sight, simple rules can be devised to respond as the future unfolds. Scenario planning serves as a reminder that planners must be responsive to changing conditions that are often beyond their control.

Critical successful factor analysis, force field analysis, present state/future state gap analysis and scenario planning can all be helpful in crafting simple rules for planning strategically. Though each approach has been conceptualized independently, integrating them appropriately provides a powerful set of tools that can be used to create a culture of planning.

Planning for Universal Design for Learning: A Case Study

One of the most powerful elements of planning strategically is that it is scalable for all sorts of issues ranging from course development to the management of the entire online initiative. This case study demonstrates how several tools associated with planning strategically and simple rules were used at Loyola University Maryland to create a roadmap for applying the principles of universal design for learning (UDL) to online courses (Alperstein 2017).

Although one of the most promising aspects of online education is its ability to reach a broad array of students, the online programs at many colleges and universities do not meet either the legal requirement or the moral obligation of making their online course content accessible to the more than 11 percent of post-secondary school students with documented disabilities. While achieving full compliance for universal accessibility for online content can be complex and costly and require an investment in technology and support, one of the key factors in moving toward that goal is faculty training (Lombardi et al. 2013).

When the Department of Communication began to develop its online M.A. programming in Emerging Media, one of its goals was to ensure that from the outset its courses were developed according to the principles of universal design for learning and were accessible to all students regardless of any physical limitations. To that end, the program's founders convened a series of meetings with key stakeholders across the university, including representatives from technology services and the disability services and support office to explore what would be needed to achieve accessibility standards. Through those meetings, it became apparent that the university was not in a position to provide the investment in technology and support needed to enable faculty to fully incorporate UDL into their course content and presentation on learning management systems. That raised the question—what to do next? On the one hand, issues of accessibility are generally managed at the university level (although they rarely appear in university strategic plans). On the other hand, over time accessibility and universal design for learning is critical. On a pragmatic basis, being in compliance with the principles of universal design ensures that no potential student's educational needs would go unmet. On an instrumental level, although senior administrators at the university were not entirely aware of the scope of the issue, the leaders of the online effort at Loyola knew that both Harvard and MIT had been sued over accessibility (specifically regarding closed captioning) to the MOOCs they were operating on the edX platform. The suit was eventually settled out of court (Hill 2015). It is clear that it was only a matter of time until online programs that do not conform to accessibility standards will be at regulatory risk.

Beyond the pragmatic and instrumental concerns, the directors of the Loyola program felt an additional urgency to incorporate UDL and accessibility standards into their online course content development process. Their M.A. program focuses on the use of emerging media so they believed it was their mandate to use best practices and to be on the leading edge in online content development and delivery. UDL should be part of the program's DNA, they reasoned. Finally, Loyola has an institutional commitment to social justice, and the founders of the online educational program saw UDL as a justice issue. It was simply wrong to impede individuals based on physical limitations.

With the incorporation of UDL standards and principles seen as a critical success factor—something that could move the needle for the program in terms of meeting its legal and moral responsibly—the next step was to conduct a force field analysis to expose the bottlenecks to moving toward UDL and to identify the forces that could help propel change. Among the factors motivating change were the law and regulations, the large population that could be positively affected by adhering to UDL standards and the justice issue. On the negative side of the ledger were, among other things, lack of awareness of UDL generally among faculty and others, limited resources in terms of both time and technology to invest into becoming compliant, lack of leadership and sponsorship from other stakeholders in the university and ongoing, entrenched practices that ignored considerations of UDL.

Force Field Analysis

Forces for Change	Forces Against Change
Sections 504, 508, WCAG2.0	2-year moratorium proposal
11 percent of students with disability	Limited resources
Variation in learning styles	One-size-fits-all classroom
Tech innovations	Added level of time and work
Recognition change is needed	Entrenched cultural practices
Accessibility on ad hoc basis	No one in charge / taking lead
Disability & UDL social justice issue	Lack of awareness/knowledge

The next step was to develop a roadmap that could ultimately lead toward accessibility compliance. Based on the force field analysis, those steps would have to be within the domain controlled by the leaders of the program. Three steps were taken. First, a vision statement was created that articulated that the program would be accessible to all persons in the university community and initiatives and services would be developed that permit students to, as independently as possible, meet the demands of the program. Second, the faculty teaching in the online program were surveyed about their understanding of UDL. The survey revealed that the greatest barriers to implementing UDL principles were a lack of awareness and a need for more time to practice how to create content using UDL. Encouragingly, the survey also found that overwhelming majority of those surveyed felt that faculty members were responsible for ensuring that their courses were compliant. In light of those results, a workshop on UDL has been developed and incorporated into the annual training for faculty who teach in the online program. Each year, faculty learn about strategies and techniques they can use immediately to improve the accessibility of their courses. Moreover, they are trained on any new technology and additional new features in existing technology that could improve compliance with accessibility and UDL standards.

The UDL example is a vivid demonstration of the power and promise of planning strategically. Universal access to online courses is an important goal that is often overlooked in general in comprehensive strategic plans. But as significant as accessibility is, many cultural and institutional barriers stand in the way of creating compliant and inclusive content based on UDL principles. The tactics associated with planning strategically helped identify the appropriate steps that could be successfully implemented at that point in time to move toward the goal, however incrementally that may be. Indeed, in this particular case, incremental progress may be appropriate and even desirable. As a presentation titled "UDL Implementation: A Process of Change" given as part of the UDL Series at the National Center for Universal Design for Learning put it, UDL is not a discrete process but an "iterative, continuously improving cycle of learning and growth" (Berquist et al. n.d., slide 5).

Conclusion

In 2006, senior executives at 156 of the world's largest companies, around 40 percent with annual sales of more than $10 billion, were surveyed about their strategic planning processes. The survey found that those who followed the traditional approach to strategic planning, in fact, made very few major strategic decisions, which the survey's authors defined as decisions that could increase profit by 10 percent. The survey led to two conclusions. First, most big decisions were being made outside of the strategic planning process. Second, strategic planning typically was more a vehicle to confirm judgments senior management had already made than as a mechanism for identifying and debating needs to allow the organization to flourish in the future (Mankins and Steele 2006).

The traditional strategic planning process is ineffective for three reasons. First, too often strategic planning is periodic, being conducted at specific pre-determined intervals. Colleges and universities may engage in a strategic planning process every five to ten years, for example. But organizations must respond to change every day. So while planning can be considered a batch process, the ongoing life of an organization is continuous. Major decisions can't necessarily wait for the next planning cycle. Opportunity can present itself at any time, as can existential threats to an institution. Secondly, most strategic decisions revolve around issues—expanding in certain areas, cutting back in others, venturing forth into new realms. But colleges and universities are structured in units, and there are few mechanisms to coordinate addressing strategic issues across units in higher education. Perhaps most importantly, however, traditional strategic planning separates planning from action. The team that creates the plan is not the same as the team that must implement it.

Planning strategically, particularly planning strategically from the middle, resolves those shortcomings. Not only is planning strategically a continuous process, by creating simple rules to address strategic decisions, managers have a useful framework for decision-making when similar issues arise. Secondly, planning strategically from the middle places the planning process in the hands of the people expected to implement the plans. But most importantly, the simple rules paradigm and the tools associated with planning strategically overtly link planning to action. The formula is simple and straightforward. Informed by vision, identify important goals that need to be accomplished. Determine the bottlenecks and barriers to achieving those goals. Create and execute a roadmap that overcomes those obstacles. Repeat as necessary. This process can be applied to issues both large and small at any level from the individual to the institution itself.

References

Abraham, S. (2012). *Strategic Planning: A Practical Guide of Competitive Success.* Bigby: Emerald Publishing Group.

Alperstein, N. (2017, June 23). Inclusiveness in the Online Classroom: A Strategic Planning Approach. *Proceedings International Conference on New Education Developments*, Lisbon Portugal.

Berquist, L, Diedrich, J., Jensen, B., Nelson, L., Plunkett, R., Ralabate, P., Rose, D. and Van Horn, G. (n.d.). *UDL Implementation: A Process of Change.* UDL Series, National Center for Universal Design for Learning. Retrieved from: http://udlseries.udlcenter.org/presentations/udl_implementation.html?plist=implement

Boynton, A. and Zmud, R. (1984, Summer). An Assessment of Critical Success Factors. *Sloan Management Review*, 25:4, pp. 17–27.

Burnes, B. and Cooke, B. (2013). Kurt Lewin's Field Theory: A Review and Re-Evaluation. *International Journal of Management Reviews*, 15, pp. 408–425.

Button, K. (2014, March 4). 7 Competency-Based Higher Ed Programs to Keep an Eye On. *Education Dive*. Retrieved from: www.educationdive.com/news/7-competency-based-higher-ed-programs-to-keep-an-eye-on/328382/

CollegeFactual.com (n.d.). Distance Learning at Florida State University. Retrieved from: www.collegefactual.com/colleges/florida-state-university/academic-life/distance-learning/

Courtney, H., Kirkland, J. and Viguerie, P. (1997, November/December). Strategy Under Uncertainty. *Harvard Business Review*. Retrieved from: https://hbr.org/1997/11/strategy-under-uncertainty

Courtney, H., Kirkland, J. and Viguerie, P. (2000, June). Strategy Under Uncertainty. *McKinsey Quarterly*. Retrieved from: www.mckinsey.com/business-functions/strategy-and-corporate-finance/our-insights/strategy-under-uncertainty#0

Crook, J. (2012, January 21). What Happened to Kodak's Moment. *Tech Crunch*. Retrieved from: https://techcrunch.com/2012/01/21/what-happened-to-kodaks-moment/

Crunchbase (n.d.). The Minerva Project. Retrieved from: www.crunchbase.com/organization/the-minerva-project#/entity

Dent, E. and Galloway Goldberg, S. (2013, March). Challenging Resistance to Change. *The Journal of Applied Behavioral Science*, 35:1, pp. 25–41.

Dunkelberger, L. (2016, October 18). Florida's University System Looks to Boost Online Classes. *Sun Sentinal*. Retrieved from: www.sun-sentinel.com/news/education/sfl-florida-s-university-system-looks-to-boost-online-classes-20161018-story.html

Eisenhardt, K. (2015, April 29). What Are Simple Rules. *Stanford E-Corner*. Retrieved from: http://ecorner.stanford.edu/videos/3520/What-Are-Simple-Rules

Eisenhardt, K. and Sull, D. (2001, January). Strategy as Simple Rules. *Harvard Business Review*, pp. 108–116.

ERM Initiative Faculty (2007, September 28). *Intersection of Strategic Planning and Risk Management*. Enterprise Risk Management Initiative, North Carolina State University. Retrieved from: https://erm.ncsu.edu/library/article/michael-raynor-roundtable

Fain, P. (2015, August 9). Digital, Verified and Less Open. *Inside HigherEd*. Retrieved from: www.insidehighered.com/news/2016/08/09/digital-badging-spreads-more-colleges-use-vendors-create-alternative-credentials

Farnum-Petronis, A. (2016, January 12). FSU Online Programs Continue to Rise in National Rankings. *Florida State University News*. Retrieved from: http://news.fsu.edu/news/university-news/2016/01/12/fsu-online-programs-continue-rise-national-rankings/

Federal Register (2016, December 19). *Program Integrity and Improvement: A Rule by the Education Department*. Retrieved from: www.federalregister.gov/documents/2016/12/19/2016-29444/program-integrity-and-improvement

Friedman, J. (2016, December 8). What Employers Think of Online, Competency-Based Degrees. *U.S. News & World Report*. Retrieved from: www.usnews.com/education/online-education/articles/2016-12-08/what-employers-think-of-online-competency-based-degrees

Fusch, D. (2016, April 28). The Current State of Competency-Based Education in the US. *Academic Impressions*. Retrieved from: www.academicimpressions.com/news/current-state-competency-based-education-us

Gates, L. (2010, November). *Strategic Planning With Critical Success Factors and Future Scenarios: An Integrated Strategic Planning Framework*. Software Engineering Institute, Carnegie Mellon University. Retrieved from: http://repository.cmu.edu/cgi/viewcontent.cgi?article=1419&context=sei

Gwinnett Daily Post (2017, February 11). University System Merges 4 South Georgia Schools. Retrieved from: www.gwinnettdailypost.com/local/university-system-merges-four-south-georgia-schools/article_cacdda34-0fa2-5ea8-bf08-c8cd8031ff2f.html

Hill, P. (2015). Miami, Harvard and MIT: Disability Discrimination Lawsuits Focused on Schools as Content Providers. eLiterate. Retrieved from: http://mfeldstein.com/miami-harvard-and-mit-disability-discrimination-lawsuits-focused-on-schools-as-content-providers/

iEdunote (n.d.). The Relationship Between Planning and Decision-Making. Retrieved from: https://iedunote.com/planning-decision-making-relation

Kahneman, D. (2011). *Thinking Fast and Slow*. New York: Farrar, Straus and Giroux.

Kelly, R. (2009, November 8). Five Steps on How to Do a Gap Analysis. *Rob Kelly Blog*. Retrieved from: http://robdkelly.com/blog/getting-things-done/gap-analysis/

King, E. (2010). *Free for All: The Internet's Transformation of Journalism*. Evanston, IL: Northwestern University Press.

Knudsen, T. (2000, June). *Beyond Predictions: An Integrated Approach to Strategy Under Uncertainty*. McKinsey & Co. Retrieved from: http://home.bi.no/fgl95002/McKinsey.PDF

Lombardi, A., Murray, C. and Dallas, B. (2013). University Faculty Attitudes Toward Disability and Inclusive Instruction: Comparing Two Institutions. *Journal of Postsecondary Education and Disability*, 26:3, pp. 221–232.

Mankins, M. and Steele, R. (2006, January). Stop Making Plans: Start Making Decisions. *Harvard Business Review*, 84:1, pp. 76–84.

McGrath, R. (2015, January 10). 15 Years Later, Lessons From the Failed AOL-Time Warner Merger. *Fortune*. Retrieved from: http://fortune.com/2015/01/10/15-years-later-lessons-from-the-failed-aol-time-warner-merger/

MIT News (2016, September 20). Thirteen Universities Adopt MicroMasters and Launch 18 New Programs via edX. Retrieved from: http://news.mit.edu/2016/thirteen-universities-adopt-micromasters-and-launch-18-new-programs-via-edx-0920

Newton, D. (2016, June 7). How Companies Profit Off Education at Nonprofit Schools. *The Atlantic*. Retrieved from: www.theatlantic.com/education/archive/2016/06/for-profit-companies-nonprofit-colleges/485930/

Obloj, T., Obloj, K. and Pratt, M. G. (2010). Dominant Logic and Entrepreneurial Firms' Performance in a Transition Economy. Entrepreneurship Theory and Practice, 34, pp. 151–170. doi:10.1111/j.1540-6520.2009.00367.x.

Parnitzke, J. (2011, March 5). *How to Build a Roadmap*. Applied Enterprise Architecture. Retrieved from: https://pragmaticarchitect.wordpress.com/2011/03/05/how-to-build-a-roadmap/

Rockart, J. (1979, March–April). Chief Executives Define Their Own Data Needs. *Harvard Business Review*, 57:2, pp. 81–93.

Ronald Daniel, D. (1961, September–October). Management Information Crisis. *Harvard Business Review*, 39:5, pp. 111–121.

Rosseter, R. (2015, March 16). *Degree Completion Programs for Registered Nurses: RN to Master's Degree and RN to Baccalaureate Programs*. American Association of Colleges of Nursing. Retrieved from: www.aacn.nche.edu/media-relations/fact-sheets/degree-completion-programs

Sherwood, D. (n.d.). Turning Innovative Scenarios Into Robust Strategies. *The Systems Thinker*. Retrieved from: https://thesystemsthinker.com/turning-innovative-scenarios-into-robust-strategies/

Smith, G., Passmore, D. and Faught, T. (2009). The Challenges of Online Nursing Education. *The Internet and Higher Education*, 12:2, pp. 98–103. Retrieved From: www.sciencedirect.com/science/article/pii/S109675160900027X

Straumshein, C. (2016a, September 20). MicroMasters on a Global Scale. *Inside HigherEd*. Retrieved from: www.insidehighered.com/news/2016/09/20/mooc-based-masters-degree-initiative-expands-globally

Straumshein, C. (2016b, November 15). University of Florida's New Plan for Online Education. *Florida Trend*. Retrieved from: www.floridatrend.com/article/21015/university-of-floridas-new-plan-for-online-education

Sull, D. and Eisenhardt, K. (2015). *Simple Rules: How to Thrive in a Complex World*. Boston, MA: Houghton, Mifflin, Harcourt.

Swanson, D. J. and Creed, A. S. (2014). Sharpening the Focus of Force Field Analysis. *Journal of Change Management*, 14:1, pp. 28–47.

Tversky, A. and Kahneman, D. (1974, September 27). Judgment Under Uncertainty: Heuristics and Biases. *Science, New Series*, 185:4157, pp. 1124–1131.

USG.edu (2011, November 8). Regents Approve Principle's for Consolidation of Institutions. University of Georgia System. Retrieved from: www.usg.edu/news/release/regents_approve_principles_for_consolidation_of_institutions

Wilkinson, L. (1995, November 1). How to Build Scenarios. *Wired*. Retrieved from: www.wired.com/1995/11/how-to-build-scenarios/

Zipper, T. (2016, June 23). *The Value of the Online Program Management Industry*. UncompromisingEDU by Learning House. Retrieved from: www.uncompromisingedu.com/2016/06/23/the-value-of-the-online-program-management-industry/

7
Getting It Done

Online education develops differently on virtually every college campus, as the mission, history and culture of the individual institution or campus shape the parameters of each program. The specific interests of the senior administration, individual faculty members and the staff supporting online education all play important roles in forging its future. At any given point in the development of an online educational program the goals and objectives may be unclear and that lack of clarity of purpose may impact the development and growth of any initiative. There is no one foolproof formula for building a vibrant and appropriate online education program at any particular college and university. However, planning strategically enables those engaged in online education to identify the next appropriate step or steps in developing online education at their institutions. An example of how different each step in the strategic process may vary from campus to campus and school to school is illustrated by the progress online education has made at the University of Southern Indiana and Tufts University.

When Megan Linos arrived at the University of Southern Indiana in 2012, she found a situation that was far from ideal but not uncommon for online education at the time. Founded in 1965 in Evansville, Indiana, USI offers 80 degree programs to approximately 10,000 undergraduate and graduate students, and the university also works with 19,000 students through its outreach and engagement programs. From most vantage points, its distance learning operation was in disarray, and morale was low. Online efforts were misaligned with the institutional goals, and nobody on campus had a vision of what the distance learning program was supposed to achieve or how. At the time, the university did offer some online courses, but they were not available to students who lived within 30 miles of the campus. Providing the technical infrastructure to offer one course two or three times a week was viewed as a primary challenge. And while the university did have a process to approve online courses, the procedure was long, laborious and not transparent. Apparently, any course could be submitted to the committee for approval, but proposals were often turned down with little explanation. Moreover, the entire process could take up 18 months.

Not surprisingly, not many faculty members were willing to run the gauntlet, so to speak, to move their course online.

There was a distance learning committee that consisted of one faculty member per college at the university, the director of information technology, the distance learning librarian, the manager of continuing education and the distance learning manager, a position that had been vacant for months. The committee's charge was to review distance learning course proposals, which could be as thick as a textbook. There were technological issues as well. The learning management system was old and not well supported. The entire educational technology infrastructure was not tightly integrated, as certain computer programs could not work with others. And the information technology help desk was not structured in a way that it could adequately meet the needs of distance learning students. In short, the situation was primed to fail from the beginning. And then there was the question of buy-in from the senior administration. While the president of the university was eager to move into distance learning, the president did not show any inclination to get personally involved in the issue or to provide specific funding to build the online program. The provost seemed to be even less engaged.

At the time, Linos, who holds a master's degree in organizational development from Case Western Reserve University and a master's in instructional technology from Georgia State University, had 12 years of experience in instructional design, faculty development, curriculum design, and learning technologies, having served as the faculty development lead and senior instructional designer in Information Technology Services at Case Western, and she served as learning technologies designer at Case's Weatherhead School of Management. She joined USI as the assistant provost for distance learning, but, given no clear mandate as to what was expected from the program or from her, Linos' start was not very promising. She found that to a large degree the faculty was opposed to distance learning. The distance learning committee was not eager to move beyond its traditional scope of approving courses and not particularly supportive of expanding the program. There were no champions for distance learning, and online education did not fit into anybody's vision, including the department of academic affairs, of the future. To complicate matters even more, Linos found herself reporting to three different administrators in her first three years. At first she reported to the provost, who at the time also supervised student affairs and simply did not have the time to focus on distance learning. Her office was then moved to the IT department with a dotted line connection to the provost's office. While the director of IT did not actually supervise Linos, that arrangement provided room for her to begin the building process by forming a good partnership. In order to build the distance learning program at USI, several steps were simultaneously taken. A market survey was conducted in order to determine the developments in distance learning specifically as they applied to each college within the university. An assessment of peer institutions and other universities around the state was conducted. The assessment, for example, found that nursing and the health professions were embracing online education. The external assessment also determined that business schools were launching certificate programs online, and continuing education programs were using online delivery for workforce development. And although online education was not high on the agendas of the deans of the various schools at the time, the assessment was shared with them, along with the president of the university. The thinking was that each college and each dean would have their own specific needs and priorities that would have to be met, and embracing that kind of diversity would be critical if the online program were to win widespread support.

While conducting what she described as a comprehensive market analysis, Linos also looked internally to see what would be needed to move online education forward. An examination of campus readiness was conducted and found that the campus was not prepared for a large-scale program in terms of technology or student readiness. The assessment looked at the organizational structures to support online education that were in place at neighboring and peer institutions to see what changes were required on the USI campus. Some of the key questions concerned staffing needs and levels of support from other offices at the university. Most critically, faculty leaders needed to be recruited and other campus champions for online education. If there was no leadership driving the program—if nobody felt passionate about online education—it would be difficult to cajole people with mixed feelings or little interest into participating. For six months, she worked to identify members of the faculty who believed in online education, and, in May 2012, Linos convened a full day meeting with faculty members representing each college, along with the distance education librarian and the staff of what had been renamed the Online Learning Office to begin to flesh out what online education at USI might look like in the future. Though they called the draft that emerged from the retreat a strategic plan, it actually consisted of a series of potential initiatives the university could take to develop online education. For example, it did not call for an increase in either the number of students studying online or the number of programs offered online, as might be expected in a traditional strategic plan. That fall, a draft of the plan was circulated throughout the university, sharing it with, among others, the president's council, the provost's council, the faculty senate, the director of IT and other departments to get feedback. The presentations were informational and interactive. The Online Learning Office was seeking endorsements and general support for their ideas. Subsequently, initiatives that were outlined in the draft proposal were launched. Perhaps the most important was a comprehensive faculty development effort. The Online Learning Office sponsored a series well-catered lunches in which faculty members could learn about online teaching tools. A typical session would be along the lines of

"10 Things You Can Do With Blackboard." While often the director made the presentations, faculty colleagues, distance education librarian and experts in the field were often called on to present. And individual meetings were held with faculty to further stimulate engagement regarding online education. Faculty engagement was surprisingly successful, with more than 100 people participating; a buzz about teaching online began to grow. It took two years working on an array of discrete initiatives and collecting data to demonstrate success. Within a year, the number of faculty members who taught at least one course online grew by 30 percent. Nearly 200 new sections of courses were offered online, which represented nearly 6,000 credit hours and more the $1 million in revenue (Linos et al. 2015).

By 2015, the Online Learning Office was ready to take the next step. An infographic was created as the basis for a presentation to the annual meeting of the United States Distance Learning Association that detailed the accomplishments from the past three years. The idea was that by promoting the online initiative's successes outside the university, they could more effectively promote their efforts internally. On a single page, the infographic laid out the four pillars on which the online program rested: the major initiatives they had launched over the past three years; the key results; and some additional background. The one-page infographic became a calling card as the director continued to solicit support from various stakeholders.

From most perspectives, the targeted approach at USI made significant progress in advancing online education. The distance education advisory board was reconstituted as the Online Learning Council with a clear mandate to chart the future of online education at USI. The council included two associate deans and the vice president of enrollment management in addition to faculty from all the schools in the university. Online education now had the clear support of the provost. There was funding for the faculty development program and the Online Education Office worked closely with the associate provost for outreach. Most important, the resistance to online education generally throughout the campus began to dissipate. Even if people still did not like distance learning, its contribution to the vitality of USI was clear.

While online education at the University of Southern Indiana developed in a positive direction, there was still clearly more work to do. The overall direction for online education was still under discussion. The process to create new online programs had to be resolved. Issues like quality and consistency were ongoing topics of debate. There was a need for more trained staff and support. But those issues could be approached in the same way—in a focused targeted manner. While the Online Learning Council had considered creating a formal strategic plan for online education, it opted to wait until the university itself had created its own new strategic plan. In the meantime, the one-page infographic served as the best description and most powerful statement for the program.

In comparison, the environment for online education in the mid-2010s was significantly different at Tufts University than it was at the University of Southern Indiana. Ranked in the top 30 national universities by U.S. News & World Report and a considered a research-intensive university according to Carnegie classifications, the university consists of ten schools, including the renowned Fletcher School of Law and Diplomacy, the oldest graduate-only school for international relations in the United States. The Fletcher School alone offers degree programs in 22 fields of study. In 2011, online education was not generally on the university's agenda. While some faculty throughout the entire university used blended learning techniques, there were very few online programs. That year, the Friedman School of Nutrition Science and Policy launched three graduate certificate programs in nutrition science and food and nutrition policy. The programs were conceptualized as continuing education programs for a global student community from a variety of career fields and disciplines. A few other initial forays into distance learning had been taken in the summer sessions offered to undergraduates and by the Poincare Institute for Mathematics Education, a joint project between Tufts and the National Science Foundation. In each case, the distance learning effort was funded by a specific school or unit, which developed their funding sources, staff and expertise.

Patrick Connell was the manager of education technology at the Friedman School. Working in a grant-funded position with few university resources, Connell began to network with others who were interested in online education to explore ways to leverage the expertise that was being developed in the individual pockets of online education sprinkled throughout Tufts. A university-wide committee made up of those interested and involved in distance learning was formed with the charge to address how the expertise being developed throughout Tufts could be better leveraged so new programs could be developed without a huge investment in resources, and so departments and individuals could avoid the duplicating capacity (Connell et al. 2011). The committee had eight members representing seven of Tufts schools. Discussions were structured around a SWOT analysis. What were the strengths and weaknesses of the distributed model of online education currently in place, and what would be the strengths and weaknesses of a more centralized model, given the institutional structure and culture at Tufts. The committee also interviewed various deans, administrators and members of the faculty at their respective schools to get their insights on the issues being raised. The goal was to develop a broad perspective that primarily represented the views of the people already engaged with distance learning and online education.

In its deliberations, the committee uncovered a confusing and apparent contradiction that would have to be resolved if online education was to grow at Tufts. On one side, the committee members and the people interviewed at the different schools agreed that it was preferable to rely on "local" staffing—that is, staff embedded specifically within each school—rather than a central unit to cultivate those services needed to support online education. There was widespread agreement that school-specific staff would better understand both the faculty and the students with whom they would be working, and could be better integrated into the school's or department's strategic planning processes. On the other side, when asked if the schools would fund a position to support distance learning, the answer was generally no. In other words, distance learning would be limited to programs that could win support from outside funding sources. However, those cross currents would have to be overcome if online education was to grow. The committee identified three specific developmental stages for online education. Phase one consisted of strategic planning, or a forward-looking activity that would allow them to stay abreast of developments in the field generally and remain current on the state of technology, pedagogy, policy and regulations. Phase two was program and course development and delivery. Maintenance, support and consultation after the program was launched were part of the final phase.

The committee proposed that Tufts develop a central unit that would focus on phase one and two. Schools and departments that wanted to explore options for moving programs and courses online could use the central unit for recommendations and guidance. Schools and departments with their own existing expertise in distance learning could access the services of the central unit as needed. The central unit would function in the same way for phase two—program and course development—activities. Schools and programs that were not in a position to hire their own distance learning experts could avail themselves of the central unit's services. Finally, phase three—maintenance and support—could also be handled centrally or at the school or department level. Once again, the choice was up to the individual school. The committee closed its report with a series of relatively modest recommendations that included that the Tufts Distance Learning Consortium (which is what the group called themselves) would continue the dialogue with deans and faculty and recommended that a university-wide committee be convened to draft a strategic plan for distance learning at Tufts. The report came at an opportune moment. The university was in the process of reviewing options to centralize several functions including human resources and information technology generally. The proposal, which was presented to the deans, vice presidents and the Administrative Council at Tufts, was well received and a larger committee was convened to work on a more formal strategic plan to scale up distance learning at Tufts.

Connell also played an important role in this effort, which took place at the moment that MOOCs captured the public attention and pushed online education onto the agendas of boards of trustees at institutions of higher education around the country. Tufts was no exception, and the question became not if Tufts should proceed with online education but how. The second committee basically reiterated the recommendations of the first. The university should establish a small centralized unit that could provide critical services, support and advice to the various schools. Working in conjunction with the schools, the office could support overall planning, program development, faculty development, and the creation of policies, publicizing the best practices and perhaps run some small pilot projects. The report also described organizationally where the new office should be located and identified the other offices at the university with which it would collaborate (Connell et al. 2013).

Over time the report's primary recommendations were accepted and the Office of Online and Blending Learning was established in the Educational Technology and Learning Spaces Unit. Its initial mandate was to support the existing online programs and to provide support for schools and departments that wished to expand their online educational presence. While the office will assist with program analysis and assessment, it does not initiate new programs; that responsibility lies with the faculty or administrations in the different schools. Nor does it try to recruit faculty to teach online. Its role is to service, support and facilitate how the schools and faculty want to nurture online education within their domain. The future of online education at Tufts University is not clear. There are no specific goals or objectives, nor are there a series of tasks outlined as the path to achieve those goals. When the Office of Online and Blending Learning was created, there was no strategic plan and the office was not charged with creating one. Indeed, the creation of the Office of Online and Blended Learning represented the next step in the evolution of online education at Tufts. What would follow would be determined by the complex interaction among many different stakeholders at the university, the various schools and the environment in which Tufts operated. But in any case, the institutional resistance to online education had begun to break down and the ship, so to speak, was sailing on the right tack.

On many levels, the road for the development of online education at Tufts was very different than the road taken at the University of Southern Indiana, as well it should be. After all, Tufts is a leading national research institution and is made up of both an undergraduate school and a series of world-class graduate schools that operate with a large degree of autonomy. The University of Southern Indiana was a regional state institution with a different mission, identity and organizational structure. The way online education would eventually be executed at Tufts would and should be far different than the nature of online education at the University of Southern Indiana. At the same time, the experiences at both institutions had several similarities. The drive for online education did not come from the senior administration but from people in the middle of the organizational structure. It was the leadership provided by those most engaged that was responsible for advancing online education. Secondly, in both cases, those pushing for online education reached out to other stakeholders and created a network with which they worked that eventually helped them achieve their next step. Third, the process both at Tufts and USI included crafting informational documents and sharing those documents with interested parties. The process of capturing specific information and sharing it helped build support for the ideas and initiatives being promoted. Fourth, in neither case did the team working to expand the footprint of online education on their campuses emerge with a full-blown classic strategic plan that they then tried to implement. Instead, they focused tactically on taking what they perceived to be the next step. At USI, that meant recruiting faculty and increasing the number of courses being offered. At Tufts, the next step was to create the Office of Online and Blended Education. And finally, the efforts at both institutions were tailored to the specific circumstances of their campuses. The leaders of online education were not following a formula nor striving to create a strategic plan or a master plan. Instead, they were interactively engaged with stakeholders for whom online education was not as high a priority as it was for them. Each of those characteristics of the processes at both Tufts and University of Southern Indiana are central to planning strategically. And in each example, the proponents of online education were able to, in the words of Simple Rules approach to planning, "move the needle."

With the experiences at Tufts and the University of Southern Indiana as a backdrop, this chapter explores the leadership needed to advance online education regardless of the starting point or the specific institutional circumstances. It investigates the need for leadership, strategic thinking and communicating strategically. Next it describes communication vehicles and approaches that can be utilized to help build support for online education and encourage faculty engagement. It concludes with an assessment of the potential for planning strategically from the middle of the organization for online education.

Leadership From the Middle

As the context for higher education has changed, so have the models for leadership at colleges and universities changed as well. During the 1970s, the organizational structure of higher education became more complex and the need for new management tools to manage that complexity became more apparent. At the time, colleges came to be seen as having few formalized structures and weak management control (Sporn 1996). In 1974, a report issued by the Stanford Project on Academic Governance argued that colleges and universities differed dramatically from traditional bureaucracies, and as a result had to develop fresh models of governance. The project itself described three alternatives, which they labeled the bureaucratic model, the collegial model and the political model (figure 7.1).

In the political model, the authors argued, colleges and universities are conceptualized as dynamic political systems with interest groups and competing centers of power that try to influence the decision making about policies that were of specific concern to them. The political frame, according to the authors, bridged the bureaucratic and collegial models. The weaknesses in

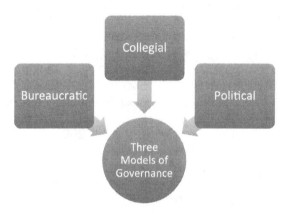

Figure 7.1 Stanford Project on Academic Governance

those models were twofold: first, while colleges and universities did have formal bureaucracies, the bureaucracies did not account for many of the ways in which decision-making authority was exercised; and, second, most colleges and universities were too complex to truly make major decisions collegially (Baldridge et al. 1974).

The pressures on contemporary higher education have also created similar stresses for management and governance. Over the past 20 years, senior leadership in higher education attempted to assert more managerial control in the face of competitive pressures and increased external scrutiny and assessment (Jones et al. 2012). As a result, colleges and universities have adopted many corporate management techniques such as strategic planning, developing key performance indicators and program evaluation (Hardy 1991). Despite the growth of corporate management techniques, colleges and universities continue to defy conforming to the conventional management structures, as decision-making processes continue to be highly fluid and idiosyncratic in many contexts. As a result, under certain circumstances, units that are located in the middle of the organizational structure can exert a significant impact. With the proper leadership, units located in the middle of the organization structure can potentially implement their plans.

In his book *Visionary Leadership*, Burt Nanus explained that leaders fill three primary roles (Nanus 1992). First, leaders have to be the spokesperson for the changes they are trying to accomplish. To that end they have to communicate the change and build a network within the organization to support the change. Second, leaders must serve as agents of change. In this regard, they must be able to think strategically and have a long-term goal of changing the organizational culture. Finally, leaders are coaches. They must be able to empower other people to implement the change they desire. The need for this brand of visionary leadership, he argued, is no less necessary at the middle levels of an organization than it is at the top. The added challenge is that people operating in the middle of the organization must be sure that their vision for their specific unit is in harmony with the overall vision for the institution. Moreover, people in the middle often see themselves more as managers than leaders. And in many cases they are called on as much to manage as to lead. Even with those caveats, Nanus believes, middle-level personnel are well positioned to lead and be agents of change within their organizations. And in the case of higher education in general and online education in particular, people in the middle may be best positioned to drive online education forward.

Implementation Strategy

From 2003 to 2008, Booz Allen Hamilton, a management consulting company, invited employees to complete an online assessment of their organization's capabilities. Over that period, they generated more than 125,000 profiles representing more than 1,000 companies, government agencies and not-for-profit organizations in more than 50 countries. The views represented all levels in the organizations, with 25 percent coming from the senior ranks. The results were not encouraging. When asked if they agreed with the statement that important strategic and operational decisions are quickly translated into action, more than 60 percent of the respondents said no (Nielson et al. 2008). The researchers identified four broad areas in which organizations could improve their ability to translate strategic and operational decisions in action. The most important was clarifying who has the authority to make a specific decision, followed by ensuring that information about the decisions are communicated appropriately throughout the organization. The next step is to provide the proper motivation for those involved to implement the decision. Restructuring—i.e., moving the boxes around on the organizational chart—was generally the last element involved in executing a strategy. While reorganizing can lead to better execution in some instances, it generally did not address the root barriers to improving execution. As Larry Bossidy, former chief executive officer of the Fortune 500 company Honeywell, noted in his book *Execution*, most strategies fail not because they were necessarily wrong but because they were poorly executed (Bossidy and Charan 2002, 15).

Understanding the barriers to successfully implementing the plans arrived at through planning strategically is a central part of the overall process—step two in using simple rules for strategy. Clearly, in most instances, those planning the future of online education, particularly if they are operating from the middle of the organization, do not have the management tools available to senior executives with the responsibility for implementing an overall strategic plan. In the most common scenario, theoretically once a strategic plan is launched at the institutional level, managers will periodically measure the progress utilizing a series of key performance indicators through formal or informal monitoring activities. If the organization or unit is not making the expected progress toward that goal, the reasons for the failure can be explored and reasonable alternatives can be developed and ultimately implemented (Luecke 2005). This approach often fails in practice, even for strategic plans developed for the entire organization. Since responsibility to execute the plan is spread throughout the organization, in many instances it is even very difficult to effectively monitor the plan on a consistent and ongoing basis. More fundamentally, however, strategic plans developed at the organizational level are not effectively communicated throughout the organization, and those on the front lines of the organization oftentimes do not understand what is expected of them to execute the plan. At other times, employees at the lower levels of the organization may actively resist the plan either because they disagree with its objectives or they fear the plan will have an adverse effect on their job, such as taking away resources. Perhaps the most common source of failure for organizational strategic plans is a lack of attention from senior administrators. Not only is it difficult to implement the appropriate monitoring structures to measure progress; in many cases, senior management does not seek out that information. According to a survey of senior executives at 197 companies conducted by management consulting firm Marakon Associates and the Economist Intelligence Unit, only 15 percent of the respondents routinely tracked how their companies perform compared to expectations. In other words, while seniors executives do track performance overall, tracking performance against plan is a lower priority, if it is done at all (Knowledge@Wharton 2005).

Planning strategically from the middle reverses the formula for executing a strategic plan. Instead of needing to ensure that the plan is communicated down to those responsible for executing it, in planning strategically from the middle, those responsible for execution of the plans are actually those formulating the plan. They decide on the goals or objectives to be achieved and are consequently already invested in accomplishing those goals. The people working from the middle do not need cajoling. They are the agents of change, not sources of resistance to change. The challenge in planning from the middle is to convincingly communicate the need for the plans to other stakeholders including the senior administration in order to obtain the needed authorizations, resources and to get buy-in from other stakeholders whose activities may need to be coordinated to achieve specific outcomes. Successfully implementing plans developed in the middle of the organization is less an exercise in management control and more of an exercise in communicating strategically.

Communicating Strategically

In his review of more than 100 companies attempting to implement large-scale transformative change, John P. Kotter, a professor at the Harvard Business School, listed "under-communication" as one of the most critical errors senior executives make (Kotter 1995). The failure of organizations to communicate strategies geared toward implementing change typically fall into three common patterns, according to Kotter. Most frequently, senior leadership does not articulate the vision for change clearly, forcefully or frequently enough. The chief executive officer may deliver a single speech, hold a single meeting or send out a single message about transformation. Not surprisingly, a single message has little impact on most employees. In the second pattern, the new vision is communicated regularly through the standard channels of communication, but employees still do not understand the new direction. The third pattern for failure comes when some senior leaders continue to act in ways that undercut the new direction. Transformation, according to Kotter, requires credible communication that convinces employees that beneficial change is possible. In the most successful examples of large-scale corporate transformation, according to Kotter, senior managers regularly and routinely turn every channel of communication to employees into a steady drumbeat promoting and underscoring, bolstering and promoting the new vision. In fact, without effective communication, organizational and corporate change is impossible (Barrett 2002).

Persuasive communication is the critical component for facilitating change from the middle of the organization as well. But communicating to facilitate change from the middle of the organization is much more complicated and involved than managing communication for change from the top leadership. People in the middle generally do not control their own channels of communication. In many instances, they do not have regular or routine mechanisms to command the attention either of their senior leadership, or the other stakeholders whose cooperation they require to achieve any specific goal. And for many stakeholders at a college or university, the priorities of one unit simply may not matter much for another. Planning, as well as promoting and supporting the growth of online education adds yet another level of complexity. In many settings, not only is online education not a priority for other stakeholders in the university, including, in many cases, key stakeholders such as academic support services and admissions, but also others may oppose online education efforts, particularly faculty. For this reason, planning and executing a communications strategy is an intrinsic part of accomplishing any specific goal or objective. Communicating strategically is key part of planning strategically. Creating and implementing an effective communication strategy rests on a multi-part foundation (Everse 2012). The first step is to understand that communication is an essential strategic undertaking and not an afterthought. Consequently, the team leading the planning process should consider the skills needed to communicate the results of their deliberations. The second part is to clearly articulate the communication plan. Planning development consists of several steps that management consultant Georgia Everse describes as the "what," "how" and "who" of communication. The "what" is what is to be communicated. The "how" represents the channels of communication that are to be utilized. The "who" refers to the potential audiences for each communication. In most cases, the "what" is the goal or objective developed through the planning strategically process. In other words, the "what" is what is supposed to get done. In most cases, effectively identifying the "who" and the "how" will determine if the "what" can be achieved.

The potential audience for any strategic communication drives the selection of the specific channels of communication needed to reach them. One of the strengths and challenges of planning strategically is that it is scalable; it can be used to communicate very broad goals as well as very targeted objectives. Each goal or objective shaped through the planning strategically process can, and in most cases will, have a different set of stakeholders. Clarifying the stakeholders for any specific plan is essential. The most common definition of stakeholder refers to any group or individual that has an interest or "stake" in, or can influence the outcome of, the achievement of an organization's objective or goal (Freeman 2010). When crafting a communication strategy, the universe of potential stakeholders must be identified and prioritized. In any given context and for any specific goal or objective the tasks are as follows: determine who are the most influential stakeholders; level of interest in the particular goal; and how they should they be approached. Generally speaking, stakeholders can be classified in several different ways: categorized according to their attributes—trustees, faculty, students, parents and so on; or they can be categorize according to their relationship to the unit, organization or issue (Rawlins et al. 2005). In the relational model, which is a central construct in public relations theory and practice, stakeholders can choose one of four relationships, or linkages to an organization—enabling linkages, functional linkages, diffused linkages and normative linkages (Bowen et al. n.d.) (figure 7.2).

Enabling stakeholders are those who exercise some kind of control over the organization. For online programs, the senior administration, funders, in some cases faculty, and others who can approve or block initiatives represent enabling stakeholders. Functional stakeholders are those who are essential to the operation of the program. In addition to faculty, this group includes all of the support offices such as admissions, student services, information technology, records and so on needed for online educational programs to operate. Normative stakeholders are those who share a common interest with the organization. They represent the broader environment within which the organization operates. Within higher education, for online education this group potentially includes other faculty who make use of educational technology in their classes as well as academic associations. Finally, there are diffused stakeholders, who only interact with the organization from time to time, based on the specific actions of the organization.

Yet a third method to categorize stakeholders is according to their relationship to a given situation. Developed by James Grunig, and considered perhaps the first "deep theory" in public relations, the situational theory of public relations

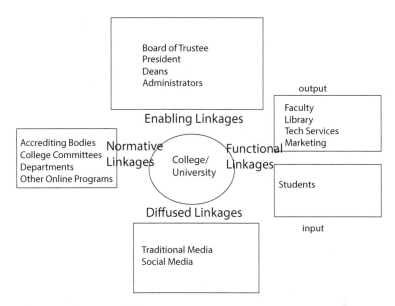

Figure 7.2 Linkages Model

proposes that the degree to which specific publics, defined as groups of people with a relationship to an issue or organization, will interact with that organization is influenced by three primary variables—the level of involvement with a particular issue, problem recognition, and constraint recognition (Aldoory and Sha 2009) (figure 7.3). The level of involvement reflects the salience and emotional connection a person has with an issue and has a major impact on whether people will pay attention to specific communication at all or act on the information they receive. Problem recognition addresses the notion that for people to attend to specific messages, they must agree that the issues represent something to which attention must be paid. Constraint recognition foregrounds the idea that if people receiving the message do not believe anything can be done to address the specific issue, they will not change their attitude and behavior. Depending on their level of interest, problem recognition and constraint recognition, publics can be classified as active, aware, latent or nonpublic.

The application of this paradigm for those responsible for nurturing online education is clear. For most people and in most institutional settings, developing online education is not a top priority. Despite its ardent, even passionate, promoters, overall many people in higher education are either indifferent to online education—it does not have an impact on what they do—or they are leery of its efficacy or blatantly opposed to it. In many contexts, for many administrators and faculty members, online education is not high on the list of priorities they perceive higher education faces, at least not on their campus.

For Categories of Publics	Active public: group is aware of the problem and organises to respond to it
	Aware public: group recognizes that a problem exists
	Latent public: problem is there, but public does not recognise it
	Nonpublic: no problem is recognised or exists

Figure 7.3 Grunig's Situational Theory of Publics

And finally, even if they are concerned or interested in the growth of online education, they are not sure what they can do to foster it. This attitude is particularly resonant among those offices that support academic programs but do not create or implement them.

Given the three ways to classify stakeholders, the challenge in creating a strategic communication plan is to prioritize the stakeholders according to their influence over, interest in, and sense of urgency about a particular issue and then develop communication mechanisms appropriate to reach them (Ogden and Wilson 2015). The top priority should be given to key stakeholders whose participation or cooperation is required to accomplish a goal. But attention must also be paid to other stakeholders who can influence the attitudes and actions of the key stakeholders. Once the key stakeholders for any specific goal or objective have been identified, the appropriate channels of communication must be selected. In general, communication from a unit or department in the middle of the organization either up toward senior management or out toward units at the same level, is episodic rather than ongoing, the appropriate and most effective communication tactics may not always be intuitively apparent.

Communication Tactics

Traditionally, the outcome of a strategic planning process is a document capturing and detailing the results of the process. The document is intended both to communicate the strategic plan to the various interested parties and to be a touchstone used to measure progress toward the different goals and objectives. And although planning strategically is a more focused and nimble process than strategic planning, crafting a comprehensive strategic plan can be a useful exercise under certain circumstances. However, other forms of permanent communication also designed to capture and publicize planning efforts might be more appropriate. The specific kind of material created to further a specific objective or goal should be determined by the nature of the goal itself and the process needed to achieve the objective. But in every kind of communication, those advancing online education should keep in mind that in many cases their audiences most likely are not paying close attention to their activities. Consequently, leaders of online education must use every opportunity to communicate their overall vision for their unit, department and program as well as their accomplishments. Communicating a clear sense of direction and purpose combined with hard evidence that progress is being made establishes a powerful context and strong support for taking the next step, whatever the next step might be.

Finally, in most situations, leaders of online education should try to make clear how their efforts and initiatives support the institution's overall strategic plan. In most cases, online educational programs are not independent of the institutions that offer and support them. For leaders of online education to win the sponsorship they need to implement their plans and ideas, they must concretely demonstrate how the growth of online education is in harmony with the overall vision of the college and university and helps reach its institutional goals. In addition to formal strategic plans, among the most common form of written materials used to advance online education include white papers, annual reports and single-page infographics. White papers are often necessary to advance major proposals through academic governance procedures. Annual reports can be important documentation when a program or unit has a broad array of external stakeholders who don't frequently communicate with each other. And an infographic is helpful to circulate to third parties as a quick snapshot of a program's goals and accomplishments. An overall report outlining the plan is the most common document of a strategic planning process. A wide variety of templates that can effectively structure and present the results of a strategic planning process are available. Most of these templates have the following elements. They start with an introductory statement that includes a description of the planning process, including who participated in the process and how the plan was crafted, and perhaps an executive summary of the plan. The report will include a mission statement, what the organization does, and a vision statement, what it hopes to achieve over time. Sometimes, the report will also include a value statement, detailing the principles that guide the organization's activities and efforts in the communities they serve. Although less common in mission statements developed by colleges and universities or strategic plans aimed primarily at an external rather than an internal audience, at least in theory, is that the report should include the results of a SWOT analysis.

The preliminary material is followed by the heart and soul of the report—the goals, objectives and tactics that support the vision. The differences between goals, objectives and tactics are often not well understood by those writing strategic plan reports. As the terms are commonly used, goals are general aspirations. For example, one of the goals in the Penn State University Outreach and Online Education Strategic Plan was to strengthen its leadership in online learning

(Penn State 2014). That goal was supported by four objectives. As opposed to goals, objectives tend to be more specific and measurable and open for more dispassionate assessment. The first objective to support the goal of strengthening its leadership in online learning at Penn State was to reinforce an unwavering commitment to academic quality. The task then is to determine the means or method by which to measure that commitment, establish a quantitative measure of commitment, and designate a time by which the commitment should have been established or reinforced. Tactics are the concrete steps that will be taken to achieve the objective; they answer the question "how." In the case of Penn State, the first tactic to achieve the objective of reinforcing an unwavering commitment to academic quality was to engage deans and chancellors throughout the systems in twice-a-year discussions about learning strategies, professional development, online program development and scholarly engagement for online faculty. The goals, objectives and tactics are cascading. For example, the Penn State plan has six goals. Each goal is supported by four to six objectives. And each objective will be achieved, according to the plan, by four to eight tactics. In recent years, in crafting the reports, some organizations moved away from the term goals and instead use the labels strategic themes or strategic initiatives to describe the broadest aspirations. The terms "themes" or "initiatives" seem to be more flexible and perhaps offer more latitude in the execution of the plan. Nonetheless, strategic planning reports structured in this way present an ambitious look to the future. A plan with six goals, for example, may ultimately be disaggregated into as many as 200 different tactics. That clearly sets a full agenda for years to come.

For reasons explained throughout the book, it is very difficult to execute a long-term strategic plan crafted by a unit in the middle of organization. That said, going through the process of drafting an overall strategic plan could have two important benefits. First, it can help the members of that unit understand each of their roles and build a group cohesiveness and camaraderie. It can serve the important function of team building. Second, a comprehensive strategic plan can form the basis or platform from which to start planning strategically. Over time, each goal, objective or tactic can come to be seen as something that can move the needle as circumstances change. While the strategic plan for the Penn State University Outreach and Online Education unit took on a traditional format, the Truman State University initiative to craft a plan for online education at Missouri's only highly selective liberal arts and sciences university opted for a variation on that approach. In April 2011, the Higher Learning Commission in Missouri extended Truman State's accreditation, authorizing it to offer limited fully online programs. The president of the university then assembled a committee made up of representatives from various schools, faculty members who were effectively teaching online, members from the instructional design staff and other stakeholder departments to explore what should come next. Kevin Minch, later associate provost for undergraduate curricula and outreach, and Donna Liss, the chief information officer, headed the effort.

It was a complicated moment in the institution's history. The university already offered several graduate certificate programs fully online that it had developed in conjunction with Boeing, a major employer in the area. As was common at the time, many faculty members were opposed to the growth of online education and questioned its value. At the same time, the students were opting to supplement their education at Truman with online course taken elsewhere, particularly during the summer. Minch knew that crafting a plan immediately would have trouble generating support. The knowledge and understanding about online education throughout the campus was not at a level needed for people to understand the next steps needed. The Truman team approached this problem systematically. They produced a draft that combined elements of a traditional strategic plan with elements of a white paper (Minch 2014). For example, the document begins by offering a definition of an online course and laying out several opportunities in online education at Truman State as well as the barriers and recommendations. The report includes the vision statement, goals, objectives and tactics usually associated with a strategic plan but also had definitions and policy suggestions often spelled out in white papers. It included a section regarding how online education could align with major divisions within the university such as undergraduate and graduate education, and continuing and professional education. And there was an entire section on the regulatory environment. The document was intended to be, in part, a plan and, in part, an educational mechanism. After Minch crafted the initial draft largely by himself, he worked with his committee to rework it to reflect broad agreement among the members. A rough draft of the plan was then shared with stakeholders across the university, including the undergraduate and graduate school councils, the faculty senate and the student senate, the president's administrative council and the deans. Based on the feedback from those groups, a final document was created and submitted to the president and the provost. The result of the plan has been incremental. Following the publication of the report, online education has grown, particularly in the summer school. But many of the objectives are still works in progress five years later. Most important, however, the document helped change the nature of the discussion about online education on the campus, for example, the awareness of the need to more actively explore online opportunities has grown. The document played an important role in educating key stakeholders about the potential for online education and the place it could hold in Truman State's academic program.

Educating key stakeholders is often the key purpose of a publishing white paper. As opposed to traditional strategic planning documents, a white paper is generally focused on a specific topic or issue. The objective is to provide the background and research needed to guide readers to a common understanding and, ideally, to reach a common conclusion. Compelling white papers have several standard features. First, they have a compelling title that describes a benefit, call to action or conclusion around which the white paper is structured.

That should be followed by a clear and concise executive summary or abstract. Unfortunately, too frequently, the executive summary may be the only part of the white paper people actually read. Under those circumstances, the best case scenario is for the executive summary to be convincing enough that readers do not need to read the rest of the paper, or better yet, to compel them to read the entire document. The body of the white paper should consist of an introduction and then the definition of the problem or the topic that the white paper addresses. In this section, it is critical to frame the topic in a way that readers understand their relationship to the issue and why they should read the remainder of the paper. Following the definition of the problem, sufficient background material should be presented, and then the solutions, the benefits of the solution, a call to action, and a summary. White papers can vary in length depending on the topic. They can be very effective in building support for major decisions that have to move through different governance processes. The best white papers are focused and targeted. They provide enough background material that people who are not generally attuned to the issue feel that they have learned enough to understand the problem and can fairly judge the adequacy of the solution.

Unlike strategic plan reports and white papers, annual reports are not instrumental—that is, they are not specifically geared toward laying the groundwork for action—but are aimed at building, nurturing and maintaining relationships. The premise behind crafting an annual report is to provide insight and information to stakeholders that have a tangential or ancillary role in online education and do not regularly monitor or track activities in the university outside of their own specific domains and areas of responsibility. An annual report can help make the gains being made in online education become more visible and in doing so build latent support for the program's development. Of course, the classic annual report is a financial document that allows stockholders to evaluate the performance of the company. While the financial performance of online education may be significant, those are not the only, or even the most significant numbers. For example, the annual report of the University of Iowa's Division of Distance and Online Education does not include any financial data at all (Rzonca 2016). In addition to, or in place of, financial data, an annual report for online education should assemble a collection of relevant metrics that demonstrate what was accomplished in the prior year. These can include the growth in the number of online programs or courses offered, the number of students enrolled in online courses, the number of students who graduated through online programs, the number of faculty members trained to teach online, and so on. The best metrics will be those that demonstrate that online education is successfully supporting the mission and vision of the university and is effectively responding to the concerns that the critics of online education may have. But insightful and significant numerical data is only part of the formula for a powerful annual report. The primary goal of an annual report is to tell an accurate story about the operation. Annual reports in the business world generally open with a letter from the chief executive officer reflecting on the past year and, as importantly, laying out a vision for the year to come. The cover letter and overview are often the most important features of the annual report. They serve to build confidence in the program and organization and assure stakeholders about the direction being pursued. The final challenge in an annual report is to humanize the numbers. While a chart reflecting the growth of the number of graduates in an online program is important, a story about one or two of the graduates may be more emotionally resonant. A statistic detailing how many faculty were trained to teach online is evidence of growing faculty acceptance of online educational tools. A profile of one or more faculty members who feel their teaching has been significantly enhanced through the use of online tools may have a greater impact on the faculty recruitment process.

Creating full strategic plan reports, white papers and annual reports are major time-consuming, labor-intensive activities. And in many cases, there is no guarantee that the intended audiences will read them. That is why condensing the information contained in those kinds of documents into an infographic can be a very efficient approach. Moreover, the infographic format is very compatible with planning strategically, as it can be tailored toward targeted goals and action. As the name implies, infographics are based on the visual display of information. Because infographics are relatively easy to create, they can be developed for very specific audiences. Ultimately, the effectiveness of an infographic relies on the quality of the underlying data. But its initial impact depends on the representation of that data. Overall, the visualization of data in an infographic should be simple and clear. The data should be focused, often several pieces of information clustered around a specific topic or theme. The headline should both grab viewers' attention and immediately communicate the subject of the infographic. And like other types of communication, an infographic should tell a story. An infographic can be a very powerful vehicle to summarize the activities of online educational programs. If used to report successes, in addition to the selected metrics for display, the infographic should include the vision for the program, the specific goals or objectives and how if fits into the university's mission or strategic vision. An infographic of this sort can be used to remind stakeholders across the university of the program's progress.

Working the Network

The need to develop written material to promote the goals of online education stems from two factors: first, like most units in the middle of an organization, managers and leaders of online education do not routinely communicate with other stakeholders; and, second, decisions that have an impact on the goals and objectives determined through the planning strategically process may be decided at multiple levels and venues in the universities. As a result, other stakeholders may not be aware on an ongoing basis regarding the successes online education at a particular college or university has achieved or the ongoing challenges and obstacles it faces.

Sometimes, a decision about a specific goal may be decided internally by the office or program charged directly with managing online program. For example, adding an ongoing workshop about the principles of universal design for learning (UDL) to the faculty training seminar for online education run by the Department of Communication at Loyola University Maryland was solely within the purview of the department. The need to adhere as much as possible to UDL principles had been identified through the planning strategically process. The leadership of the department itself decided to add a component to the yearly training program. Sometimes, an online educational program or department will need the approval of a single administrator. For example, since the online educational training seminar in the Department of Communication at Loyola was the only department-based faculty development program and faculty members were offered stipends to attend, the department's leadership secured the approval of the associate vice president for graduate and online education as well as the associate dean who would have to approve the payment of the stipends.

In many cases, however, the proposed steps needed to expand and improve online education in a given context might need to go through complex governance and approval processes. Policy changes, for example, may need to be approved by the academic senate. New programs might need to be submitted to the board of trustees. In most of those situations, the decision-makers will not be fully aware of the scope of the activity associated with online education that is already in place. Consequently, the written material developed has primarily an educational and informational objective. One of the primary principles in planning from the middle is that managers and leaders have to identify their location in the organization and build bridges to those whose support and assistance they will need to achieve their goals. Strategic plan reports, white papers, annual reports and infographics can be used to keep those in the network aware of the program even if they are not being called on to make a specific decision at the moment.

Cultivating Faculty Support

Over time, the faculty is the most important constituency for online education; however, faculty resistance to online education has been one of the most significant impediments to its growth. In 2014, a survey of more than 3,000 faculty members from throughout the United States and a cross-section of institutions of higher education found that only about 9 percent of the respondents felt that the outcome of online courses was the equivalent of the outcome of traditionally delivered face-to-face courses, and while around one-third reported that their institutions planned to increase the number of online educational programs, only half that percentage, a paltry 16 percent, supported the expansion (Jaschik and Lederman 2014).The opposition or resistance of regular, tenured and tenure-track faculty members to online education has been well publicized and well documented since online education began to edge its way into traditional colleges and universities in the late 1990s. In 1997, for example, the Kentucky Virtual University was created by an act of the state legislature to offer distance learning classes throughout the entire state higher education system. Four years later, 1,500 faculty members at nine colleges and universities in Kentucky ranging from doctoral degree granting universities to community colleges were surveyed about their attitude about online education. The results indicated that faculty members were not convinced of the efficacy of online education and they were not persuaded that they wanted to participate (Wilson 2001). Faculty skepticism about online education has not changed much over time. Regular faculty members are hesitant about online education for several reasons. The most common objection is that they are simply not convinced that the outcomes in the online environment will match those in face-to-face learning situations (Allen and Seaman 2012). But faculty members also worry that online courses will require too much of their time; they will not receive the necessary support or guidance from their institution; and they have little incentive, other than internal motivation, to do so (Lloyd et al. 2012; Miller and Ribble 2010).

But the pedagogical and instrumental objections are not the only factors in faculty resistance. Not uncommonly, professors believe that online education undercuts the very reasons they entered the academic work by diminishing the interaction they have with students. They fear that methods used in online education devalue the role of the professor, and the economics of online education may hurt their ability to shape their courses as they see fit or force them to have more students in their classes than they think appropriate. Finally, many are concerned that over time the growth of online education will lead to a reduction in faculty ranks overall (Bacow et al. 2012). Resistance to online education among some faculty is real, deep-seated and ongoing and may be the most important single barrier to the growth of online education generally. After all, at the bottom line, colleges and universities are about teaching and learning, and if the teachers are not interested in exploring teaching online, that puts a limit on an institution's growth.

While deep-rooted, faculty objections to online education are not insurmountable. In a 2015, Peter Shea, an associate provost of online learning at the University at Albany, part of the State University of New York system, replicated Jachik and Lederman's study drawing a sample from the Center for Online Teaching Excellence in the integrated Open SUNY system of online education. The successor to the SUNY Learning Network, Open SUNY has been operating for nearly two decades. In that period, thousands of professors have gone through its faculty development program. It has also built a robust approach to course design. And it provides central services for student support (Shea et al. 2016). The contrast between the two studies was striking. Perhaps the most important finding: while in the national survey only 26 percent of the respondents agreed or strongly agreed with the statement that online learning outcomes are the equivalent to classroom outcomes, in the SUNY sample 57 percent agreed or strongly agreed with that statement. On the other end of the scale, in the national sample, fully 20 percent strongly felt that online outcomes could not match face-to-face outcomes. In the SUNY sample, that number fell to 7 percent. When Shea and his team drilled down into the data, the contrasts between the SUNY sample and the national survey became even more pronounced. For example, they compared the results from their sample and the national survey for specific institutions (comparing faculty who have been involved with Open SUNY and those who had not) and found that twice as many respondents with the online experience felt that online outcomes could equal classroom outcomes. When the data was parsed by discipline, the gap in perception was even greater. Looking at the other end of the scale in this case, in the national sample, 53 percent of the respondents felt that online outcomes could not be as effective as face-to-face outcomes in their specific discipline. Among Open SUNY respondents, that number dropped to 16 percent.

The Shea study is not the only research that suggests that as faculty members gain experience with teaching online, their perceptions change in a positive direction. A small study by the Center for Teaching, Research and Learning at American University found that attitudes about the effectiveness of online education climbed after their teachers' first experience teaching online. In general, after teaching online, a larger percentage of respondents felt that online education was a viable alternative to face-to-face learning and online students could learn as much as face-to-face students. And fewer faculty members felt there was less teacher-student interaction in the online setting than in the face-to-face environment (Lee et al. 2015).

Cultivating faculty support for online education is an ongoing challenge and responsibility for the leadership of online educational programs. The primary task is to facilitate faculty becoming more comfortable with teaching with technology in general. Not surprisingly, comfort with educational technology is a significant predictor of faculty attitudes toward online education (Kopczynski et al. 2012). Offering ongoing faculty training is an essential element in building faculty support for online education. Over time, many schools have developed a wide array of faculty development programs for teachers interested in teaching online or using educational technology (McQuiggan 2012). Most of the successful approaches, however, have several elements in common. They start with the faculties' needs and goals. The development programs are individualized. The environment is one in which the faculty member feels respected, accepted and supported. They require active participation and make use of faculty members' experiences. Faculty training can be offered in many formats. A key to building faculty support for online education generally is to offer ongoing training to professors even if they are not teaching online at that moment. Many faculty members have an uneasy relationship to educational technology generally and many continue to doubt that the use of educational technology leads to better outcomes in the classroom (Straumshein 2016). In addition to understanding the promise, potential and mechanics of online education, people managing online educational programs are most engaged with new learning tools. They are in the best position to share their knowledge with faculty members, which may encourage instructors to incorporate educational technology into the classroom. The steps from a traditional face-to-face classroom to one in which some technology is incorporated into a blended or hybrid class to a fully online class are much smaller than the leap from fully face-to-face to fully online.

For faculty members to invest the time to incorporate technology into their teaching, they must see clear benefits and the costs of learning the new tools must not seem overwhelming. The challenges involved in cajoling faculty to use new technology can be seen in the difficulty campuses have had in facilitating the adoption of learning management systems. A comprehensive 2014 survey revealed that while 74 percent of faculty members say they believe that LMSs are useful tools for enhancing teaching, and 85 percent say they use LMSs at least a bit, the overwhelming majority of the use is only to "push out" information such as syllabi and handouts to students. Only about 40 percent of the respondents used the features of their LMS that support student interaction. Less than half of the faculty members surveyed believe they can engage in meaningful student interaction via the LMS. And even fewer believe LMSs can serve as meaningful platforms for student-to-student interaction (Dahlstrom et al. 2014). The message is that after nearly 20 years, many of the features in learning management systems—which are the core platforms for online learning—are under-utilized despite countless training opportunities. It is difficult to convince a faculty member who only uses the LMS to post a syllabus to trust that an LMS can be the platform through which a meaningful educational experience can be delivered.

But while targeted training that demonstrates specific, tangible and immediate benefits can be a critical tactic to building faculty support for online education, the overall goal is to help faculty see that not only is online education not, a priori, a threat but, in fact, it can enhance their experience as well as the experience of their students. Devoney Looser, a professor of English at Arizona State University, began teaching online primarily because her husband had a serious disease and she felt that the option to teach asynchronously would provide her the flexibility she needed to care for him. She was very familiar with all the arguments her colleagues had lodged against online education, and before she started teaching online, she agreed with most of them. But what she found through her experience was that her online students were every bit as engaged and motivated as her face-to-face students had been (Looser 2017). In short, Looser began teaching online because it fit her schedule and needs. As she became comfortable with the approach generally, eventually through her experience she became an advocate for online education.

Building on successes of the existing online program is the last part of the process in building faculty support. As more faculty achieve online outcomes that equal or exceed those of face-to-face classroom, the resistance and opposition to online education will begin to mitigate. In truth, online education is not an existential threat to traditional colleges and universities. Universities and colleges are not going to abandon their buildings, and students still like being on campus and having a campus experience. Face-to-face education can be both powerful and comfortable. But if faculty support can grow, online education can assume a more significant role in higher education overall, opening more options and opportunities for both teachers and students.

Conclusion

In the early 1970s, the Harvard paleontologist Stephen Jay Gould and Niles Eldridge, a paleontologist at the Museum of National History, electrified the world of evolutionary biology with their theory of punctuated equilibrium (Gould and Eldridge 1977). In it, they argued that evolution was not a continuous process. Instead, punctuated change dominated the history of life. While species did change slowly over time due to natural selection, as Darwin postulated, for long stretches of time, those changes are imperceptible and did not move in any particular direction. Change and natural selection was random and many different kinds of changes survived. In Gould and Eldridge's view, the primary drivers of large-scale evolutionary change were concentrated in major, often rapid events that favored heretofore marginalized species, and in effect, transforming the evolutionary line. The norm, over time, is equilibrium. But the real work of evolution takes place in concentrated bursts.

Critics often suggest that higher education has been static for 1,000 of years. But any human institution that has survived for such a long time has had to evolve. Over the past millennia, colleges and university have proven to be remarkably resilient and adaptable to new conditions and contexts. The road from the nine students who graduated from the first class at Harvard University in 1642 to the more than 60,000 students who attend the Ohio State University in the mid-2010s was neither straight nor gradual. Instead, growth in higher education was marked by several major turning points, watershed moments. Among other factors, the spread of the Internet and network-based technologies have plunged higher education into period of tremendous turbulence. In the language of punctuated equilibrium, higher education is in a period of punctuation.

Prior to the growth of the Internet and online education, that last great period of change in academia occurred in the 1950s and 1960s, a time in which the doors to higher education were opened wider than ever before. Following World War II, for the first time, the ability to attend college was seen as appropriate for people from all walks of life including women, not just men from the elite or the urban middle class. State university systems rapidly expanded and changed their mission, increasing the number of seats available. Federal and state funding mechanisms were put in place that made a college education affordable to a much larger percentage of the population. And a college degree was seen as a ticket to upward social mobility. At the same time, colleges and universities expanded in several other directions. Federal research support became an important stream of revenue for some universities. Many institutions of higher learning created professional and graduate schools that attracted more students and generated more tuition dollars. And college sports became a big business at some institutions. Finally, starting in the late 1960s, many more students began to live on campus, at least for the first couple of years of their education. In response, colleges and universities scurried to build and operate residential dormitories, dining facilities, health clubs and other accouterments that enhanced student life, and generated revenue.

The multifaceted growth in higher education increased both the complexity of managing colleges and universities and the pressure to change. If administrations did not respond appropriately, their institutions fell into financial trouble and suffered other maladies. In response to the complexity that followed in the wake of the access revolution, some senior administrators began to turn to management tools more commonly used in the corporate world. One of those tools was strategic planning, an approach to planning for the future that had been developed as corporations have become larger and more complex in the post–World War II period. As senior management became more distant from the actual operation of any of the individual units under the corporate umbrella, strategic planning was a mechanism that allowed top executives to maintain control of the direction of the corporation overall. Despite its promise, strategic planning has had a mixed record, at best, in the corporate world. Its impact in guiding the future in higher education is even more open to debate. As loosely coupled organizations without clear lines of hierarchical authority, it is has proven difficult to cajole competing elements in the university to coalesce around a meaningful single vision or even a set of specific objectives. In short, even in the corporate world planners find it difficult to carry out their strategic plans. Given the amorphous structure of most colleges and universities, that process is more mired in complexity.

The social proposition that a college or university degree, and even additional post-B.A. certifications, is essential to career development in the twenty-first-century economy has proven tenuous. The skyrocketing cost of education, fueled in part by access to loans, has place limits on growth. Growth of the Internet and related communication network infrastructure has brought us to the point in higher education whereby students can access college-level courses without actually having to travel to campus. These factors have attracted a new wave of heretofore "non-traditional" students as well as new kinds of institutions or programs to meet their needs. Finally, established colleges and universities can now provide services to students well beyond their traditional geographic reaches, potentially putting a premium on reputations and branding.

In the same way that, in the 1960s, colleges and universities had to respond to the explosion in access, they must decide how to manage their relationship with online education. That process is ongoing, complicated, and risky, and it carries added layers of complexity due to the structure of the university itself. The primary conundrum is this: on the one hand, unlike a decision for a college to become co-ed in the 1960s, for example, in most cases, senior administrators or boards of trustees cannot simply mandate an effective online educational program. Even if an overt initiative to develop online education is incorporated into an institution's strategic plan—and it rarely is—the path to effectively implementing the plan may not be clear or straightforward. Many parts of the university would have to be convinced to participate.

Complicating matters, for the first 15 years of the growth of online education, for the most part, full-time faculty have largely resisted online education, although in an ideal world, we would anticipate that faculty would be the primary promoters of online education. In the actual world, however, in many cases faculty represent a primary source of resistance. Within this scenario, while many of the components of strategic planning such as creating a vision and assessing the potential for online programs within a competitive environment is important, relevant and valuable to the overall traditional strategic planning process, such a formal process may not be a good fit in some situations. Traditional strategic planning is typically a tool of senior executives. Online education is largely being driven from the middle of the organization—by individual departments, programs or centers. Groups planning from the middle do not have the time or latitude to engage in time-consuming, labor-intensive planning processes that can extend for several months or more. Nor do they have the management levers and authority to align the university's resources with their plans.

The concepts embodied in planning strategically from the middle coupled with the idea of Simple Rules provides an alternative planning paradigm for leaders of online education on any campus. Grounded by a common vision and an acute understanding of the specific internal and external context in which they operate, this paradigm is focused on identifying both what is important and what is achievable for any specific program. The planning process is nimble and geared toward action. Perhaps most importantly, it conceives of planning as an ongoing process managed by those most responsible for ultimately executing the plan and allows those operating at any level in an organization to build a culture of planning. When Stephen Jay Gould first presented his theory of punctuated equilibrium, he did not postulate how long the periods of turbulence would last. At some point, online education will be full incorporated into the ongoing operations of those colleges and universities that have embraced it. And at that point, at least on this dimension, colleges and universities may return to a point of equilibrium. Or they may not. Since the underlying technology that supports online education continues to improve, enabling more exciting and successful educational experiences and outcomes. As this happens, the professionals managing online education on their campuses will have to remain engaged in ongoing planning focused on identifying and implementing what is important and what is achievable.

In his letter to shareholders in 2017, Jeff Bezos, the chairman and chief executive officer at Amazon, responded to an inquiry regarding what "day 2" looked like, which refers to the period of time that follows rapid innovation or stasis. Amazon had been disrupting the traditional retail industry for two decades. For the entire time, Bezos continued to aggressively invest in new ventures and ideas. Day 1—disruption—Bezos opined, is followed by day 2, stasis, the equivalent of Gould's equilibrium. Day 1 could last for decades and companies could also function profitably for a long period of time in day 2. But day 2, in Bezos' view, is inevitably followed by painful decline, irrelevance and ultimately death. The existential question, he suggested, was what were the tactics, techniques and paths that would allow a large corporation to maintain the vitality of day 1 (Del Ray 2017). It is day 1 for online education. It is a period of rapid change and innovation and holds the potential for generating significant disruption in higher education. Planning strategically is an effective tool for managing that change, and its use will ensure that online education remains, to borrow Bezos' term, in day 1 for the foreseeable future.

References

Aldoory, L. and Sha, B. (2009). The Situational Theory of Publics: Practical Applications, Methodological Challenges and Theoretical Horizons. In Toth, E. (Ed.), *The Future of Excellence in Public Relations and Communication Management: Challenges for the Next Generation.* New York: Routledge, pp. 339–341.

Allen, I. E. and Seaman, J. (2012). *Conflicted: Faculty and Online Education.* Babson Survey Research Group 2012. Retrieved from: www.insidehighered.com/sites/default/server_files/files/IHE-BSRG-Conflict.pdf

Bacow, L., Bowen, W., Guthrie, K., Lack, L. and Long, M. (2012, May 1). Barriers to Adoption of Online Learning Systems in U.S. Higher Education. *Ithaka S+R.* Retrieved from: www.sr.ithaka.org/wp-content/uploads/2015/08/barriers-to-adoption-of-online-learning-systems-in-us-higher-education.pdf downloaded

Baldridge, J., Curtis, D., Ecker, G. and Riley, G. (1974, November). *Alternative Models of Governance in Higher Education.* Stanford Center for Research and Development in Teaching. Retrieved from: http://files.eric.ed.gov/fulltext/ED109937.pdf

Barrett, D. (2002). Change Communication: Using Strategic Employee Communication to Facilitate Major Change. *Corporate Communications*, 7:4, p. 219.

Bossidy, L. and Charan, R. (2002). *Execution: The Discipline of Getting Things Done.* New York: Crown Books.

Bowen, S., Rawlins, B. and Martin, T. (n.d.). *Stakeholder Management and Prioritizing Publics.* Mastering Public Relations. V. 1.0. Retrieved from: http://catalog.flatworldknowledge.com/bookhub/reader/5573?e=bowen_1.0-ch07_s01

Connell, P., Giguere, P., Gay, P., Williams, W., Mehta, D., Sanderson, N., Brogan, S. and Heffern, E. (2011, October 20). *Strategic Planning and Support of Distance Learning Programs: A Model to Centrally Develop and Locally Support Online and Blended Programs at Tufts.* Tufts Distance Learning Consortium Meeting. Retrieved from: https://wikis.uit.tufts.edu/confluence/display/TuftsDistanceLearningConsortium/Meeting+Agenda+October+20%2C+2011

Connell, P., Siesing, G. and Purkayastha, S. (2013, January 11). *Distance and Blended Learning at Scale: How Tufts Can Move From Grassroots Practice to University-Wide Strategy and Service Model.* Retrieved from: http://sites.tufts.edu/ets/files/2013/05/Tufts_Distance_Learning_Service_Strategy_Report.pdf

Cotter, M. and Paris, M. (2007). *Strategic Planning Processes in Higher Education, Office of Quality Improvement.* Madison, WI: University of Wisconsin. Retrieved from: http://oqi.wisc.edu/resourcelibrary/uploads/resources/Survey%20of%20Strategic%20Planning%20in%20Higher%20Education%20DEC%202007.pdf

Dahlstrom, E., Brooks, C. and Bischel, J. (2014). *The Current Ecosystem of Learning Management Systems in Higher Education: Student, Faculty, and IT Perspectives.* Educause Center for Analysis and Research. Retrieved from: https://net.educause.edu/ir/library/pdf/ers1414.pdf

Del Ray, J. (2017, April 12). This Is the Jeff Bezos Playbook for Preventing Amazon's Demise. *Recode.* Retrieved from: www.recode.net/2017/4/12/15274220/jeff-bezos-amazon-shareholders-letter-day-2-disagree-and-commit

Everse, G. (2012, March 7). Four Steps to Building a Strategic Communications Capability. *Harvard Business Review.* Retrieved from: https://hbr.org/2012/03/four-steps-to-building-a-strat

Freeman, R. E. (2010). *Strategic Management: A Stakeholder Approach.* Cambridge: Cambridge University Press.

Gould, S. J. and Eldridge, N. (1977). Punctuated Equilibria: The Tempo and Mode of Evolution Reconsidered. *Paleobiology,* 3, pp. 115–151. Retrieved from: www.blc.arizona.edu/courses/schaffer/182/Punct-Equilib/Gould%20Eldredge%20PE77.pdf

Hardy, C. (1991). Pluralism, Power and Collegiality in Universities. *Financial Accountability and Management,* 7:3, pp. 127–142.

Jaschik, S. and Lederman, D. (2014). Faculty Attitudes on Technology. *Inside Higher Education.* Retrieved from: www.insidehighered.com/system/files/media/IHE-FacTechSurvey2014%20final.pdf

Jones, S., Lefoe, G., Harvey, M. and Ryland, K. (2012, February). Distributed Leadership: A Collaborative Framework for Academics, Executives and Professionals in Higher Education. *Journal of Higher Education Policy and Management,* 34:1, pp. 67–78.

Knowledge@Wharton (2005, August 10). *Three Reasons Why Good Strategies Fail: Execution, Execution.* Retrieved from: http://knowledge.wharton.upenn.edu/article/three-reasons-why-good-strategies-fail-execution-execution/

Kopczynski, L., Green, M. and Gibson, A. (2012, Winter). A Study of Faculty Technology Use in Online Learning: Is There a Disconnect? *Journal of Technology in the Classroom,* 4:1. Retrieved from: http://digitalcommons.apus.edu/facultySAH/8/

Kotter, J. (1995, March–April). Leading Change: Why Transformation Efforts Fail. *Harvard Business Review.* Retrieved from: https://cb.hbsp.harvard.edu/resources/marketing/docs/95204f2.pdf

Lee, J., March, L. and Peters, R. (2015, November). *Faculty Training and Approach to Online Education: Is There a Connection?* Center for Teaching, Research and Learning, American University. Retrieved from: https://edspace.american.edu/online/wp-content/uploads/sites/504/2016/03/FacultyTrainingAndApproachToOnlineEducation.pdf

Linos, M., Bierley, V., Bordelon, J. and Suero, L. (2015). *A Case Study: Developing a Holistic Distance Learning Readiness Plan.* Presentation at United States Distance Learning Association. Retrieved from: www.usi.edu/media/2806505/USDLA-poster-letter-size.pdf

Lloyd, S., Bryne, M. and McCoy, T. (2012, March). Faculty-Perceived Barriers of Online Education. *MERLOT Journal of Online Learning and Teaching,* 8:1. Retrieved from: http://jolt.merlot.org/vol8no1/lloyd_0312.pdf

Looser, D. (2017, March 20). Why I Teach Online. *Chronicle of Higher Education.* Retrieved from: www.chronicle.com/article/Why-I-Teach-Online/239509

Lozier, G., Oblinger, D. and Choa, M. (2002, January 22). Organizational Models for Delivering Distance Learning. *ECAR Research Bulletin,* 2.

Luecke, R. (2005). *Strategy.* Boston, MA: Harvard Business School Press.

McQuiggan, C. (2012, March). Faculty Development for Online Teaching as a Catalyst for Change. *Journal of Asynchronous Learning Networks,* 16:2. Retrieved from: https://eric.ed.gov/?id=EJ971044

Miller, T. and Ribble, M. (2010). Moving Beyond Bricks and Mortar: Changing the Conversation on Online Education. *Educational Considerations*, 37:2, pp. 3–6. Retrieved from: https://eric.ed.gov/?id=EJ889185

Minch, K. (2014). *Truman State University Strategic Plan for Online Learning*. Retrieved from: http://online.truman.edu/files/2014/12/Online-Strategic-Planning-Document-final.pdf

Nanus, B. (1992). *Visionary Leadership*. San Francisco, CA: Jossey-Bass Publishers.

Neilson, G., Martin, K. and Powers, E. (2008). Successful Strategy Execution. *Harvard Business Review*, 86:6, pp. 61–71.

Ogden, J. and Wilson, L. (2015). *Strategic Communications Planning for Public Relations and Marketing*. Dubuque, IA: Kendall Hunt.

Penn State Outreach and Online Education Strategic Plan 2014–2015 Through 2018–2019 (2014). Retrieved from: www.opia.psu.edu/sites/default/files/unit_sp/OutreachAndOnlineEducation.docx

Rawlins, B., Plowman, K. and Stohlton, E. (2005, March). A Comprehensive Approach to Prioritizing Stakeholders: A Synthesis of Stakeholder and Public Relations Literature on Identifying and Prioritizing Stakeholders for Strategic Management. *8th International Public Relations Research Conference*.

Rzonca, C. (2016). *A Year of Transitions: One Story at a Time*. Division of Distance and Online Education, University of Iowa. Retrieved from: https://issuu.com/distance.iowa/docs/annualreport2016_final?e=0/42252064

Shea, P., Bidjerno, T. and Vickers, J. (2016). Faculty Attitudes Toward Online Learning: Failures and Successes. *SUNY Research Network*. Retrieved from: www.sunyresearch.net/hplo/wp-content/uploads/2016/03/AERA-2016-w-new-analysis-3.pdf

Sporn, B. (1996, July). Managing University Culture: An Analysis of the Relationship Between Institutional Culture and Management Approaches. *Higher Education*, 32:1, pp. 41–61.

Straumshein, C. (2016, October 4). Doubts About Data: 2016 Survey of Faculty Attitudes on Technology. *Inside Higher Ed*. Retrieved from: www.insidehighered.com/news/survey/doubts-about-data-2016-survey-faculty-attitudes-technology

Wilson, C. (2001). Faculty Attitudes About Distance Learning. *Educause Quarterly No 2*. Retrieved from: https://net.educause.edu/ir/library/pdf/eqm0128.pdf

Index

3